D1435123

PRINCE2

PLANNING AND CONTROL

USING

MICROSOFT® PROJECT

UPDATED FOR MICROSOFT OFFICE

PROJECT 2007

BY

PAUL EASTWOOD HARRIS

Windows, XP, Microsoft® Project 2000, Microsoft® Project Standard 2002, Microsoft® Project Professional 2002, Microsoft Project Standard 2003, Microsoft® Project Professional 2003, Microsoft® Office Project 2007, PowerPoint, Word, Visio and Excel are registered trademarks of Microsoft Corporation. Primavera Project Planner, P3, SureTrak Project Manager, SureTrak, Primavera Enterprise, TeamPlay, P3e and P3e/c are registered trademarks of Primavera Systems, Incorporated.

Adobe® and Acrobat® are registered trademarks of Adobe Systems Incorporated.

All other company or product names may be trademarks of their respective owners.

PRINCE2™ is a project management methodology developed, owned and published by the UK Office of Government Commerce (OGC), an office of H M Treasury. PRINCE2™ products published by the Office of Government Commerce (OGC) are © Crown Copyright, and have the status of Value Added Products which falls outside the scope of the HMSO Click Use Core Licence. PRINCE® is a Registered Trade Mark and a Registered Community Trade Mark of the Office of Government Commerce and is Registered in the US patent and Trademark office. PRINCE2™ is a Trade Mark of the Office of Government Commerce (OGC) and is used here under licence and with the kind permission of OGC.

There is no endorsement implied or association between the author of this book and the Office of Government Commerce the owners of the Trade Mark PRINCE2.

Screen captures were reprinted with authorization from Microsoft Corporation.

This publication was created by Eastwood Harris Pty Ltd (ABN 18 133 912 173) and is not a product of Microsoft Corporation or the Office of Government Commerce.

DISCLAIMER
The information contained in this book is to the best of the author's knowledge true and correct. The author has made every effort to ensure accuracy of this publication, but cannot be held responsible for any loss or damage arising from any information in this book.

PUBLISHER, AUTHOR AND DISTRIBUTOR
Paul E Harris
Eastwood Harris Pty Ltd
PO Box 4032
Doncaster Heights 3109
Victoria, Australia
Email: harrispe@eh.com.au
Website: http://www.eh.com.au
Tel: +61 (0)4 1118 7701
Fax: +61 (0)3 9846 7700

25 September 2008

ISBN 978-1-921059-17-9 - B5 Perfect

SUMMARY

The book is an update of my PRINCE2™ Planning and Control Using Microsoft® Project book and has been written so it may be used as:

- ➤ A training manual for a two-day training course,
- ➤ A self teach book, or
- ➤ A reference manual.

The screen shots for the book are taken from Microsoft Project Standard 2007 but the book may be used to learn Microsoft Project Professional 2007 and all versions of Microsoft Project 2003, 2002 and 2000 as the differences between the versions is described in this book

The book has been written to be used as the basis for a two-day training course and includes exercises for the students to complete at the end of each chapter. Unlike many training course publications this book may be used by the students as a reference book after the course.

This publication is ideal for people who would like to quickly gain an understanding of how the software operates and explains how the software differs from Primavera P3 and SureTrak, thus making it ideal for people who wish to convert from these products.

SPELLING

This book is written in US English to be compatible with the software menu. PRINCE2 terms have been spelt in British English spelling so not to contradict the British spelling of PRINCE2 terms.

AUTHOR'S COMMENT

As a professional project planner and scheduler and an Approved PRINCE2 Trainer I have used a number of planning and scheduling software packages for the management of a range of project types and sizes. There appeared to be very little literature aimed at the professional who understands how to run projects, however require a practical guide on how to use Microsoft Project in a PRINCE2 project environment. The first books I published were user guides/training manuals for Primavera SureTrak and P3 users. These were well received by professional project managers and schedulers, so I decided to turn my attention to Microsoft Project 2000, 2002 and 2003. To produce this book I edited my Microsoft Project 2003 book to explain how Microsoft Project may be used with PRINCE2. I trust this book will assist you in understanding how to use Microsoft Project on your PRINCE2 projects. Please contact me if you have any comments on this book.

I would like thank my daughter Samantha Harris and Peter Whitelaw of Rational Management Pty Ltd, Victoria, Australia for their assistance in the production of this publication.

COVER PHOTOGRAPHS

Top right   Photograph of the Endeavour Replica in Melbourne Docklands, Australia.
Middle right   Iron bridge at Lower Landing on the West Coast Wilderness Railway Tasmania, Australia.
Bottom right   ConocoPhillips Ltd, Humber Refinery, UK.

CURRENT BOOKS PUBLISHED BY EASTWOOD HARRIS

99 Tricks and Traps for Microsoft® Office Project
Including Microsoft® Project 2000 to 2007, published May 2007
ISBN 978-1-921059-19-3 - A5 - Paperback

Planning and Scheduling Using Microsoft Office Project 2007
Including Microsoft Project 2000 to 2003, published March 2007
ISBN 978-1-921059-15-5 - B5 Paperback, ISBN 978-1-921059-16-2 - A4 Spiral

PRINCE2 Planning & Control Using Microsoft Project
Updated for Microsoft Office Project 2007, published March 2007
ISBN978-1-921059-17-9 - B5 Paperback

Planning and Control Using Microsoft Project and PMBOK® Guide Third Edition
Updated for Microsoft Office Project 2007, published March 2007
ISBN 978-1-921059-18-6 - B5 Paperback

Planning Using Primavera Project Planner P3® Version 3.1
Revised 2006, published March 2000
ISBN 1-921059-13-3 - A4 Spiral Bound

Planning Using Primavera® SureTrak Project Manager Version
3.0 Revised 2006, published June 2000
ISBN 1-921059-14-1 - A4 Spiral Bound

Project Planning and Scheduling Using Primavera® Contractor Version 4.1
For the Construction Industry, published January 2005
ISBN 1-921059-04-4 - A4 Paperback, ISBN 1-921059-05-2 A4 Spiral Bound

Project Planning & Control Using Primavera® P6
For all industries including Versions 4 to 6, published February 2008
ISBN 978-1-921059-20-9 - B5- Paperback, ISBN 978-1-921059-21-6 - A4 - Spiral Bound

SUPERSEDED BOOKS BY THE AUTHOR

Planning and Scheduling Using Microsoft® Project 2000
Planning and Scheduling Using Microsoft® Project 2002
Planning and Scheduling Using Microsoft® Project 2003
PRINCE2™ Planning and Control Using Microsoft® Project
Planning and Control Using Microsoft® Project and PMBOK® Guide Third Edition
Project Planning and Scheduling Using Primavera Enterprise - Team Play Version 3.5
Project Planning and Scheduling Using Primavera Enterprise - P3e & P3e/c Version 3.5
Project Planning and Scheduling Using Primavera® Version 4.1 for IT Project
Project Planning and Scheduling Using Primavera® Version 4.1 or E&C
Planning and Scheduling Using Primavera® Version 5.0 - For IT Project Office
Planning and Scheduling Using Primavera® Version 5.0 - For Engineering & Construction
Planning Using Primavera Project Planner P3® Version 2.0
Planning Using Primavera Project Planner P3® Version 3.0
Planning Using Primavera Project Planner P3® Version 3.1
Project Planning Using SureTrak® for Windows Version 2.0
Planning Using Primavera SureTrak® Project Manager Version 3.0

1   INTRODUCTION

1.1 Purpose

The purpose of this book is to provide you with methods of using Microsoft Project and the PRINCE2 Planning and Controlling components in a single project environment. The PRINCE2 Product Based Planning Technique is not simply transposed to Microsoft Project; this book makes some suggestions on how to best handle these areas of incompatibility.

The screen shots in this book were captured using Microsoft Project Standard 2007 and Windows XP. Readers using Microsoft Project Professional 2007 will have additional menu options to those shown in this book, which will operate when their software is connected to Microsoft Project Server software. Users of Microsoft Project 2003, 2002 and 2000 will find some minor differences in how the software functions which are outlined in **Chapter 23 WHAT IS NEW IN MICROSOFT PROJECT** and in the relevant sections of this book.

By the end of this book, you should be able to:
- Understand the steps required to create a project plan using PRINCE2
- Set up the software
- Define calendars
- Add tasks which will represent the PRINCE2 **Products** and/or **Activities**
- Organize tasks and format the display
- Add logic and constraints
- Use Tables, Views and Filters to present PRINCE2 **Project Plans, Stage Plans, Exception Plans** and **Team Work Package Plans**
- Print reports
- Record and track progress, producing PRINCE2 **Highlight Reports** and **Checkpoint Reports**
- Customize the project options
- Create and assign resources
- Understand the impact of task types and effort driven tasks
- Analyze resource requirements and resource level a schedule
- Status projects that contain resources, producing resourced **Highlight Reports** and **Checkpoint Reports**
- Understand the different techniques for scheduling

The book does not cover every aspect of Microsoft Project, but it does cover the main features required to create and status a project schedule. It should provide you with a solid grounding, which will enable you to go on and learn the other features of the software by experimenting, using the Help files and reviewing other literature.

This book has been written to minimize superfluous text, allowing the user to locate and understand the information contained in the book as quickly as possible. It does NOT cover functions of little value to common project scheduling requirements. If at any time you are unable to understand a topic in this book, it is suggested that you use the Microsoft Project Help menu to gain a further understanding of the subject.

1.2 Required Background Knowledge

This book does not teach you how to use computers or to manage projects. The book is intended to teach you how to plan and control a project using Microsoft Project in a PRINCE2 project environment. Therefore, to be able to follow this book you should have the following background knowledge:

- An understanding of the PRINCE2 Project Management Methodology.

- The ability to use a personal computer and understand the fundamentals of the operating system.

- Experience using application software such as Microsoft Office, which would have given you exposure to Windows menu systems and typical Windows functions such as copy and paste.

1.3 Purpose of Planning

The ultimate purpose of planning is to build a model that allows you to predict which tasks and resources are critical to the timely completion of the project. Strategies may then be implemented to ensure that these tasks and resources are managed properly, thus ensuring that the project will be delivered within **Tolerances**, or more traditionally described as delivered **On Time** and **Within Budget**.

A PRINCE2 **Tolerance** is the permissible deviation from plan without bringing the deviation to the attention of the next higher authority. This may be negative or positive and be defined in values such as costs, time, quality, scope and risks.

Planning aims to:
- Identify the Products and Activities required to deliver a project

- Evaluate different project delivery methods

- Identify and optimize the use of resources

- Optimize time and evaluate if target dates may be met

- Identify risks and set priorities

- Provide a baseline plan against which progress is measured

- Communicate the plan to all stakeholders, including what is to be done, when and by whom

- Provide early warning of potential problems and enable proactive and not reactive action to be taken

- Assist management to think ahead and make informed decisions

Planning helps to avoid:

- Increased project costs or reduction in scope and/or quality

- Additional changeover and/or operation costs

- Extension of time claims

- Loss of your client's revenue

- Contractual disputes and associated resolution costs

- The loss of reputation of those involved in a project

- Loss of a facility or asset in the event of a total project failure

1.4 Definition of a Plan

PRINCE2 defines a plan as a document identifying all the Products to be delivered by a project and their associated timescale, cost, quality and targets for the production of each.

A PRINCE2 Project Plan must at all times be able to deliver the expected benefits identified in the Business Case.

PRINCE2 also states that all plans must have the approval and commitment of all the appropriate management levels.

A plan is therefore not just a Microsoft Project Gantt Chart (bar chart), although a Gantt Chart is an important output of the planning process.

Microsoft Project is also able to record resource hours, costs and targets, and other basic information that can be kept in the Notes or Custom (user defined) Fields. It is neither a quality assurance nor a document management software package. Specialist packages should be considered for those processes.

1.5 Elements of a Plan

PRINCE2 defines the elements of a plan as:

- Products to be produced, both Specialist and Management

- Activities required to produce the Products

- Activities to validate the Products' quality

- Resources required to produce the Products, including management and quality

- The relationships or dependencies between the Products and Activities

- External dependencies that will influence Product creation

- Timings for the Products

- Control points to measure progress

- Tolerances in time, cost and any other agreed variable

All these elements may be entered into Microsoft Project, as well as additional information such as Notes and links to documents.

A Plan must be supported with a document that explains:

- The scope of the Plan

- The method to be used to execute the project

- Methods to measuring progress and report

- Quality control techniques

- Assumptions and risks

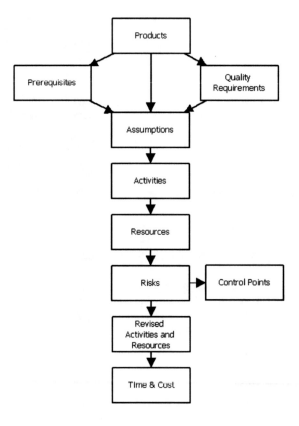

Note the above picture was created using Microsoft Project 2007.

1.6   Plan Levels

PRINCE2 defines four levels and five types of plans:

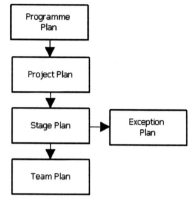

- **Programme Plan**, a Project Plan may be a stand-alone plan or part of a portfolio of multiple projects within a programme.

- **Project Plan**, this is mandatory and updated throughout the duration of a project.

- **Stage Plan**, there are a minimum of two Stage Plans: an **Initiation Stage Plan** and **First Stage Plan**. (There would be usually one Stage Plan for each Stage.)

- **Exception Plan**, which is at the same level and detail as a Stage Plan and replaces a Stage Plan at the request of a Project Board when a Stage is forecast to exceed Tolerances.

- **Team Plan** is optional and would be used on larger projects where Teams are used for delivering Products which require detailed planning. A typical example is a contractor's plan that would be submitted during the bidding process.

1.6.1   Programme Plan

A **Programme Plan** contains a large amount of information including:

- The **Vision Statement**, a statement of the target or targets of an organisation and the performance measurements of the new capabilities.

- The **Blueprint**, the outline of practices, processes, information and technology required to deliver the Vision Statement.

- **Benefits**, a statement of the benefits that the programme will deliver the Organisation. Benefits may be scheduled and monitored using Microsoft Project with tasks in a programme level.

- **Projects**, which may be grouped under **Tranches**.

- **Resources**, which outlines the people, equipment, funding and all other assets required to deliver the Projects. This allows the management of resources amongst projects; it is possible to share a Microsoft Project Resource pool over more than one project.

- **Stakeholders**, identification and communication with the stakeholders to ensure that the right products are delivered; their acceptance is very important.

- **Risks**, managed at both Programme and Project level. A sound Risk Management Plan and supporting processes are required to successfully manage a Programme.

- **Timetable**, this outlines deadlines and the timeline that the programme must work to. This timeline would usually impose start and completion dates for projects. The programme work may be scheduled with Microsoft Project and include tasks for Benefits Realisation.

- **Progress monitoring**, established in a programme. Programmes may be divided into **Tranches**, which are distinct steps of a Programme, they may be tied to a financial instalment and provide a point where the business benefits of completed projects may be evaluated.

- **Transition** addresses the cultural changes required in an organisation from the Project Approach through to the smooth operation of a new process.

Programme planning steps are as follows:

- The Portfolio of projects should be designed.

- The Projects and the Programme Benefits Realisation are scheduled and the Benefits Realisation should be aligned with the programme strategic objectives.

- The Project plans should show an increasing level of detail as they are executed and progress is reflected back into the Programme Plan.

- The Programme schedule will have to be monitored, reviewed and revised as the projects progress and the effects of external events and emerging risks impact on the Programme.

Below is a very simple example of a programme plan produced with Microsoft Project to demonstrate how Microsoft Project may be used to assist in the management of Programmes:

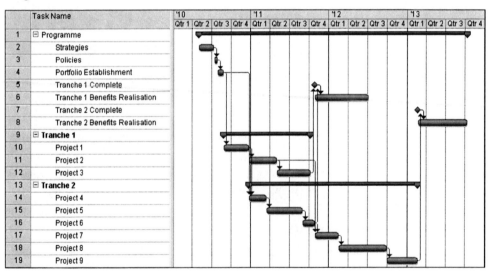

1.6.2   Project Plan

The Project Plan is the overall control document for the **Project Board**, who is responsible for directing and monitoring the project in terms of Product, Cost, Timing, Resources and Control Points. Quality is documented in the Project Quality Plan. The Project Plan is part of the Project Initiation Document (PID) and the Project Plan is Baselined after the project has been authorised in **DP2 – Authorising a Project**.

The Project Plan is updated at least:

- At the end of each Stage, and

- When a Project has exceeded Tolerances and the Project Board has requested the Exception Plan.

1.6.3   Stage Plan

There are a minimum of 2 Stages in a PRINCE2 project and each have a plan:

- Initiation Stage Plan, created during Starting Up a Project, and

- First Stage Plan, created during the Initiation Stage.

A **Next Stage Plan** is created towards the end of the previous Stage and approved by the Project Board before the next Stage commences.

A Stage Plan provides the Project Manager with a tool for day-to-day management of the project. It would have a greater level of detail than the Project Plan and would fit into the timing of the Project Plan. A Stage Plan may be created in Microsoft Project in several ways:

- Granulating the Project schedule into more detail in the Projects schedule file , thus creating a single schedule that contains both Project and Stage schedules, or

- Creating a stand-alone schedule for each Stage that is manually aligned to the Project Plan. This allows the Project Manager to set tighter time Tolerances on a Stage schedule than the Project schedule. Thus creating a Stage schedule with a tight Stage Tolerances to force Team Managers to deliver the products on time, or

- Creating a stand-alone schedule for each Stage that is inserted into a Project Schedule.

1.6.4   Exception Plan

When a Stage exceeds Tolerances, normally identified as a breach of time or cost but could include Scope, Quality, Risk or Benefit, then the project is in Exception. If a Stage breaks Tolerances:

- The Project Manager may create an Exception Report in the sub-process **CS8 – Escalating Project Issues** and would submit the Exception Report, which should include options for the future course of the project, to the Project Board.

- The Project Board may request an Exception Plan from the Project Manager in **DP4 – Giving Ad Hoc Direction**.

- The Project Manager would produce an Exception Plan in **SB6 – Producing an Exception Plan** and submit it for approval by the Project Board,

- Should the Project Board approve the Exception Plan in **DP3 – Authorising a Stage or Exception Plan**, this plan would replace the current failed Stage Plan.

1.6.5 Team Plan

Team Plans are optional plans for detailing out the delivery of one or more products included in a **Work Package** and would typically be represented by:

- A subcontractor plan for the delivery of a product which could be submitted with a bid for work, or

- A plan supplied by another team, group or department for the internal delivery of products.

A Team Plan should be approved as part of **Accepting a Work Package** and progress would be reported in **Checkpoint Reports** from a **Team Manager** to the **Project Manager**. In a similar way to the development of a Stage Plan from a Project plan, a Team Plan may be integrated into a Stage Plan in several ways. For example:

- A single task may be manually inserted in the Stage schedule to represent all the tasks from a Team schedule, and manually updated.

- A single task representing each of the Team schedule summary tasks may be manually inserted into the Stage schedule and manually updated, thus providing a summary of the Team schedule with more than one task.

- When a Team schedule is received electronically it may have all its tasks copied and pasted into the Stage plan as long as all the activities and resources are common.

- When a Team schedule is received electronically it may be inserted into the Stage schedule and look like a sub-project.

1.7 Controlling a Project

Controlling a project ensures:

- The work is being authorised in accordance with the plan

- The required products are being produced

- The required quality is being met

- The products are being produced on time, with the planned resources and to the planned costs

- The project products will achieve the **Business Case**

Controlling a project provides the next level of management with information allowing them to:

- Monitor the progress of products

- Compare the progress with the plan

- Review options

- Forecast problems as early as possible enabling corrective action to be taken as early as possible

- Authorise further work

1.7.1 Project Board Controls

The Project Board controls the project using the following processes:

- **DP1 – Authorising Initiation** where an Initiation Stage Plan would be reviewed and approved.

- **DP2 – Authorising a Project** where the Project Plan and First Stage would be reviewed and approved.

- **DP3 – Authorising a Stage Plan** where:

  - ➢ A Stage would be reviewed and approved, or
  - ➢ After receiving an Exception Plan and holding an Exception Assessment meeting, the Exception Plan would be reviewed and approved.

- **DP4 – Giving Ad Hoc Direction** after reviewing:

  - ➢ Highlight Reports from the Project Manager produced in **CS6 – Reporting Highlights** which would include an update of the Stage Plan, or
  - ➢ Review Exception Reports created by the Project Manager in **CS8 – Escalating Project Issues**, which would show Tolerances being exceeded.

- **DP5 – Confirming Project Closure** where the Actual Duration and Costs would be compared to the Planned Duration and Costs.

1.7.2 Project Manager Controls

The Project Manager controls the project through the normal day-to-day management activities which should be recorded on the **Daily Log**. The Project Manager controls Product delivery through:

- The definition of Products in **PL2 – Defining and Analysing Products**,

- Authorising work to commence in **CS1 – Authorising Work Packages**,

- **CS2 – Assessing Progress** where the Project Manager would review Checkpoint Reports created by Team Managers, and

- **CS9 – Receiving Completed Products**.

1.8 Project Planning Metrics

There are four components that are usually measured and controlled using planning and scheduling software:

- Time
- Effort (resources)
- Cost
- Scope

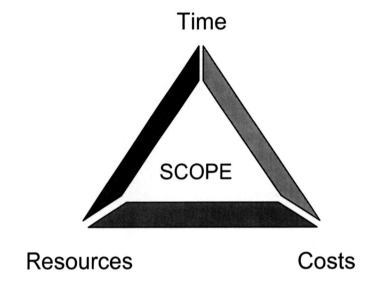

A change in any one of these components normally results in a change in one or both of the other two.

Other project management functions that are not traditionally managed with planning and scheduling software but may have components reflected in the schedule include:

- Document Management and Control,
- Quality Management,
- Contract Management,
- Issue Management,
- Risk Management,
- Industrial Relations, and
- Accounting.

The development of Enterprise Project Management systems has resulted in the inclusion of more of these functions in project planning and scheduling software.

1.9 Planning Cycle

The planning cycle is an integral part of managing a project. A software package such as Microsoft Project makes this task much easier.

When the original plan is agreed to, either Project or Stage, the **Baseline** is set. The **Baseline** is a record of the original plan. The **Baseline** dates may be recorded in Microsoft Project in data fields titled **Baseline Start** and **Baseline Finish**.

After project planning has ended and project execution has begun, the actual progress is monitored, recorded in **CS2 – Assessing Progress** and compared to the **Baseline** dates in **CS5 – Reviewing Stage Status**.

The progress is then reported in **Checkpoint Reports** produced by **Team Managers** for the **Project Manager** or **Highlight Reports** produced by the Project Manager for the **Board**.

The plan may be amended by adding or deleting tasks and adjusting Remaining Durations or Resources. A revised plan is then published as progress continues.

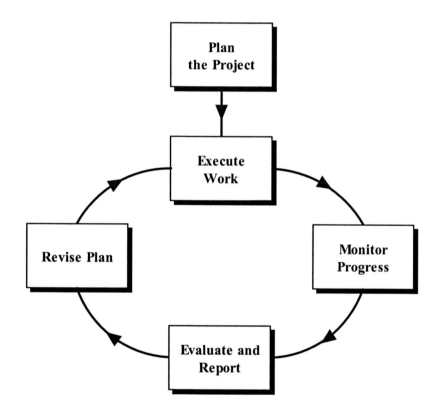

1.10 PRINCE2 Planning Component and Microsoft Project

The picture below shows the PRINCE2 processes:

Directing a Project

DP1 Authorising Initiation	DP2 Authorising a Project	DP3 Authorising a Stage Plan or Exception Plan	DP4 Giving ad hoc Direction	DP5 Confirming Project Closure

Starting up a Project	Initiating a Project	Controlling a Stage			Managing Stage Boundaries	Closing a Project
SU1 Appointing a PB Executive and a PM	IP1 Planning Quality	CS1 Authorising a Work Package	CS2 Assessing Progress	CS3 Capturing Project Issues	SB1 Planning a Stage	CP1 De-commissioning a project
SU2 Designing a PM Team	IP2 Planning a Project	CS4 Examining Project Issues	CS5 Reviewing Stage Status	CS6 Reporting Highlights	SB2 Updating a Project Plan	CP2 Identifying Follow on Actions
SU3 Appointing a PM Team	IP3 Refining the Business Case and Risks	CS7 Taking Corrective Action	CS8 Escalating Project Issues	CS9 Receiving Completed Work Package	SB3 Updating a Project Business Case	CP3 Evaluating a project
SU4 Preparing a Project Brief	IP4 Setting up Project Controls				SB4 Updating the Risk Log	
SU5 Defining a Project Approach	IP5 Setting up Project Files	**Managing Product Delivery**			SB5 Reporting Stage End	
SU6 Planning an Initiation Stage	IP6 Assembling a PID	MP1 Accepting a Work Package	MP2 Executing a Work Package	MP3 Delivering a Work Package	SB6 Producing an Exception Plan	

Planning

PL1 Designing a Plan	PL2 Defining and Analysing Products	PL3 Identifying Activities and Dependencies	PL4 Estimating	PL5 Scheduling	PL6 Analysing Risks	PL7 Completing a Plan

It is possible to use Microsoft Project to support most PRINCE2 processes, as presented in the table below:

SU2	Designing a PM Team	There are some functions in Microsoft Project that allow Organisation information to be recorded. This may be achieved by using either a Resource Customized Field or a Resource Customized Outline Code to record the Organisation Structure and assign these codes to resources.
SU6	Planning an Initiation Stage	The Initiation Stage plan may be prepared and presented in Microsoft Project.
PL1	Designing a Plan	Microsoft Project may be nominated as the planning tool in this process. However it would not be used to define this process, normally a word processor software package such as Microsoft Word to create the Plan Design document.
PL2	Defining and Analysing Products	The **PRINCE2 Product Based Planning** technique is a good technique and is used to define and analyze products. Products may be represented as Tasks, or Summary Tasks using the Outlining feature, or by using a Custom Outline Code.

	Product Based Planning	1. Defining the **Product Breakdown Structure** may not be duplicated exactly in Microsoft Project due to formatting limitations. Graphical flow charting tools or specialist PRINCE2 tools may be used to duplicate this process exactly. Only a close approximation of a Product Breakdown Structure may be duplicated using Outlining or a Custom Outline Code structure. 2. **Product Descriptions** may be recorded in Microsoft Project using a number of methods including: ➤ Notes, as an attached file, or ➤ Custom Fields. When data such as Product Descriptions are entered into Notes or in User Defined Fields in Microsoft Project, this information is no longer accessible to those who do not have access to the software. This may deter the use of Microsoft Project to record such data. 3. A PRINCE2 type **Product Flow Diagram** may be created in Microsoft Project by using the Network Diagramming function; however, users may find this software function a little time consuming to use for this purpose.
PL3	Identifying Activities & Dependencies	Microsoft Project will handle this process as it is the primary purpose of the product.
PL4	Estimating	Microsoft Project may be used for estimating and has a number of functions that would assist including Labor Resources, Material Resources, Cost Resources (new to Microsoft Project 2007) and Fixed Costs. A user must be aware that a detailed schedule with many resources and costs is very difficult to update and maintain as the project progresses. Consider the use of an external estimating system or a spreadsheet with the summary costs then transferred to Microsoft Project.
PL5	Scheduling	Microsoft Project is designed to handle this function.
PL6	Analysing Risks	Microsoft Project is not a Risk Analysis tool. It may be used to evaluate options and include risk countermeasure activities; however, it is recommended that Risk Analysis data be recorded outside Microsoft Project.
PL7	Completing a Plan	The output from Microsoft Project would form part of the plan, but it should not be the only element in the plan. Microsoft Project Views and Tables would be used to create reports for stakeholders to review the schedule.
DP1	Authorising Initiation	The Initiation Stage schedule would be created in Microsoft Project and form part of the Initiation Stage Plan authorised in this PRINCE2 sub-process.
DP2	Authorising a Project	During this process a project schedule created in Microsoft Project would be analyzed. Microsoft Project Views and Tables would be used to create reports for the Project Board to review.
DP3	Authorising a Stage or Exception Plan	The review of a Microsoft Project Stage schedule would form part of this review.

DP5	Confirming Project Closure	The Project and Last Stage Plan should be reviewed to ensure all activities are complete.
CS1 and MP1	Authorising and Accepting a Work Package	The Timing and Costs aspects of a Work Package may be calculated and recorded in Microsoft Project. When there is more than one task per Work Package then tasks associated with a Work Package may be tagged with a Custom Field and all the WP tasks viewed with a filter when the WP tasks are separated by other activities, or if the activities are in one location they may be demoted under a summary task.
CS2 and CS5	Assessing Progress and Reviewing Stage Status	These processes could be managed in Microsoft Project by statusing the schedule in the normal way. Microsoft Project Filters would assist in isolating Stage activities and the Baseline function would show deviation from the Approved Stage Plan.
MP2	Executing a Work Package	Microsoft Project may be used to record and report the progress of a Work Package.
CS6	Reporting Highlight	Microsoft Project Views, Tables and Filters may be used to create elements of a Highlight Report.
MP3 and CS9	Delivering a Work Package and Receiving Completed Work Package	A Microsoft Project Schedule would be updated when a Work Package is completed and delivered.
SB1	Planning a Stage	Microsoft Project may be used in the way identified in PL1 to PL7 above.
SB2	Updating a Project Plan	The Project schedule would be updated as part of this process. Activities would be updated with progress and compared to the Approved Project Plan.
SB5	Reporting Stage End	The Stage schedule would be updated as part of this process.
SB6	Producing an Exception Plan	The replacement Stage schedule and possibly the Project schedule would be updated as part of this process.
CP3	Evaluating a Project	The Baseline schedule should be compared to the actuals and the performance evaluated from this comparison.

2 CREATING A PROJECT SCHEDULE

The aim of this chapter is to give you an understanding of what a schedule is and some practical guidance on how your schedule may be created and statused during the life of a PRINCE2 project.

2.1 Understanding Planning and Scheduling Software

A project is essentially a set of unique operations or tasks to be completed in a logical order to achieve a defined outcome by a definitive end time. A schedule is an attempt to model these tasks, their durations and their relationships to other tasks. These tasks take time to accomplish and may employ resources that may have a limited availability such as people, materials, equipment, and money.

Planning and scheduling software allows the user to:

- Enter the **Product Breakdown Structure** (PBS) of the project deliverables or products and any other coding structures into the software,

- Break a project down into activities required to create the deliverables and that are entered into the software as **Tasks** under the appropriate PBS node,

- Assign, calendars, durations, constraints, predecessors and successors of the activities and then calculate the start and finish date of all the activities,

- Assign resources and/or costs, which represent people, equipment or materials, to the activities and calculate the project resource requirements and/or cash flow,

- Optimize the project plan,

- Set Baseline Dates and Budgets to compare progress against,

- Use the plan to approve the commencement of work,

- Record the actual progress of activities against the original plan and amend the plan when required allowing for scope changes, etc.,

- Record the consumption of resources and/or costs and re-estimate the resources and/or costs required to finish the project, and

- Produce management reports.

There are four modes or levels in which planning and scheduling software may be used:

	Planning	Tracking
Without Resources	**LEVEL 1** Planning without Resources	**LEVEL 2** Tracking progress without Resources
With Resources	**LEVEL 3** Planning with Resources	**LEVEL 4** Tracking progress with Resources

As the level increases, the amount of information required to maintain the schedule will increase. More importantly, your skill and knowledge in using the software will also need to increase. This book is designed to take you from Level 1 through Level 4.

2.2 Understanding Your Project

Before you start the process of creating a project plan, it is important to have an understanding of the project and how it will be executed. On large, complex projects, this information is usually available from the following types of documents:

- A PRINCE2 project should have a **Project Mandate** to commence the **SU – Starting up a Project** process

- Project scope

- Functional specification

- Requirements baseline

- Contract documentation

- Plans and drawings

- Project execution plan

- Contracting and purchasing plan

- Equipment lists

- Installation plan

- Testing plan

It is important to gain a good understanding of the project before starting to plan your project. A PRINCE2 Project would begin to define these parameters during the **IP – Initiating a Project** process.

You should also understand what level of reporting is required. Providing too little or too much detail will often lead to the schedule being discarded and not being used. Again, a PRINCE2 project should clearly define these requirements in **IP4 – Setting Up Project Controls**.

There are three processes required to create or maintain a plan at each of the four levels:

- Collecting the relevant project data

- Entering and manipulating the data in software

- Distributing the plan, reviewing and revising

The ability of the scheduler to collect the data is as important as the ability to enter and manipulate the information using the software. On larger projects, it may be necessary to write policies and procedures to ensure accurate collection of data from the various people, departments, stakeholders/companies, and sites.

2.3 Level 1 – Planning Without Resources

This is the simplest mode of planning.

2.3.1 Creating Projects

To create the project, you will require the following information:

- Project Name

- The Project Start Date (and perhaps the Finish Date)

It would be helpful to know other important information such as:

- Client name

- Other project data such as location, project number and stakeholders.

2.3.2 Defining the Calendars

Before you start entering tasks into your schedule it is advisable to set up the calendars. These are used to model the working time for each task in the project. For example, a six-day calendar is created for those tasks that will be worked for six days a week. The calendar should include any public holidays and any other exceptions to available working days such as planned days off.

The finish date and time of an activity (when there are no resources using a resource calendar assigned to an activity) is calculated from the start date and time plus the activity duration over the calendar assigned to the activity.

The pictures below show the effect of nonwork days on the finish date of a 13-day duration activity assigned a 5-Day Working Week. The elapsed duration is 19 days due to the three weekends where work does not take place.

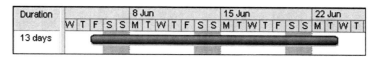

2.3.3   Product Based Planning with Microsoft Project

The PRINCE2 Product Based Planning Technique has three steps:

- Defining the **Product Breakdown Structure**. This process may not be displayed exactly in Microsoft Project, as it does not allow the creating of a hierarchical tree structure report. Graphical flow charting tools such as Visio, or the Organization Chart function in Excel, or specialist PRINCE2 tools like P2WORLD, may be used to duplicate this process exactly. A close approximation of a Product Breakdown Structure may be duplicated either using **Outlining**, see below:

	Task Name
1	⊟ **Specialists Products**
2	⊟ **Collective Group 1**
3	Product 1
4	Product 2
5	Product 3
6	⊟ **Collective Group 2**
7	Product 4
8	Product 5
9	Product 6

or using **Custom Outline Codes**, see below:

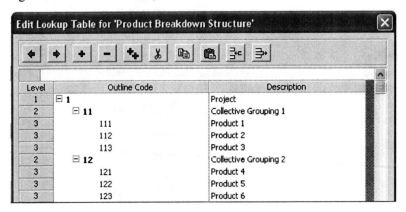

But neither of these may be displayed in a tree structure from within Microsoft Project and when a **Custom Outline Code** is used a **Product Flow Diagram** may not be created in Microsoft Project..

- **Product Descriptions** may be recorded in Microsoft Project in **Notes**, or as an attached file, or by using **Custom Fields**. When data is recorded in Microsoft Project, this information is no longer accessible to those who do not have access to the software. This may deter the use of Microsoft Project to record such data.

- A **Product Flow Diagram (PFD)** may be created in Microsoft Project, see picture below, using the Network Diagramming function as the Products have been entered as tasks. Users may find the Network Diagramming function too time consuming to create a **PFD,** and there are some restrictions on the formatting of the boxes around the task descriptions which is required by PRINCE2 for **External Products**.

The **Project Approval External Product** below is formatted with a stretched octagon and not an ellipse.

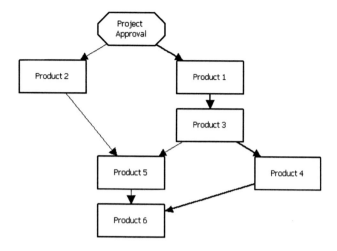

2.3.4   Defining Project Breakdown Structures

Project breakdown structures are coding structures that are used to Group, Summarize and/or Filter activities that meet set criteria and therefore are used to provide clarity when working on or reviewing parts of the project schedule. These coding structures may include:

- PBS   **Product Breakdown Structure**, the method used by the **PRINCE2** Product Based Planning Technique.
- WBS   **Work Breakdown Structure**, breaking down the project into the elements of work required to complete a project.
- OBS   **Organization Breakdown Structure**, showing the hierarchical management structure of a project.
- CBS   **Contract Breakdown Structure**, showing the breakdown of contracts.
- SBS   **System Breakdown Structure**, showing the elements of a complex system.

Other coding structures may be required to identify items:

- Project Phases such as design, procure, install and test

- Physical locations such as sites, buildings or floors in a building

- Disciplines such as Civil, Electrical, Mechanical

- Stakeholders, responsibility, who the work has been assigned to and who reports progress.

The principal method to assign a project breakdown structure to a project in Microsoft Project is through the Outlining function. The Outlining function may be used to define some but often not all of the coding structures listed above.

When Outlining is NOT used to represent the PRINCE2 Product Breakdown Structure and is used to represent another project breakdown structure, then a Custom Outline Code may be used the represent the Product Breakdown Structure. Other codes may be assigned to tasks using Custom Outline Codes, which are hierarchical code structures, or Custom Fields.

Before creating a project, you should decide which is your primary project breakdown structure and design your other project breakdown structures by asking the following types of questions:

- What are the most suitable primary project breakdown structures? In a PRINCE2 project it would normally be the Product Breakdown Structure.

- Which phases are involved in the project? (E.g., Design, Procure, Install and Test)

- Which disciplines are participating? (E.g., Civil, Mechanical and Electrical)

- Which departments are involved in the project? (E.g., Sales, Procurement and Installation)

- What work is expected to be contracted out and which contractors are used?

- How many sites or areas are there in the project?

Use the responses to these and other similar questions to create the project breakdown structures required to plan and control the project.

The main decision at this point in time is to decide if:

- The Product Breakdown Structure the primary breakdown of the project, and

- Is the Product Breakdown Structure to be represented with Outlining or a Customized Code.

2.3.5 Adding Tasks

Microsoft Project is a "top down" scheduling tool and is ideally suited to project planning using summary activities, created using the Outlining function, as Stages and Products in a Project Plan as per the example below:

PRINCE2 Project Schedule

If Products are entered as single activities as per the picture above, the Network Diagram may be used to create a Product Flow Diagram. When **Collective Groupings** are added as Summary Activities then these may be filtered out to produce a Product Flow Diagram. On the other hand, when a Custom Outline Code is used to create a Product Breakdown Structure, then a Product Flow Diagram may not be created utilizing the Network Diagram function.

In a PRINCE2 project the **Activity List** is created in the sub-process **PL3 – Identifying Activities and Dependencies** and the **Estimate** is created in the sub-process **PL4 – Estimating**. This information should be used to breakdown the project schedule into tasks, resources and costs and may provide an indication of how long the work will take. These two processes could be completed using Microsoft Project.

As Stage Plans are created the Activities or more Activities that are required to produce the Products may be added below the Product Summary tasks. This Product task is treated as a parent task and the Activities required to deliver the Products are entered as detailed tasks. See the following example:

PRINCE2 Project Schedule and Stage 1 Schedule Combined

This is a typical example of using Outlining as a project breakdown structure with the hierarchy of Stage and Product. A Product Breakdown Structure does not show the Stages.

Summary tasks in Microsoft Project may be used to represent PRINCE2 Stages and Products, as per the example above and this is the simplest way to use Microsoft Project. Custom Fields are an alternative function which may also be used to identify Stages and/or the Product Breakdown Structure. Other options include using Milestones to identify the completion of products when the schedule is organised using Outlining under a different coding structure to the PBS. These alternative methods require more knowledge of the software and the display options are not as simple to use. An example is shown in **Chapter 16 GROUPING, OUTLINE CODES AND WBS**.

PRINCE2 Activities must be defined before they are entered into the schedule as Tasks. It is important that you consider the following factors carefully:

- What is the scope of the task? (What is included and excluded?)
- How long is the task going to take?
- What resources are required?

Activities may have variable durations depending on the number of resources assigned. You may find that one activity that takes 4 days using 4 workers may take 2 days using 8 workers or 8 days using 2 workers.

Usually **Checkpoint Reports** are issued on a regular basis, such as every week or every month. It is recommended that, if possible, a task should not span more than two reporting periods. That way the tasks should only be **In-Progress** for one report. Of course, it is not practical to do this on long duration activities that may span many reporting periods, such as procurement and delivery.

It is also recommended that you have a measurable finish point for each group of tasks such as a Stage. These may be identified in the schedule by **Milestones** and are designated with zero duration. Documentation may be used to officially highlight the end point of one task and the start point of another, thereby adding clarity to the schedule. Examples of typical documents that may used are:

- Issue of a drawing package

- Completion of a specification

- Placing of an order

- Receipt of materials (delivery logs or tickets or dockets)

- Completed testing certificates for equipment

2.3.6 Adding the Logic Links

The PRINCE2 Product flow diagram will provide the basis of the Project Plan logic.

There are two methods that planning software uses to sequence activities:

- Precedence Diagramming Method (PDM), and

- Arrow Diagramming Method (ADM).

Most current project planning and scheduling software, including Microsoft Project, use the Precedence Diagramming Method. Product based planning is similar to the Precedence Diagramming Method. A PDM diagram may be produced with the Network Diagram function and therefore a PFD may be created from within Microsoft Project.

There are several types of dependencies that may be used when planning a project:

- **Mandatory dependencies**, also known as **Hard Logic**, are relationships between activities that may not be broken. For example, a hole has to be dug before it is filled with concrete or a computer delivered before software is loaded onto it.

- **Discretionary dependencies**, also known as **Sequencing Logic** or **Soft Logic**, are relationships between activities that may be changed when the plan is changed. For example, if there are five holes to be excavated and only one machine available, or five computers to be assembled and one person available to work on them, then the order of these activities could be set with sequencing logic but changed at a later date.

Both **Mandatory dependencies** and **Discretionary dependencies** are entered into Microsoft Project as activity relationships or logic links. The software does not provide a method of identifying the type of relationship because notes or codes may not be attached to relationships. A **Note** may be added to either the predecessor or successor activity to explain the relationship.

External dependencies are usually events outside the control of the project team that impact the schedule. An example would be the availability of a site to start work. This is usually represented in Microsoft Project by a Milestone which has a constraint applied to it. This topic is discussed in more detail in the next section.

The software will calculate the start and finish dates for each activity. The end date of the project is calculated from the start date of the project, the logic amongst the activities, any **Leads** (often referred to as **Negative Lag**) or **Lags** applied to the logic and durations of the activities. The pictures below show the effect of a lag and a lead on the start of a successor activity:

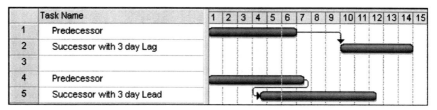

It is good practice to create a **Closed Network** with the logic. In a **Closed Network**, all tasks have one or more predecessors and one or more successors except:

- The project start milestone or first task which has no predecessors, and

- The finish milestone or finish task which has no successors.

The project's logic must not loop back on itself. Looping would occur if the logic were stated that A preceded B, B preceded C, and C preceded A. That's not a logical project situation and will cause an error comment to be generated by the software during network calculations.

Thus, when the logic is correctly applied, a delay to a task will delay all its successor tasks and delay the project end date when there is insufficient spare slippage time to accommodate the delay. This spare time is normally called **Float** but Microsoft Project uses the term **Slack**. The picture below shows Product 4 has **2 days Total Float**.

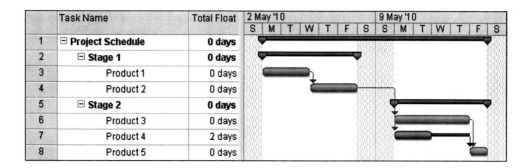

2.3.7   Constraints

Constraints may model the impact of events outside the logical sequence of tasks. A constraint would be imposed to specific dates such as the availability of a facility to start work or the required completion date of a project. Constraints should be cross-referenced to the supporting documentation, such as Milestone Dates from contract documentation. Typical examples of constraints would be:

- **Start No Earlier Than** for the availability of a site or building, and

- **Finish No Later Than** for the date that a product must be delivered by.

In PRINCE2 a constraint may well be used to fix in time the availability of an External Product.

2.3.8 Risk Analysis

The process of planning a project may identify risks and in a PRINCE2 model this is formalized in both **PL6 – Analysing Risks** and **IP3 – Refining Business Case and Risks**. These processes may identify risk mitigation activities that should be added to the schedule before it is submitted for approval.

2.3.9 Scheduling the Project

The software calculates the shortest time in which the project may be completed. Unstatused tasks without logic or a constraint will be scheduled to start at the Project Start Date.

Scheduling the project will also identify the **Critical Path(s)**. The Critical Path is the chain(s) of tasks that take the longest time to accomplish. This chain defines the Earliest Finish date of the project. The calculated completion date depends on the critical tasks starting and finishing on time. If any of them are delayed, the whole project will be delayed.

Tasks that may be delayed without affecting the project end date have **Float**.

Total Float is the amount of time a task may be postponed without delaying the project end date. The delay of a task with a positive Total Float value may delay other tasks with positive Total Float but will not delay the end date of the project unless the delay is greater than the Total Float. The delay of any task with a zero Total Float value (and is, therefore, on the **Critical Path)** will delay other subsequent tasks with zero Total Float and extend the end date of the project.

Free Float is the amount of time a task may be delayed without delaying the start date of any of its immediate successor tasks.

Product 2 may be delayed 4 days before it will delay Product 5 (work will not take place over the weekend) therefore has 4 days Free Float. Product 2 may also be delayed 6 days before it will delay the end of the project and therefore has 6 days Total Float.

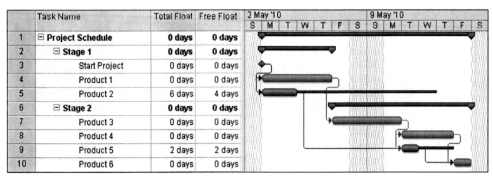

The Critical Path flows through tasks with 0 days Total Float.

The Microsoft Project term **Slack** has been replaced by **Float** in the column titles in the picture above, as **Float** is the more commonly accepted term.

2.3.10   Tolerances

Tolerances are agreed upon when the plan is approved. Time tolerances may be represented in a schedule in a number of ways:

- Adding a Tolerance task to a Project and/or Stages. The Tolerance tasks are reduced in duration to keep the project on time as delays are incurred. After a Tolerance task has been reduced to zero, a subsequent forecast delay will put the project in Exception and an Exception Report would be raised by the Project manager.

- By adding additional non-work days to the calendar.

- By increasing the duration of all or some of the tasks by a percentage to allow for the total amount of tolerance.

The method used to account for time Tolerance and how it is managed when activities are delayed should be clearly documented. The first option above is the easiest to manage.

When there is a schedule of several years' duration and a tolerance of several months is added at the end of a project, then the tasks may be scheduled out of season. This situation should be avoided in weather dependent projects by spreading the tolerance throughout the schedule so all activities are scheduled in their correct season.

2.3.11   Formatting the Display – Views, Tables and Filters

There are tools to manipulate and display the tasks to suit the project reporting requirements to create Programme, Portfolio, Project, Stage and Team Plans, Highlight and Checkpoint Reports, plus any special reports required for Stakeholders. These functions are covered in **Chapter 12 FILTERS** and **Chapter 13 VIEWS, TABLES AND DETAILS**.

2.3.12   Printing and Reports

There are software features that allow you to present the information in a clear and concise manner to communicate the requirements to all project members. These functions are covered in **Chapter 14 PRINTING AND REPORTS**.

2.3.13   Issuing the Plan

All members of the project team should review the project plan in an attempt to:
- Optimize the process and methods employed, and
- Gain consensus among team members as to the project's logic, durations, and Product Breakdown Structure.

Correspondence should be used to communicate expectations of team members while providing each with the opportunity to contribute to the schedule and further improve the outcome.

2.4   Level 2 – Monitoring Progress Without Resources

2.4.1   Setting the Baseline

The optimized and agreed-to plan is used as a baseline for measuring progress and monitoring change. The software can record the baseline dates of each activity for comparison against actual progress during the life of the project. These planned dates are stored in the **Baseline date** fields and displayed as the upper bars in the picture below:

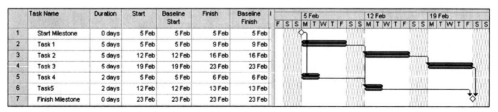

In a PRINCE2 project a schedule would be Baselined when the Project Plan or Stage Plan is approved by the Board.

2.4.2   Tracking Progress

The schedule should be **Statused** (updated or progressed) on a regular basis and progress be recorded at that point in time. The date as of which progress is reported is known by a number of different terms such as **Data Date**, **Update Date**, **Time Now** and **Status Date**. The Status Date is the field used in Microsoft Project to record this date. Whatever the frequency chosen for statusing, you will have to collect the following activity information in order to status a schedule:

- Completed activities
  - ➢ Actual Start date and
  - ➢ Actual Finish Date
- In-progress activities
  - ➢ The Actual Start Date
  - ➢ Percentage Completed
  - ➢ The Duration or Expected Finish Date of the Activity
- Un-started work
  - ➢ Any revisions to activities that have not started
  - ➢ New activities representing scope changes
  - ➢ Revisions to logic that represent changes to the plan

The schedule may be statused after this information has been collected. The recorded progress is compared to the **Target** dates, either graphically or by using columns of data such as the **Finish Variance** column:

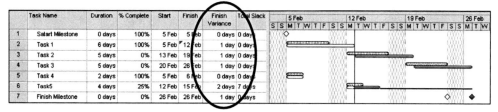

Whatever the frequency chosen for statusing, you will have to collect the following information in order to status a schedule:

- Actual Start Dates of tasks that have begun, whether they were planned to start or not,

- Percentage Complete and Remaining Duration or Expected Finish date for started, but incomplete tasks,

- Actual Finish Dates for completed tasks, and

- Any revisions to tasks that have not yet started.

The schedule may be statused after this information has been collected in **CS2 – Assessing Progress** and **CS5 – Reviewing Stage Status**. The recorded progress is then compared to the **Baseline Dates**.

At this point, it may be necessary to further optimize the schedule to meet the required end date by discussing the schedule with the appropriate project team members. The **Data Date** is **NOT** the date that the report is printed out but rather the date that reflects when the status information was gathered.

2.5   Level 3 – Planning With Resources

2.5.1   Estimating or Planning for Control

There are two modes that the software may be used at Level 3.

- **Estimating**. In this mode the objective is to create a schedule with costs that are being used as an estimate and the schedule will never be statused. Activities may have many resources assigned to them to develop an accurate cost estimate and include many items that would never be updated in the process of statusing a schedule.

- **Planning for Control**. In this mode the intention is to assign actual units (hours) and costs to resources, then calculate units and costs to completion, and possibly conduct an Earned Value analysis. In this situation it is important to ensure the minimum number of resources are assigned to activities, and preferably only one resource assigned to each activity. The process of statusing a schedule becomes extremely difficult and time consuming when a resourced schedule has many resources per activity. The scheduler is then in threat of becoming a timekeeper and may lose sight of other important functions, such as calculating the forecast to complete and the project finish date.

2.5.2   The Balance Between the Number of Activities and Resources

When Planning for Control on large or complex schedules, it is important to maintain a balance between the number of activities and the number of resources that are planned and tracked. As a general rule, the more activities a schedule has, the fewer resources should be created and assigned to activities.

When there is a schedule with a large number of activities and a large number of resources assigned to each activity, the result may be a schedule that members of the project team cannot understand and that the scheduler cannot maintain.

Instead of assigning individual resources, such as people by name, consider using Skills or Trades, and on very large projects use Crews or Teams.

This technique is not so important when you are using a schedule to estimate the direct cost of a project (by assigning costs to the resources) or if you will not use the schedule to track a project's progress (such as a schedule that is used to support written proposals).

Therefore, it is more important to minimize the number of resources in large schedules that will be updated regularly, since updating every resource assigned to each activity at each schedule update is very time consuming.

2.5.3   Creating and Using Resources

First, establish a resource pool by entering all the project resources required on the project into a table in the software. You then assign the required quantity of each resource to the tasks.

A resource in planning and scheduling software may represent an individual person, a skill or trade, individual pieces of equipment, fleets of equipment, a team or crew, material, space or funds. Each resource may have a quantity and an associated cost.

Entering a cost rate for each resource enables you to conduct a resource cost analysis, such as comparing the cost of supplementing overloaded resources against the cost of extending the project deadline.

Costs may also be assigned to tasks without the use of resources by using the Fixed Cost function, or with out a quantity in Microsoft Project 2007 using the Cost Resource function..

Time-phased cash flows and budgets may be produced from this resource/cost data.

2.5.4   Resource Calendars, Activity Types and Driving Resources

These are additional features that enable the user to more accurately model real-life situations. These features add a level of complexity that should be used only when the environment demands their use and should be avoided by inexperienced schedulers.

2.5.5   Task Types

Tasks may be assigned a **Type**, which affects how resources are calculated. There are additional software features that enable the user to more accurately model real-life situations. These features are covered in **Chapter 18 CREATING RESOURCES**.

2.5.6   Resource Graphs and Usage Tables

These features allow the display and analysis of project resource requirements both in tables and graphically.

The data may be exported to Excel for further analysis and presentation.

2.5.7   Resource Leveling

The schedule may now have to be resource leveled to:

- Reduce peaks and smooth the resource requirements, or

- Reduce resource demand to the available number of resources, or

- Reduce demand to an available cash flow when a project is being financed on a customer's income.

The process of leveling is defined as delaying activities until resources become available. There are several methods of delaying activities and thus leveling a schedule, which are outlined in the **RESOURCE HISTOGRAMS, TABLES, S-CURVES AND LEVELING** chapter.

2.6   Level 4 – Monitoring Progress of a Resourced Schedule

2.6.1   Statusing Projects with Resources

When you status (update) a project with resources you will need to collect some additional information that may include:

- The quantities or costs spent to date per activity for each resource, and

- The quantities or costs required per resource to complete each activity.

You may then status a resourced schedule with this data.

Once the schedule has been statused then a review of the future resource requirements, Project and Stage end dates, cash flows and performance may be made.

Statusing a resourced schedule is time consuming and requires experience and a good understanding of how the software calculates. It should ideally be attempted by experienced users or novice under the guidance of an experienced user.

2.7   Managing PRINCE2 Project, Stage and Work Package Plans

Microsoft Project may be used for the management of Programmes, Portfolios, Projects, Stages and Work Packages. When using Microsoft Project there are several options for managing these plans and the same techniques may be applied to programmes and portfolios:

- Each Project, Stage and Work Package are managed as individual schedules. The Project schedule is manually updated from the Stage schedules and the Stage schedules manually updated from the Work Package schedules. This is technically the simplest procedure. The advantage of having two separate schedules is the ability of the Project Manager to provide a tight schedule, with a small Tolerance at Stage level, which allows the Project Manager to pressure contractors to supply Products earlier than indicated by the Project Plan. Also, different people may manage each schedule.

- All Project, Stage and Work Package products and activities could be entered into and managed as one schedule and, if resourced, share a resource pool. This situation is beneficial when one person is updating all the levels of schedule.

- The Stage and Project schedules could be separate schedules and the Stage could be inserted into the Project schedule. In this Master Project and Subproject environment, resources may be shared from a Resource pool. This method only should be attempted once a scheduler has a high level of experience with Microsoft Project, as this is not a simple process to administer.

- **Microsoft Project Server** could be implemented when the project personnel are in different locations or access is required over the Internet by subcontractors.

3   CREATING PROJECTS AND SETTING UP THE SOFTWARE

Ensure to check the Internet for the latest software updates, as some critical functions such as Outlining did not perform correctly in the original release of Microsoft Project 2003.

There are three principal methods of creating a new project:

- Start with a blank project, or

- Use a template that contains default data and formats, or

- Open an old project and save it with a new file name.

Before creating a project file it is important to understand the file types that Microsoft Project will open and save.

3.1   File Types

Microsoft Project is compatible and will operate with the following file types:

- **Microsoft Project (*.mpp)**. This is the default file format for Microsoft Project 2007,
  - ➢ Microsoft Project 98, 2000, 2002 and 2003 will not open or save a **Project (*.mpp)** file created by Microsoft Project 2007.

- **Microsoft Project 2000 – 2003 (*.mpp)**. This is the default file format for Microsoft Project 2000, 2002 and 2003. This is a different format than the ***.mpp** file created by Microsoft Project 2007 and Microsoft Project 98.
  - ➢ Microsoft Project 2007 may open and save to this format.

 When a project file is saved from 2007 format to 2000 – 2003 format all the calendar notes are lost and each repeating nonwork period becomes an individual nonwork period without the note. See the **CALENDAR** chapter for more detail.

- **Microsoft Project 98 (*.mpp)**. This is the format created by Microsoft Project 98.
  - ➢ Microsoft Project 98 will not open or save a **Project (*.mpp)** file created by Microsoft Project 2000, 2002, 2003 and 2007.
  - ➢ Microsoft Project 2000, 2002 and 2003 will open and save to a **Microsoft Project 98 (*.mpp)** file.
  - ➢ Microsoft Project 2007 will not save to a **Microsoft Project 98 (*.mpp)** file.

- **MPX (*.mpx)**. This is a text format data file created by Microsoft Project 98 and earlier versions of Microsoft Project.
  - ➢ This format may be opened by Microsoft Project 2000 – 2003 and 2007 but cannot be created by Microsoft Project 2000, 2002, 2003 and 2007.
  - ➢ mpx is a format that may be imported and exported by many other project scheduling software packages.
  - ➢ Some third-party software will convert mpx files to and from Microsoft Project 2000 – 2003 mpp format files. You may search the Internet for the latest available products.

- **Template (*.mpt)**. This format is used for creating project templates.

- **Project Database (*.mpd)**. This is a Microsoft Project database format that may be used for exporting data and is intended to replace the mpx format in Microsoft Project 2000 – 2003, but is not available in Microsoft Project 2007.

- **Microsoft Access Database (*.mdb)**. This is the Microsoft Access format in Microsoft Project 2000 – 2003 that is not available in Microsoft Project 2007.

- Data may be saved to (and imported from) files in the following additional formats using **File/Save**, **File/Save As** and **File/Open**:
  - ➢ Excel (*.xls)
  - ➢ Excel **Pivot Table** (save only)
  - ➢ Web page (save only) (*.html; *.htm)
  - ➢ Tab delimited text files (*.txt)
  - ➢ Comma delimited text files (*.csv)

- **XML format (*.xml)**. Introduced in Microsoft Project 2002, this enables files to be saved in XML (eXtended Markup Language) format allowing data to be shared with other applications.

3.2   Starting Microsoft Project 2000 – 2003

When opening Microsoft Project 2000 – 2003, you will be presented with a blank project that you may start working with immediately. The **Startup Task** pane shown in the picture below with a heading **Getting Started** may be displayed on the left-hand side of the screen; this may be closed by clicking on the icon ☒ as shown below, and you may start work immediately.

Close the **Startup Task** pane by clicking here

Getting Started menu

Getting Started pane

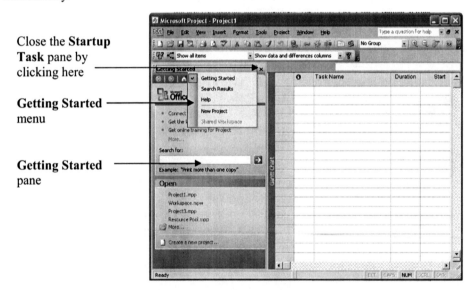

To prevent the pane titled **Getting Started** from being displayed every time Microsoft Project is opened select **Tools**, **Options…**, select the **General** tab and uncheck the **Show Startup Task pane** box.

3.3   Starting Microsoft Office Project 2007

After closing the **Getting Started** pane in Microsoft Project 2000 – 2003 or opening Microsoft Office Project 2007, your screen may look like the picture below showing a pane on the left-hand side titled **Tasks**. This is the called the **Project Guide**. This guide may be used to assist in the creation of project schedules.

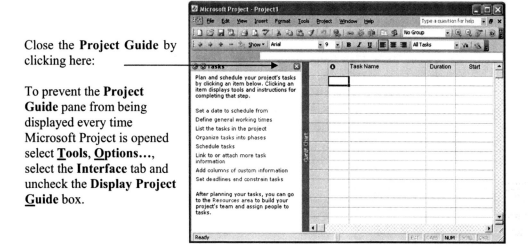

Close the **Project Guide** by clicking here:

To prevent the **Project Guide** pane from being displayed every time Microsoft Project is opened select **Tools, Options…**, select the **Interface** tab and uncheck the **Display Project Guide** box.

3.4   Creating a Blank Project

A blank project may be created from the **New Project** pane, which is displayed by:

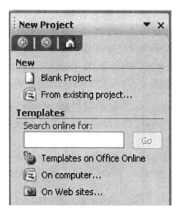

- Keying in **Ctrl+N**, or

- Clicking on the **New** toolbar icon, or

- Selecting **File**, **New**, or

- Selecting **New Project** from the **Startup Task** drop-down menu in Microsoft Project 2000 – 2003, see picture on the previous page. Select **Blank Project** and a new blank project will be created.

At this point the Project **Start date** is normally set in the **Project Information** form. Select **Project, Project Information…** to open this form:

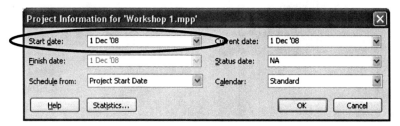

- The **Project Information** form may be set to be displayed when a new project is created by selecting **Tools**, **Options**, **General** tab and checking the **Prompt for project info for new projects** check box.

- When **Schedule from:** is set to the **Project Start Date**, which is the usual method of scheduling projects:
  - ➢ Enter the **Start date:** – This is the date before which no task will be scheduled to start.
  - ➢ The **Finish date:** – This is a calculated date and is the date of the completion of all tasks.

- When **Schedule from:** is set to the **Project Finish Date**:
  - ➢ All new tasks are set with a constraint of **As Late As Possible**, and
  - ➢ Therefore, all new tasks are scheduled before the **Project Finish Date** and not after the start date which is now calculated by the software.

- **Current Date:** – This field defaults to **today's date**; it represents the date today and may be changed at any time. This date has no effect on most calculations and reverts back to the system date each time a schedule is opened.

> As the Current Date will revert back to the system date each time a schedule is opened it is suggested that this date not be used for identifying the **Data Date**.

- **Status Date:** – This is an optional field used when statusing a project. This topic is covered in the **TRACKING PROGRESS** chapter.

- **Calendar:** – This is the project **Base** calendar that is used to calculate the durations of all tasks unless they have:
  - ➢ A resource with an edited resource calendar, or
  - ➢ A different task calendar assigned.

- **Priority:** – This is the project priority when sharing resources over a number of projects. 1000 is highest priority and 0 the lowest.

- Click on the ⬛ Statistics... button to open the **Project Statistics** form, which outlines statistical information about the project.

A new blank project copies default values such as the Standard Calendar from the **Global.mpt** file. The **Global.mpt** file may be edited using the **Tools, Organizer...** utility.

> The default Microsoft Project 2007 blank project has a Standard calendar based on 5 days per week without any holidays, which will not suit many projects. It is recommended that the **Global.mpt** Standard calendar be replaced with a project calendar that has been edited to represent your local public holidays using the **Tools, Organizer...** utility or consider using Templates to create new projects which have had the calendar edited to suit your organization's work periods.

3.5   *Opening an Existing Project*

Another method of creating a new project is to open an existing project, saving with a new name and then modifying it. To open an existing project display the **Open** form by selecting:

- **File**, **Open**, or

- **Ctl+O**, or

- Click on the New
  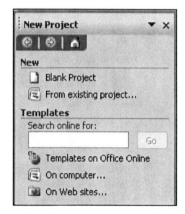 toolbar icon

Then select the file you want to open.

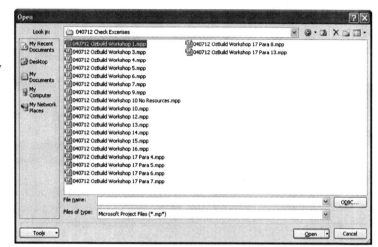

The **New Project** form may be used to open an existing project:

- Select **File**, **New** and this will always display the startup **Task Pane** menu,
  - ➢ Then select the **Choose project...** item under the **New from existing project** heading, or
  - ➢ Select **More projects...** item under the **Open a project** heading.

Then use **File**, **Save As** to save the file under a different name:
- ➢ Enter a new Project Name,
- ➢ Select in which **Current Folder** you want to save the project, and
- ➢ Click on [**Save**] to save the new project.

You may now alter the contents of this existing plan to reflect the scope of your new project.

3.6   Creating a New Project from a Template

Project templates allow organizations to create project models containing default information applicable to the organization and, in particular, a calendar with the local public holidays. It is normal for organizations to create their own templates to save time when creating a new project.

To create a new project from a template:
- Select **File**, **New** to open the startup **Task Pane**. There are three options for template locations:
  - ➤ **Templates on Office Online**, this will take you to a Microsoft web page through Microsoft Explorer.
  - ➤ **On my computer...**, this will allow you to open templates on your computer and is covered in the next paragraph.
  - ➤ **On my Web sites...**, this opens an Explorer-style window where web site addresses may be recorded and templates from these sites used to create projects and templates saved to the sites.
- Click on the **On my computer...**, item under the **New from template** heading to open the **Templates** form to select a Microsoft template. After you have created your own templates these will be available from the **General** tab.

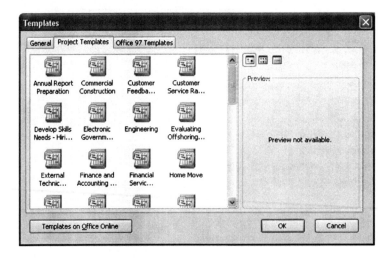

- Select the required template from the form by double-clicking on the template icon or selecting the template by clicking on it and clicking on the ☐ OK ☐ button.

At this point you would normally set the Project **Start date** in the **Project Information** form. Select **Project**, **Project Information...** to open this form.

3.7 Creating a Project Template

To save time when you create new projects, you should create your own templates to suit the different types of projects your organization undertakes. Create a template by saving a project, with or without tasks, in **Template (*.mpt)** format. This template will be available when you select **File**, **New**.

This directory where user templates are saved may be changed by selecting the **Tools**, **Options…**, **Save** tab.

Templates may be deleted by right-clicking to open a menu.

3.8 Saving Additional Project Information

Often additional information about a project is required to be saved with the project such as location, client and type of project. This data may be saved in the **File**, **Properties** form:

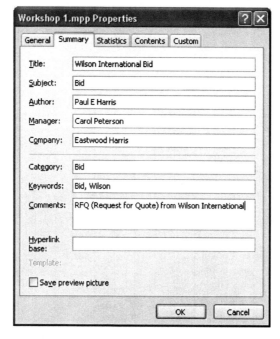

- **Hyperlink base:** This allows you to enter the path to a file or web page.

- **Save preview picture**. This saves a thumbnail sketch, which may be seen when viewing files in Windows Explorer.

WORKSHOP 1

Creating Our Project

Background

You are an employee of OzBuild Pty Ltd and are responsible for planning the Bid preparation required to ensure that a response to an RFQ (Request For Quote) from Wilson International is submitted on time.

While short-listed, you have been advised that the RFQ will not be available prior to 1 December 2008.

NOTE: The date format will be displayed according to a combination of your system default settings and the Microsoft Project Options settings. You may adjust your date format under the system Control Panel, Regional and Language Options and the Microsoft Project settings in the Options form, which is covered in the **OPTIONS** chapter.

Assignment

1. Create a new project and set the **Start date:** to **Mon 01 Dec 08** with the **Project, Project Information...** form but do not edit the **Current date**. Press the **OK** button to save the input data.

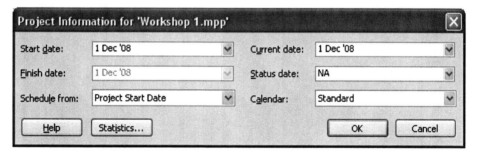

continued over...

NOTE: Completed workshops may be downloaded from the Eastwood Harris web site at www.eh.com.au.

2.   Add the following project information in the **File**, **Properties** form.

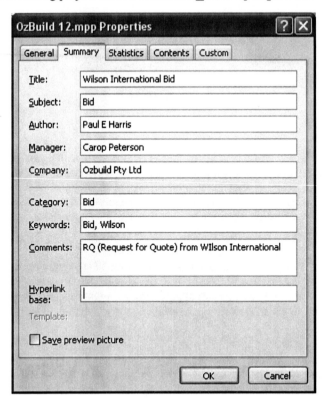

3.   **S**ave your project as **OzBuild Bid**.

4 NAVIGATING AROUND THE SCREEN

4.1 Identify the Parts of the Project Screen

After a blank project has been created from a template, the default Microsoft Project 2007 screen will look like this:

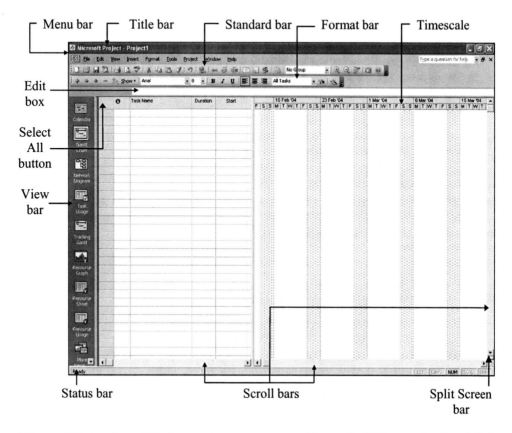

Microsoft Project has a Windows-style menu system with a typical Windows look-and-feel.

- The project name is displayed after **Microsoft Project** at the top of the left-hand side of the screen.

- The drop-down menus are just below the project name.

- The toolbars are displayed below the menu.

- The left-hand side of the line underneath the toolbars is the **Entry Bar** and **Edit Box**. Any editable data may be edited in the **Edit Box** or directly in the field.

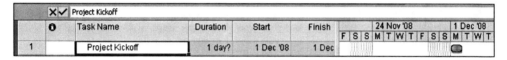

The ⬛ and ⊠ icons are displayed on the left of the **Edit Box** only when performing editing, and may be used for accepting and not accepting data changes that are made from within the edit box.

- The main display has the **Bar Chart** or **Gantt Chart** on the right-hand side, with the **Timescale** above, and the **Data Columns** on the left-hand side with their column titles above them. The divider between the two areas may be dragged from side to side by holding down the left mouse button.

- The **View Bar** displays the same options as the **View** menu and is located on the far left of the screen. This may be hidden or displayed by:

  ➢ Selecting **View**, **View Bar**, or
  ➢ Holding the mouse pointer over the **View Bar**, right-clicking to display a menu, and selecting **View Bar**.

- The horizontal **Scroll Bars** are at the bottom of the screen and the **Status Bar** is below the **Scroll Bars**. The vertical **Scroll Bar** is at the right-hand side of the screen.

It is recommended screens to hide the **View Bar** when using computers with small as it consumes valuable screen space that is often better utilized showing project data.

4.2 Customizing the Screen

The screen may be customized in a number of ways to suit your preferences. The toolbars and menu bar may be moved around the screen by holding down the right mouse button and dragging them to a new position on the screen.

4.2.1 Toolbars

Toolbars will not be covered in detail but significant productivity improvements may be made by ensuring that functions frequently used are available on a toolbar.

- There are many built-in toolbars in Microsoft Project. These may be displayed or hidden by:

  ➢ Using the command **View**, **Toolbar** or **Tools**, **Customize**, **Toolbars...** and selecting the **Toolbar** tab, then checking or un-checking the required boxes to display or hide the toolbars, or
  ➢ Right-clicking the mouse in the toolbar area to display a Toolbar menu.

- Icons may be added to a bar by selecting **Tools**, **Customize**, **Toolbars...**, **Commands** tab. **Toolbar Icons** may be selected from the dialog box and dragged onto any toolbar.

- Icons may be removed from the toolbars after the **Customize** (Toolbar) form is opened by holding down the left mouse button on the icon and dragging them off the toolbar.

- Icons may be reset to default by selecting **Tools**, **Customize**, **Toolbars...**, selecting the **Toolbar** tab and clicking on Reset....

- Other toolbar display options are found under **Tools**, **Customize**, **Toolbars...** and then selecting the **Options** tab.

It is recommended to check the **Always show full menus** option in the **Tools**, **Customize**, **Toolbars...**, **Options** tab to ensure full menus are always displayed. This saves time waiting for the menu item you require to be displayed.

4.2.2 Menu Bar

The **Menu Bar** display options are found under **Tools**, **Customize**, **Toolbars...** and then selecting the **Options** tab.

4.3 Setting up the Options

The basic parameters of the software must be configured so it will operate the way you desire. In order for the software to operate and/or calculate the way you want, some of the defaults must be turned on, or off, or changed. These configuration items may be found under **Tools, Options…**.

We will discuss some of the more important options now. All the Options are discussed in the **OPTIONS** chapter. Select **Tools, Options…** to display the **Options** form.

Select the **View** tab:

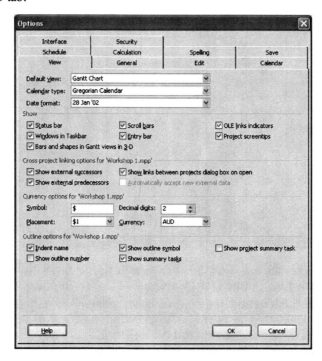

- **Date format:** This is used to select the display style of the dates for all projects. The date format will be displayed according to a combination of your system default settings and the Microsoft Project Options settings. You may adjust your date format under the system Control Panel, Regional and Language Options and the Microsoft Project settings in the Options form, which are covered in the **OPTIONS** chapter.

 There is often confusion on international projects between the numerical US date style, mmddyy and the numerical European date style, ddmmyy. For example, in the United States 020710 is read as 07 Feb 10 and in many other countries as 02 Jul 10. Consider always adopting the ddmmmyy style, **06 Jan '07** or mmmddyy style, **Jan 06 '07**.

- Select the **Schedule** tab:

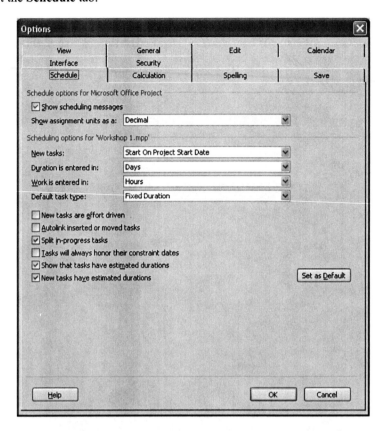

- **New tasks:** - When the option of **Start on Current Date** is selected new tasks are assigned an Early Start constraint as they are added to the schedule.

 It is not desirable to have activities assigned constraints as they are created in a Critical Path schedule, therefore Start On Project Start Date should always be selected when creating a Critical Path schedule.

- **Duration is entered in:** – This option specifies the format in which durations are entered via the keyboard. If **Day** is selected as the default, then a duration of 2 days is entered as 2 (without the d). If **Hours** is selected as the default, then a 2-hour duration should be entered as 2h.

- It is important that both the **Autolink inserted or moved tasks** and the **Tasks will always honor their constraint dates** are both unchecked.

  ➤ **Autolink inserted or moved tasks** option will result in relationships being changed when tasks are dragged to another position.

  ➤ **Tasks will always honor their constraint dates** results in the possibility of tasks being scheduled earlier than it is technically possible.

4.4 Splitting the Screen Views and Details Forms

The screen may be split horizontally into two panes. A different **View** may be displayed in each pane. This is termed **Dual-Pane view**. To open or close the dual-pane view:

- Select **Window**, **Split** or **Window**, **Remove Split**, or

- Grab the horizontal dividing bar at the bottom of the screen (see the picture in paragraph 4.1) by holding down the left mouse button and dragging the line to resize the panes.

- Right-click in the right-hand side of the top pane and you will, in most views, be able to display a menu to open or remove the split.

- Double-click the dividing line or drag it to also remove or open the split window.

Active pane has dark band

Grab this line with the mouse to split and resize the screen

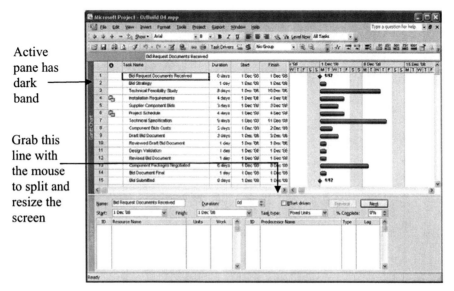

A pane needs to be **Active** before menu items pertaining to that pane become available. A dark blue band (with the standard Windows color scheme) on the left-hand side is displayed in the **Active Pane**.

The menu options will often change when different **Views** are selected in a pane.

A **Pane** is made **Active** just by:

- Clicking anywhere in the pane, or

- Pressing **F6** to swap active panes.

Not all panes may be printed and only the **Active Pane** may be printed, thus it is not possible to create a printout with a Gantt Chart and a Resource Sheet (Table) or Graphs (Histograms) with Microsoft Project.

Some **Views** displayed in **Panes** have further options for displaying data. These are titled **Details** forms. The **Details** forms may be selected, when available, by:

- Making the pane active, then

- Selecting:
  - ➢ **Format**, **Details**, or
  - ➢ Right-clicking in the right-hand side of the screen and clicking the required form.

The example below is for the **Task Information** form:

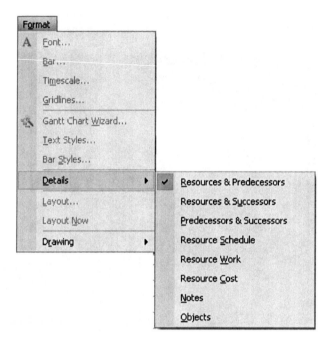

4.5   Right-clicking with the Mouse

It is very important that you become used to using the right-click function of the mouse as this is often a quicker way of operating the software than using the menus. The right-click will normally display a menu, which is often different depending on the displayed View and which pane is the Active Pane. It is advised that you experiment with each view to become familiar with the menus.

WORKSHOP 2

Setting Your Project Options

Background

For control purposes it is expected that all tasks will be entered in days.

Assignment
1. Select **Tools**, **Options...** and open the **Project Options** form. Click on each tab and familiarize yourself with the forms. set your options as follows:
    ➢ Select **View** tab, set the **Date format** to:
       1. "**ddmmmyy**" i.e., 28 Jan '02, or
       2. "**mmmddyy**" i.e., Jan 28 '02.
       The available date format will depend on your system settings.
    ➢ Select the Schedule tab and set the Schedule Options as per the picture below:

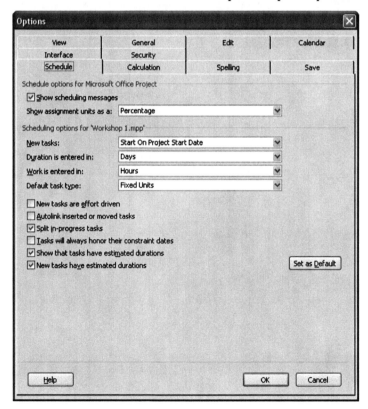

Continued over....

2. Hide and display the **Standard** and **Formatting** toolbars using the **View** menu.

3. To ensure full menus are always displayed (and thus save time waiting for the menu item you require to be displayed) check the **Always show full menus** option in the under **Tools**, **Customize**, **Toolbars…**, **Options** tab.

4. Experiment by dragging the toolbars around the screen with your mouse.

5. Hide and display the **View** bar by selecting **View**, **View Bar**.

6. Split the screen into two panes by right-clicking with the mouse in the right-hand side of the screen, and selecting **Split** from the menu.

7. Activate the lower pane by clicking in it; note the blue bar (or a different shade of bar if you do not have the default Windows colors) on the left-hand side of the screen has moved from the top pane to the bottom pane.

8. Activate the upper pane, by clicking in it.

9. Resize the panes by dragging the Split screen bar.

10. Close the Split screen by double-clicking on the horizontal dividing line.

11. Split the screen by double-clicking on the small bar in the bottom right-hand corner of the screen.

12. Save your **OzBuild Bid** Project.

5   DEFINING CALENDARS

The finish date (and time) of a task is calculated from the start date (and time) plus the duration over the calendar associated with the task. Therefore, a five-day duration task that starts at the start of the work day on a Wednesday, and is associated with a five-day workweek calendar (with Saturday and Sunday as nonwork days) will finish at the end of the workday on the following Tuesday.

Microsoft Project is supplied with three calendars, which are termed **Base Calendar**s:

- **Standard** – This calendar is 5 days per week, 8 hours per day.

- **24 Hour** – This calendar is 7 days per week and 24 hours per day.

- **Night shift** – This calendar is 7 days per week and 8 hours per day during the night.

You may create new or edit existing Base Calendars to reflect your project requirements, such as adding holidays or additional work days or adjusting work times. For example, some tasks may have a 5-day per week calendar and some may have a 7-day per week calendar.

A **Base Calendar** is assigned to each project. Microsoft Project uses the term **Project Calendar** to describe this calendar. By default all un-resourced tasks use the **Project Calendar** to calculate the end date of the task. Any un-resourced task may be assigned a different calendar and the end date will be calculated using the assigned calendar.

This chapter will cover the following topics:

Topic	Menu Command
• Assigning a base calendar to a project	**P**roject, **P**roject Information…
• Editing a calendar's working days	**T**ools, C**h**ange Working Time…
• Creating a new calendar	**T**ools, C**h**ange Working Time…, N**e**w…
• Renaming an existing calendar	**T**ools, **O**rganizer…, **Calendars** tab, Re**n**ame…
• Deleting a calendar	**T**ools, **O**rganizer…, **Calendars** tab, **Delete**
• Copying a calendar to Global.mpt for use in future projects	**T**ools, **O**rganizer…, **Calendars** tab, **C**opy >>
• Copying calendars between projects	**T**ools, **O**rganizer…, **Calendars** tab, **C**opy >>

Microsoft Project 2007 introduces significant changes in the way calendars are created and edited and which now allows for each non-default work period to have a name or note explaining the purpose of the non-default work period. These periods could be due to holidays or changes to working hours for a planned shutdown or system upgrade requiring people to work different or longer hours.

5.1   Assigning a Calendar to a Project

In all versions of Microsoft Project a new blank project is assigned the **Standard** calendar as the **Project Calendar** when the project file is created. The **Project Calendar** is changed using the **Project Information** form by:

- Selecting **P**roject, **P**roject Information…, and

- Selecting the alternative calendar from the **Ca**lendar: drop-down box:

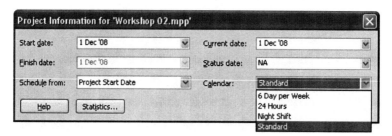

The **Project Calendar** is identified in the **Change Working Time** form as the calendar with **(Project Calendar)** written after the calendar name. The forms below are from Microsoft Project 2007 and from Microsoft Project 2000 – 2003 and they are different. This book will explain both versions.

Microsoft Project 2007   **Microsoft Project 2000 – 2003**

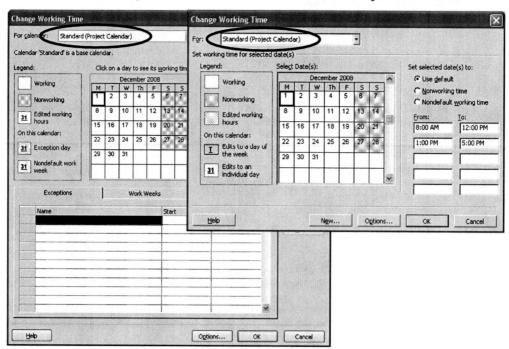

> *i*   When a **Project Calendar** is changed or edited, the end date of all tasks assigned with the **Project Calendar** will be recalculated based on the new calendar. This may make a considerable difference to your project schedule dates.

5.2 Editing Calendars in Microsoft Office Project 2007

5.2.1 Editing Working Days

To edit a calendar, select **Tools**, **Change Working Time...** to open the **Change Working Time** form:

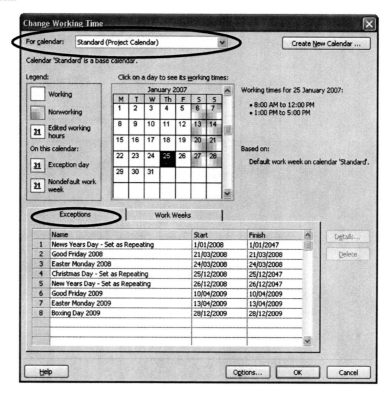

- Select the calendar to be edited from the **For calendar:** drop-down list at the top of the form,

- Click on the **Exceptions** tab and highlight the days to be made nonwork days,

- To make **Nonwork Days** into **Work Days**, add the following information in the first blank line in the lower half of the form:

  ➢ Name of the Nonwork Day,
  ➢ The Start Date, and
  ➢ The Finish Date

  The Start and Finish Dates of a one-day holiday are identical.

- When the Holiday is Recurring, such as the annual Christmas Day and New Year's Day, these days may be made recurring by clicking on the Details... button to open the calendar **Details:**

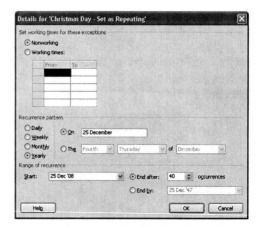

  > In the **Recurrence pattern** set the occurrence of the holiday to use the Daily, Weekly, Monthly or Yearly options. The options are displayed below:

Daily

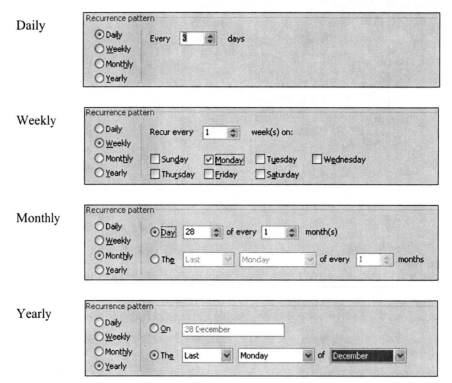

Weekly

Monthly

Yearly

  > The **Range of recurrence** option allows the specification of the number of times the holiday occurs up to the year 2049. The picture below shows Christmas Day is scheduled for the next 40 years.

Daily

i The author found by experimentation that only single day nonwork periods could be made repeating. This problem may be rectified with patches.

5.2.2 Adjusting Calendar Default Working Hours

To adjust the standard working hours of a calendar:

- Select **Tools**, **Change Working Time…** to open the **Change Working Time** form:

- Select the calendar to be edited from the **For calendar:** drop-down list,

- Click on the **Work Weeks** tab,

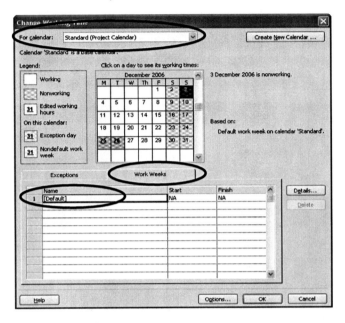

- Select the **[Default]** line in the **Work Weeks** tab,

- Click on the **Details…** button to open the **Details for 'Calendar'** form,

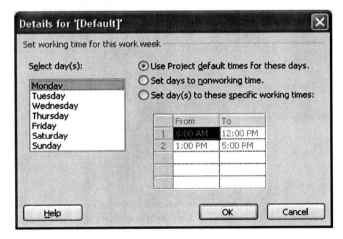

- Days that are to be set the same working hours may be **Ctrl-Clicked** or **Dragged** to select them,

- The working hours for select day/s may be edited in the **From** and **To** cells on the right of the form.

5.2.3 Creating Calendar Periods with Alternate Working Hours

This **Work Weeks** tab may be used to create a period of one or more days where the working hours are different from the default working hours. Longer working hours may be required during a system upgrade or shutdown period. To create a period with different working hours from the default:

- Select the calendar that is required to have a special work period. The example below uses the Standard calendar,

- Select the **Work Week** tab,

- Select the first blank line in the **Workweek** tab and type in the description of the period. The example below has a unique set of working hours for a February Shutdown,

- Enter the Start and Finish dates of the period in the **Workweek** tab,

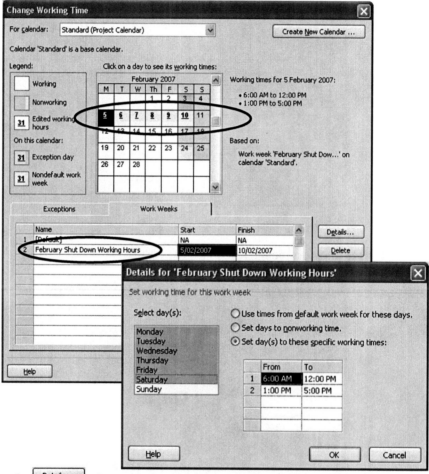

- Click on the [D̲etails...] tab to open the **Calendar, Details for 'Calendar'** form,

- Select the days to be edited by dragging with the mouse pointer or **Ctl Clicking**,

- Click on the appropriate radio button and edit the hours as required:

> *i* When this option is used and the hours per day are not the same for each day then the durations displayed in days may not be correct. Options to manage this issue is discussed later in this chapter

5.3   Editing Calendars in Microsoft Project 2000 – 2003

5.3.1   Editing Working Days

To edit a calendar, select **Tools, Change Working Time…** to open the **Change Working Time** form:

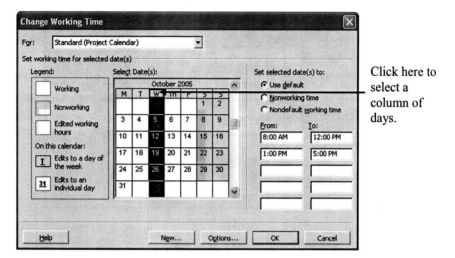

- To make **Work Days** into **Nonwork Days**, highlight the day(s) you want to edit:
  - ➢ Click on an individual day, or
  - ➢ Ctrl-click to select multiple days, or
  - ➢ Click and drag to select multiple days, or
  - ➢ Click on a column or columns of days by clicking the day of the week box, which is located below the month and year,
  - ➢ Then click on the **Nonworking time** radio button to make these days Nonworking.
- To make **Nonwork Days** into **Work Days**, highlight the day(s) you want to edit as described in the paragraph above and then click on the **Nondefault working time** radio button to make these days working days.

5.3.2   Adjusting Working Hours

To adjust the working hours of one or more days:

- Open the **Change Working Time** form,
- Highlight the days you want to edit, and
- Edit the working hours in the **From:** and **To:** section on the right-hand side of the screen.

There are some workable options to ensure that the durations in days are calculated and/or displayed correctly:

- All the calendars used on a project schedule should have the same number of hours per day for each day. This value is entered in the **Hours per day:** field in the Options form below. Then all durations in days will calculate correctly.

- When there is a requirement to use a different number of hours per day (in either the same calendar or in different calendars) then all durations should only be displayed in hours and the Task Calendar displayed, as per the picture above. Two examples of how this may occur are when:

  ➢ There is an 8-hour working day Monday to Friday and a 4-hour working day on Saturday, or
  ➢ Different calendars are required on a project, for example when some activities are assigned an 8-hour per day calendar and some a 24-hour per day calendar.

  Then the **Duration is entered in:** field in the **Tools**, **Options**, **Edit** tab should be set to **Hours**.

- A Customized Field may be used to calculate and display the correct duration by using a formula. The example below uses the **Duration1** field to calculate and display the correct duration in days of a 24-hour per day calendar using a formula.

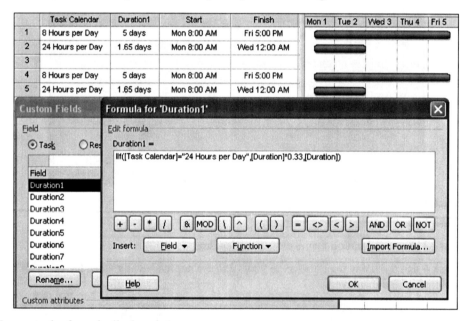

To create the formula displayed above:

- Select **Tools**, **Customize**, **Fields…** to open the **Custom Fields** form,

- Select **Duration 1** from the **Type** drop-down box in the top left-hand side of the form,

- Click on the [Formula…] button to open the **Formula** form and enter the formula as required.

- The formula in the picture above will work for a schedule that has two calendars in use.

- The formula above is

  IIf([Task Calendar]="24 Hours per Day",[Duration]*0.33,[Duration])

To display durations in hours:

- The **Duration is entered in:** field in the **Tools**, **Options**, **Edit** tab should be set to **Hours** and then

- Existing durations in days are changed to hours by overtyping the original durations.

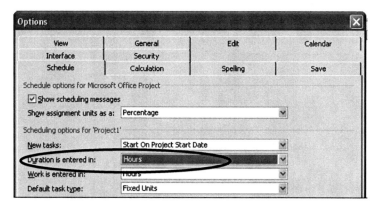

5.6 Understanding Default Start and Default End Time

The **Default start time:** and **Default end time:** are the times that the software uses when a date is entered and a time is not entered. These times should be aligned to the **Project** calendar and they are used in Microsoft Project when:

- Constraints are assigned to tasks, and

- Actual Start or Actual Finish Dates are assigned.

These times are set in the **Options, Calendar** which may be accessed by:

- Clicking the [Options...] button from the **Change working time** form, or

- Selecting the **Tools, Options, Calendar** tab:

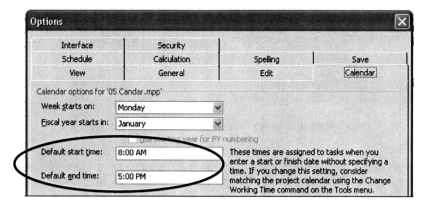

If these times are not aligned then tasks may be displayed one day longer than the duration as per the picture below, where the calendar start time is 8:00am and the Default start time is 9:00am.

5.7 Effect on 2007 Calendars When Saving to 2000 – 2003

When a project file is saved from 2007 format to 2000 – 2003 format all the calendar notes are lost and each repeating nonwork period becomes an individual nonwork period without the note. The pictures below show the effect before and after saving to 2000 – 2003 format and then reopening with 2007:

Before saving to 2000 – 2003 format

	Name	Start	Finish
1	New Years Day	1/01/2006	1/01/2045
2	Easter 2006	14/04/2006	17/04/2006
3	Christmas Day	25/12/2006	25/12/2045
4	Boxing Day	26/12/2006	26/12/2045
5	Easter 2008	21/03/2007	24/03/2007
6	Easter 2007	6/04/2007	9/04/2007
7	Easter 2009	10/04/2009	13/04/2009
8	Christmas 2009	28/12/2009	28/12/2009

After saving to 2000 – 2003 format

	Name	Start	Finish
1	[Unnamed]	1/01/2006	1/01/2006
2	[Unnamed]	14/04/2006	17/04/2006
3	[Unnamed]	25/12/2006	25/12/2006
4	[Unnamed]	26/12/2006	26/12/2006
5	[Unnamed]	1/01/2007	1/01/2007
6	[Unnamed]	21/03/2007	24/03/2007
7	[Unnamed]	6/04/2007	9/04/2007
8	[Unnamed]	25/12/2007	25/12/2007

5.8 Renaming a Calendar

To rename a calendar:

- Select **Tools**, **Organizer...**, and select the **Calendars** tab.

- Highlight the calendar you want to rename and click on the ⎡Re**n**ame...⎤ button to open the **Rename** form and type in the new name.

5.9 Deleting a Calendar

To delete a calendar:

- Select **Tools**, **Organizer...**, and select the **Calendars** tab.

- Highlight the calendar you want to delete and click on the ⎡**D**elete...⎤ button.

5.10 Copying Calendars between Projects

To copy a calendar between projects:

- Open both projects,

- Select **Tools**, **Organizer...**, and select the **Calendars** tab,

- From the drop-down boxes at the bottom of the tab under Calendars available in: select the projects that you want to copy to and from, and

- Select the calendar you want to copy and click on the ⎡**C**opy >>⎤ button.

  To save time when multiple calendars have the same nonwork periods, such as religious holidays, one calendar should be created and all of its nonwork periods entered. Then copy this calendar to create new calendars showing the same nonwork days. .

5.11 Resource Calendars

Individual Resources are allocated a Base Calendar when they are created. The resource Base Calendar may be changed and edited to reflect the availability of the resource. This feature is covered in the **CREATING RESOURCES** chapter.

5.12 Copying a Base Calendar to Global.mpt for Use in Future Projects

Global.mpt is the default project template and all new projects created from a **Blank Project** copy their default settings from the Global.mpt. Once you have set up a calendar with all the holidays for your location or business, it is suggested that you copy it to the Global.mpt.

- Select **Tools**, **Organizer…**, and select the **Calendars** tab.

- Select the **Standard** calendar from your project and click on the [<< Copy] button.

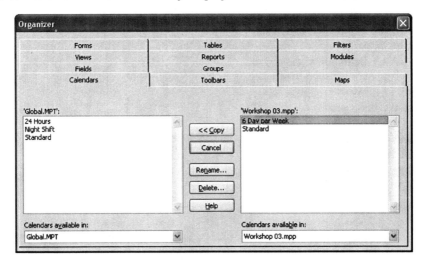

 If more than one person needs to use a tailored calendar, another alternative to copying the calendar to the Global.mpt is to create a template and make this available to all users.

5.13 Selecting Dates

With the introduction of Microsoft Project 2007 there is a slight loss of functionality in selecting dates in a column.

5.13.1 Selecting Calendar Dates in Microsoft Office Project 2007

A calendar form is displayed by clicking on a date cell with the mouse pointer:

- The month may be scrolled forward or backward by clicking on the blue arrows,

- A date is selected by clicking on it, and

- When a date is selected an Early Start Constraint will be set.

5.13.2 Selecting Calendar Dates in Microsoft Project 2000 – 2003

Microsoft Project 2000 – 2003 has a function to enable the user to quickly scroll through days, months and years when editing dates from a column. A calendar form is displayed by clicking on a date cell with the mouse pointer:

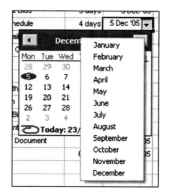

- To change the day, click on the required day.

- To change month either:
  - ➢ Scroll a month at a time by clicking on the arrows on the top left-hand or top right-hand side of the form, or
  - ➢ Click on the month at the top of the form and a drop-down list will be displayed to allow any month of the year to be selected.

- To change the year, click on the year in the top of the form and scrolling arrows will be displayed allowing scrolling one year at a time.

When a date is selected from a column Microsoft Project will set a constraint without informing the user. This may result in an incorrect constraint being set.

5.14 *Printing the Calendar*

It is always useful to be able to print out the calendar for people to review the working hours and Nonwork periods. The options are:

- Display the Calendar View which is discussed in the **VIEWS, TABLES AND DETAILS** chapter, or

- Print a report using the **Report** (**Views** in 2000 – 2003), **Reports…**, **Overview**, **Working Day** report which is preferred by the author.

It is useful to print the report to a pdf format so it may be saved and emailed.

WORKSHOP 3

Maintaining the Calendars

Background

The normal working week at OzBuild Pty Ltd is Monday to Friday, 8 hours per day excluding Public Holidays. The installation staff works Monday to Saturday, 8 hours per day.

Assignment

The company observes the following Australian holidays:

	2007	2008	2009	2010
New Year's Day	1 January	1 January	1 January	1 January
Good Friday	6 April	21 March	10 April	2 April
Easter Monday	9 April	24 March	13 April	5 April
Christmas Day	25 December	25 December	25 December	27 December*
Boxing Day	26 December	26 December	28 December*	28 December*

* These holidays occur on a weekend and the dates in the table above have been moved to the next weekday.

Boxing Day is a religious holiday, the day after Christmas, celebrated in many countries.

Assignment

1. Edit the **Standard Calendar** to ensure that only the holidays above in 2008 and 2009 are present by selecting **Tools, Change Working Time...**, see pictures over the page.
2. Exit the **Calendar** form to save the calendar edits.
3. Create a new calendar titled **6-Day Working Week** for the 6-day week by:

   ➤ Copying the **Standard (Project Calendar),** and then

   ➤ Microsoft Project 2000 – 2003, clicking on the **S** for Saturday in the **Change Working Time** form and then clicking on the **Nondefault working time** radio button to make all Saturdays work days.

   ➤ Microsoft Project 2007, selecting the **Work Weeks** tab, clicking on the ⬚ Details... tab and making Saturdays work days with the same working hours as the other days, see the picture over the page.
4. Save your **OzBuild Bid** project.

Answers over the page......

ANSWERS TO WORKSHOP 3

In the edited **Standard (Project Calendar)** of the **Change Working Time** form below, the dates are displayed in the ROW (Rest of World) date format of dd/mm/yyyy. Computers configured with the US date format will see the dates in the mm/dd/yyyy format.

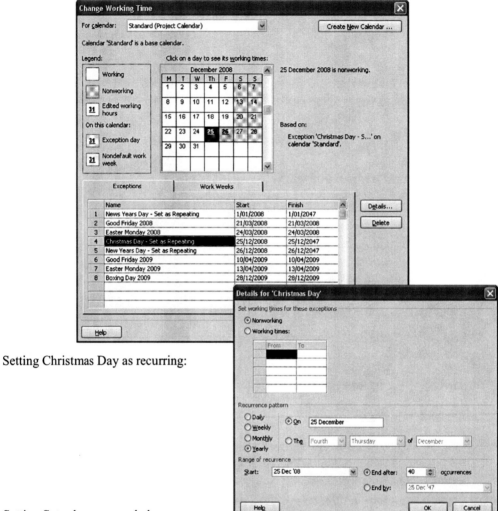

Setting Christmas Day as recurring:

Setting Saturday as a work day:

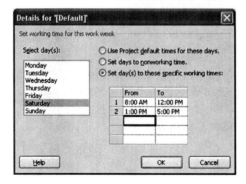

6 ADDING TASKS

The PRINCE2 Planning Process develops the PBS first and the activities second, but it is easier to teach Microsoft Project by showing task addition first and then the PBS.

Tasks, or Activities, should be well-defined, measurable pieces of work with a measurable outcome. Task descriptions containing only nouns such as "Specification" have confusing meanings. Does this mean Draft, Review, Approve, Issue, or all of these? Adequate task descriptions always have a noun-verb structure to them. A more appropriate task description would be "Specification Approved" or "Specification Issued." The limit for task names is 255 characters, but try to keep task descriptions meaningful yet short and concise so they are easier to print.

When tasks are created they may be organized under Summary tasks, which may represent the PRINCE2 Product Breakdown Structure and have logic added to calculate their start and finish dates. Summary or Detailed tasks may be created first and logic added once the relevant tasks have been created.

The creation and sequencing of Detailed and Summary tasks are discussed in the following chapters:

- Creating **Detailed** tasks in this chapter,

- Creating **Summary** tasks, which may represent the WBS Nodes, in the **ORGANIZING TASKS USING OUTLINING** chapter, and

- Adding the logic in the **ADDING THE DEPENDENCIES** chapter.

This chapter will cover the following topics:

Topic	Menu Command
• **Adding New Tasks**	Select a line in the schedule and strike the **Ins (Insert Key)** or click on a blank line.
• **Reordering** tasks	Select and drag the task(s) or cut and paste in the required location.
• **Copying** tasks in Microsoft Project	Select the tasks and copy and paste to the required location.
• **Copying** tasks from other programs	Display the required columns and paste the data.
• **Elapsed** duration tasks	Type "e" after the duration and before the Units, e.g., 5 edays.
• **Milestones**	Assign a zero duration, or Check the **Mark task as milestone** box on the **Advanced** tab in the **Task Information** form.
• **Task Information** form	Double-click anywhere on the task line, or Highlight the task line click on the ▣ button.
• Assigning **Calendars** to tasks	Set a task calendar in the **Advanced** tab in the **Task Information** form or display the **Task Calendar** column.

6.1   Adding New Tasks

Method 1

The first and easiest is to:

- Click on the first blank line under the title **Task Name** and type the task description.

- The duration of the new task is assigned a default duration of 1 day and may have a "?" after to indicate it has been assigned an **Estimated Duration**. Overtyping the default duration with the required duration task will remove the "?".

- The option of assigning and/or displaying a new task with an **Estimated Duration** is controlled in the **Schedule** tab of the **Options** form by checking or un-checking **New tasks have estimated durations**.

Task Name	Duration	Start	Finish	1 Dec S S M T W T F S S
First Task	1 day?	1 Dec '08	1 Dec '08	

- Click into the second row and enter a second Task Name. A sequential **Task Number** starting from "**1**" will be created in the column to the left of the **Task Name**.

Task Name	Duration	Start	Finish	1 Dec S S M T W T F S S
First Task	5 days	1 Dec '08	5 Dec '08	
Second Task	1 day?	1 Dec '08	1 Dec '08	

The task **Start** and **Finish** dates will be calculated from the **Project Start Date** and the task duration. This information is displayed in the **Start** and **Finish** columns.

Understanding Change Highlight

The Second Task in the picture above has the Start and Finish dates highlighted and the First Task no longer does. This is due to the new Microsoft Project 2007 feature titled **Change Highlighting** that highlights any changed dates and durations as a result of an edit, addition or deletion of another task. This function highlights all date and duration fields that will change when another field has been changed.

- The menu **View, Show/Hide Change Highlight** or clicking on the ⬛ icon will hide/display the highlighting.

- Remove the highlighting produced by the last change by:
  - ➢ Pressing the **F9** key which will also recalculate the project, or
  - ➢ Saving the project, or
  - ➢ Entering a value into a changed cell twice.

- To change the color of the highlighting select **Format, Text Styles…** and select **Changed Cells** from the **Item to change** list

This is a very good feature as it highlights changes in date and duration fields of all tasks, thus making it simpler to see what tasks have moved as a result of the change.

Method 2

The second method of adding a task, which is used for inserting a task between two other tasks, is to highlight a task where you want to insert a new task. The highlighted task will be moved down one line after the new task is inserted. Inserting may be achieved by:

- Select **Insert**, **New Task**, or

- Press the **Insert Key** on the keyboard, or

- Highlight the entire task row by clicking on the Task ID, then right-click and select **New task** from the sub-menu.

Task Name	Duration	Start	Finish	1 Dec
First Task	5 days	1 Dec '08	5 Dec '08	
Inserted Task	3 days	1 Dec '08	3 Dec '08	
Second Task	2 days	1 Dec '08	2 Dec '08	

 Do not type a Start or Finish date into the **Start** or **Finish** column unless you want to set a constraint, which may override the logic.

6.2 Reordering Tasks by Dragging

You may move one or more tasks up or down the schedule by:

- Highlighting any one or more adjacent tasks by using the Task ID column; this will ensure you have selected the whole task and not just cells of the task,

- Moving the cursor to the top line of the selected tasks until it changes to an ⊹ icon,

- Then left-clicking and holding down the mouse to drag the row up or down. A gray line will indicate where the tasks will be inserted:

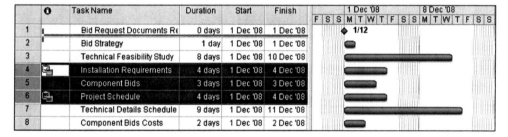

The tasks will be renumbered when in their new location.

6.3 Copying and Pasting Tasks

Tasks may also be copied from another project or copied from within the same project using the normal Windows commands **Copy** and **Paste**, by using the menu commands **Edit**, **Copy Task** and **Edit**, **Paste** or **Ctrl+C** and **Ctrl+V**.

You may also copy one or more adjacent tasks by using the **Ctrl Key** and dragging as follows:

- Select the whole task or tasks, not just a cell,

- Hold down the **Ctrl Key**, and

- Drag the tasks to the location you want to insert them. This will create a copy of the original tasks.

6.4   Copying Tasks from Other Programs

Task data may be copied to and from, or updated from other programs such as Excel, by cutting and pasting. The columns and rows in your spreadsheet will need to be formatted in the same way as in your schedule before they may be pasted into your schedule.

It is recommended that you first display the data columns that you want to import or update in your schedule. If you have no tasks then create a dummy task and data, then copy and paste this dummy data into your spreadsheet, update the data and paste it back into the schedule. The data headings are not brought across from the schedule; therefore it is also recommended that you type the column headings into the spreadsheet above the imported data, which will assist you in typing the data in the correct columns.

When you copy and paste dates into the schedule, you may find that activities are assigned constraints, which you may not desire. It is recommended that you display the **Indicators** column, which will show an icon if a constraint has been applied. There is no warning message that these constraints have been set, except when using Windows XP and a Graphical Indicator or Smart Tag that will warn you that a constraint has been set.

6.5   Dynamically Linking Cells to Other Programs

It is also possible to dynamically link data to other programs such as an Excel spreadsheet:

- Copy the data from the spreadsheet,

- Select the cell position in the table where the data is to be pasted in Microsoft Project,

- Select <u>E</u>dit, **Paste Special** and then select the **Paste Link** and **Text Data** options,

- The data will be pasted into the cell(s) and changes to linked cell in the spreadsheet or other program will be reflected in the Microsoft Project schedule.

- The linked cell will have a little triangle in the bottom right-hand side indicating that the cell is linked. The top three cells in the picture below are linked.

		Task Name	Duration	Start
		Component Bids Costs	6 days	1 Dec '08
		Revised Bid Document	1 day	20 Dec '06

Little triangle

- Be careful when linking dates as this sets constraints. Because the Start date is linked in the picture above this task also has a constraint which indicated by the ▦ in the indicator column.

- When reopening the project schedule at a later date you will be asked if you wish to refresh the data from the other application.

- To remove a link delete or change the data in the cell.

- To open the linked document double-click on the little triangle in the bottom left-hand side of the cell.

It is also possible to link one or more cells in a schedule with another cell in the same schedule so a change in one cell will change all the other linked cell(s) using the **Paste Link** option.

6.6   Task Information Form

The Task Information form may be opened by double-clicking on a task line, or by clicking on the ▣ button when the task is highlighted, or right-clicking, or Shift+F2. You are able to make changes to a number of task parameters from this form. Once the form is open, it is not possible to move to another task without closing the form. There are several tabs on the form:

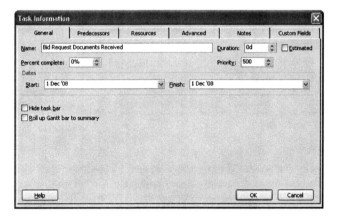

- **General** – This form contains the basic information about a task:
  - ➢ The **Estimated** check box is used to indicate the task has an **Estimated Duration**. The task duration will be displayed with a "?" which disappears when a duration is entered against a task.
  - ➢ **Priority** is used in resource leveling. 1000 is the highest and 0 the lowest.
  - ➢ The **Bar** options are covered in the **Formatting Bars** section.

- **Predecessors** – This is where the task's predecessors are displayed. This is covered in the **ADDING THE DEPENDENCIES** chapter.

- **Resources** – This is where resources may be created, assigned to tasks and assignment information displayed. This topic is covered in the **RESOURCES** chapters.

- **Advanced** – Options are covered in the **CONSTRAINTS** chapter.

- **Notes** – This is where notes about a task may be recorded.

- **Custom Fields** – Any **Custom Fields** that have been customized will be displayed in this tab. They are existing but undefined fields that may be customized by selecting **Tools**, **Customize**, **Fields…**. These fields may hold different types of project information such as text, times, values, etc. There are options to define how these fields are summarized at the summary activity level and may be assigned formulae to calculate their values.

- When multiple tasks are selected then the task form may be opened by right-clicking and some of the attributes of all the tasks may be edited at the same time.

6.7   Indicators Column

The **Indicators** column, which has an ⓘ icon in the column header, will display an icon in the column when a task contains a non-default setting such as a Note, Constraint, or a Task calendar. Placing the mouse over the icon will display information about the task.

6.8 Elapsed Durations

A task may be assigned an **Elapsed** duration. The task will ignore all calendars and the task will take place 24 hours a day and 7 days per week. A 24-hour, 7-day per week calendar does not need to be created for these tasks. This is useful for tasks such as curing concrete but the Total Float will calculate three times longer than a task on an 8-hour a day calendar and this may be misleading.

To enter an elapsed duration, type an "**e**" between the duration and units. The example below shows the difference between a 7-**Elapsed Day** task and a 7-day task on a **Standard** (5 day per week) calendar.

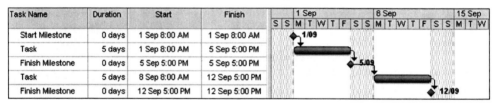

6.9 Milestones

A Milestone normally has a zero duration and is used to mark the start or finish of a major event. Microsoft Project does allow the user to nominate if a Milestone is a **Start** or **Finish Milestone** as with other products. A Milestone is a Start Milestone when it has no predecessors and is scheduled at the start of a work day, and a Finish Milestone when it has predecessors and is scheduled at the end of a work day.

Task Name	Duration	Start	Finish
Start Milestone	0 days	1 Sep 8:00 AM	1 Sep 8:00 AM
Task	5 days	1 Sep 8:00 AM	5 Sep 5:00 PM
Finish Milestone	0 days	5 Sep 5:00 PM	5 Sep 5:00 PM
Task	5 days	8 Sep 8:00 AM	12 Sep 5:00 PM
Finish Milestone	0 days	12 Sep 5:00 PM	12 Sep 5:00 PM

A Task is assigned a zero duration to create a milestone and is then normally displayed in the bar chart with a ◆.

Microsoft Project also has the ability to display a task with a non-zero duration. The duration may be elapsed or a calendar calculated duration as a Milestone:

- Highlight the task with a duration that you want to mark as a milestone,

- Open the **Task Information** form by double-clicking on the task,

- Select the **Advanced** tab, and

- Click the **Mark task as milestone** check box.

The picture above shows that the Milestone point is displayed at the end of the task duration.

6.10 Assigning Calendars to Tasks

Tasks often require a different calendar from the **Project Calendar**. This is assigned in the **Project Information** form. Microsoft Project allows each task to be assigned a unique calendar. A Task Calendar may be assigned by using the **Task Information** form or displaying the **Task Calendar** column.

6.10.1 Assigning a Calendar Using the Task Information Form

- Select one or more tasks that you want to assign to a different calendar by using Shift-click or Ctrl-click.

- Open the **Task Information** form when selecting a single task by double-clicking on a task.

- Open the **Task Information** form when selecting multiple tasks by:
  - ➢ Select **Project**, **Task Information**, or
  - ➢ **Shift+F2**, or
  - ➢ Right-click and select **Task Information**.

- Then select the **Advanced** tab:

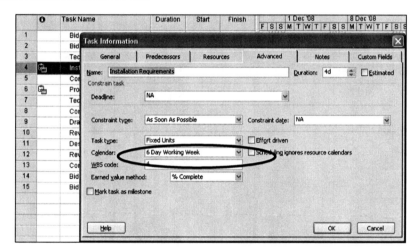

- From the **Calendar:** drop-down box select the calendar you want to assign to the task or tasks.

6.10.2 Assigning a Calendar Using a Column

You may also display the **Task Calendar** column and edit the task calendar from this column. The process of displaying a column is covered in the **FORMATTING THE DISPLAY** chapter. After a calendar has been assigned, an icon will appear in the **Indicators** column as displayed beside the **Installation Requirements** activity below:

	❶	Task Name	Task Calendar
3		Technical Feasibility Study	None
4	📅	Installation Requirements	6 Day Working Week
5		Component Bids	None

Note the **Indicators** column icon indicating a Task Calendar has been assigned to Task 4.

WORKSHOP 4

Adding Tasks

Background
If you do not have the default Microsoft Project settings loaded on your computer or your Global.mpt has been edited then you may not have the same results as displayed in these workshops.

Assignment
1. We will assume that the Planning Process is complete and we are to produce a schedule with one task per Product. We will enter the Products as Microsoft Project tasks in this workshop.
2. The PBS was created in Excel using the **Organization Chart** function with the External and Collective Groupings Products outline created with the **Drawing Toolbar**:

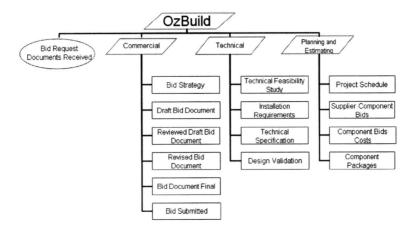

3. The PFD (created with Microsoft Project) is:

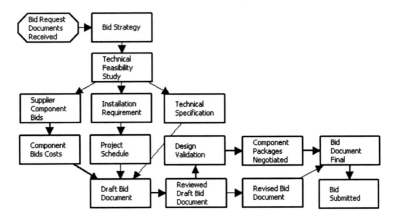

4. We will not enter the Collective Grouping Products of Commercial, Technical or Planning and Estimating in this workshop.
5. Use the columns to enter the Name and Original Duration of the tasks as below.
6. Assign the 6-Day Working Week calendar using the **Task Information** form. Double-click on the task to open this form and select the **Advanced** tab.
7. The task will become a milestone when assigned a zero duration.

ID	Task Name	Duration	Task Calendar
1	Bid Request Documents Received	0 days	
2	Bid Strategy	1 day	
3	Technical Feasibility Study	8 days	
4	Installation Requirements	4 days	Assign the 6 Days Working Week calendar
5	Supplier Component Bids	3 days	
6	Project Schedule	4 days	Assign the 6 Days Working Week calendar
7	Technical Specification	9 days	
8	Component Bids Costs	2 days	
9	Draft Bid Document	3 days	
10	Reviewed Draft Bid Document	1 day	
11	Design Validation	1 day	
12	Revised Bid Document	1 day	
13	Component Packages Negotiated	6 days	
14	Bid Document Final	1 day	
15	Bid Submitted	0 days	

8. Save your **OzBuild Bid** project.
9. Your schedule should look like this:

	❶	Task Name	Duration	Start	Finish	
1		Bid Request Documents Received	0 days	1 Dec '08	1 Dec '08	◆ 1/12
2		Bid Strategy	1 day	1 Dec '08	1 Dec '08	
3		Technical Feasibility Study	8 days	1 Dec '08	10 Dec '08	
4	📅	Installation Requirements	4 days	1 Dec '08	4 Dec '08	
5		Supplier Component Bids	3 days	1 Dec '08	3 Dec '08	
6	📅	Project Schedule	4 days	1 Dec '08	4 Dec '08	
7		Technical Specification	9 days	1 Dec '08	11 Dec '08	
8		Component Bids Costs	2 days	1 Dec '08	2 Dec '08	
9		Draft Bid Document	3 days	1 Dec '08	3 Dec '08	
10		Reviewed Draft Bid Document	1 day	1 Dec '08	1 Dec '08	
11		Design Validation	1 day	1 Dec '08	1 Dec '08	
12		Revised Bid Document	1 day	1 Dec '08	1 Dec '08	
13		Component Packages Negotiated	6 days	1 Dec '08	8 Dec '08	
14		Bid Document Final	1 day	1 Dec '08	1 Dec '08	
15		Bid Submitted	0 days	1 Dec '08	1 Dec '08	◆ 1/12

The icon in the Information column on the left-hand side indicates that Tasks 4 and 6 have a non-standard calendar, which is the 6-Day Working Week calendar set in the last workshop.

7   ORGANIZING TASKS USING OUTLINING

Outlining is used to summarize and group tasks under a hierarchy of **Parent** or **Summary Tasks**. They are used to present different views of your project during planning, scheduling and statusing. These headings are normally based on your project breakdown structure. In a PRINCE2 project these Summary Tasks may be used to represent the project Stages and/or the Product Breakdown Structure.

Defining the project's breakdown structure can be a major task for project managers. The establishment of templates makes this operation simpler because a standard breakdown is predefined and does not have to be typed in for each new project.

Projects should be broken into manageable areas by using a structure based on a breakdown of the project deliverables, systematic functions, disciplines or areas of work. The Outline structure created in your project should reflect the primary breakdown of your project, normally as the PBS and Stages.

Microsoft Project 2000 introduced a new feature titled **Grouping**, which is similar to the **Organize** function found in Primavera software. This feature allows the grouping of tasks under headings other than the Outline Structure. Unlike Primavera software, **Grouping** is not the primary method of organizing tasks. It is covered in the **GROUPING, OUTLINE CODES AND WBS** chapter.

7.1   Creating an Outline

To create an **Outline**:

- Insert a new **Summary** task above the **Detailed tasks**:

- Then **Demote** the **Detailed tasks** below **Summary task**. (Demoting is explained in the next section.):

The Start and Finish dates of the **Summary task** are adopted from the earliest start date and latest finish date of the **Detailed tasks**.

The duration of the **Summary** is calculated from the adopted start and finish dates over the **Summary** task calendar, which is initially the **Project Calendar**.

The Duration and Finish dates of the Summary task are shaded because these were changed after Tasks 1 to 3 were demoted. This shading may be removed by pressing F9 to recalculate the schedule or saving the file.

7.2   Promoting and Demoting Tasks

Demoting or **Indenting** tasks may be achieved in a number of ways. Select the task or tasks you want to **Demote**. Ensure you have selected the whole task and not just some cells. You may use any of the following methods to **Demote a selected task**:

- Click on the Indent [⇨] button, or

- Right-click on the **Task ID** column to open the task shortcut menu, click on the [⇨ Indent] button, or

- Move the mouse until you see a double-headed horizontal arrow in the task name, left-click and drag the task right. A vertical line (see lower of the two pictures below) will appear indicating the outline level you have dragged the task(s) to, or

ⓘ		Task Name	Duration	1 Sep		8 Sep	
				S S M T W T F	S S	M T W T F	
1		Summary	1 day?				
2		Task 1 ⟵⟶	3 days				
3		Task 2	2 days				
4		Task 3	3 days				

ⓘ		Task Name	Duration	1 Sep		8 Sep	
				S S M T W T F	S S	M T W T F	
1		⊟ **Summary**	**8 days**				
2		Task 1	3 days				
3		Task 2	2 days				
4		Task 3	3 days				

- Hold down the **Alt** and **Shift keys** and press the **Right Arrow Key** on your keyboard.

Promoting or **Outdenting tasks** uses the same principle as demoting tasks. Select the task or tasks you want to demote, ensure you have selected the whole task and not just some cells, then you may:

- Click on the Outdent [⇦] button, or

- Right-click on the **Task ID** column to open the task shortcut menu, click on the [⇦ Outdent] button, or

- Move the mouse until you see a double-headed horizontal arrow in the task name column, left-click and drag the tasks left, or

- Hold down the **Alt** and **Shift keys** together and press the **Left Arrow Key** on your keyboard.

Tasks may be added under a **Detailed** task and demoted to a third level and so on.

ⓘ		Task Name	Duration	1 Sep		8 Sep	
				S S M T W T F	S S	M T W T F	
1		⊟ **Summary**	**8 days**				
2		Task 1	3 days				
3		Task 2	2 days				
4		⊟ **Task 3**	**3 days**				
5		Task 3.1	1 day				
6		Task 3.2	1 day				
7		Task 3.3	1 day				

7.3 Summary Task Duration Calculation

The Summary Task duration is calculated from the Start to the Finish over the calendar assigned to the task, thus changing the summary task calendar will change the displayed duration of the Summary Task:

7.4 Summarizing Tasks

Once you have created summary tasks, the detailed tasks may be rolled up or summarized under the summary tasks. Rolled up tasks are symbolized by the + sign to the left of the summarized task description:

- This picture shows **Detailed Task 3** rolled up.

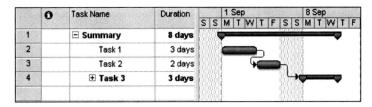

- This picture shows **SUMMARY TASK** rolled up.

7.4.1 To Roll Up Summary Tasks and Show Tasks

The Outline Symbols, ⊞ and ⊟, in front of the tasks may be hidden and displayed from the **Tools**, **Options…**, **View** tab, **Show outline symbol**.

Select the task you want to roll up:

- Click on the ⊟ to the left of the Task Name, or

- Click on the **Hide Subtasks** 「−」 icon, or

- Double-click on the **Task ID** (not the **Task Name** as this will open the **Task** form).

Displaying rolled-up tasks is similar to rolling them up. To do this, select the task you want to expand. Then:

- Click on the ⊞ to the left of the Task Name, or

- Click on the **Show Subtasks** 「+」 icon, or

- Double-click on the **Task ID**.

7.4.2 Roll Up All Tasks to an Outline Level

A schedule may be rolled up to any Outline Level by selecting the desired Outline Level from the ⌊Show ▾⌋ drop-down box on the **Formatting Toolbar**.

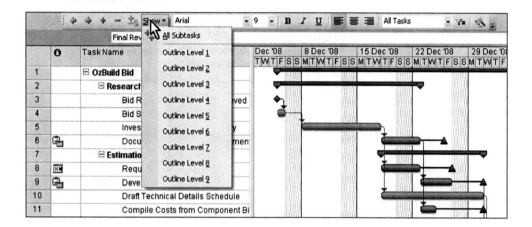

7.4.3 Show All Tasks

Select the ⌊ All Subtasks ⌋ option at the top to display all tasks.

7.5 Project Summary Task

A Project Summary Task may be displayed by checking the **Show project summary task** box from the **Tools**, **Options…**, **View** tab. This task spans from the first to the last task in the project and is in effect a built-in Level 1 outline. The description of the Summary Task is the Project Title entered in the **File**, **Properties** form. A Project Summary Task is a virtual task and may not have resources, relationships or constraints assigned.

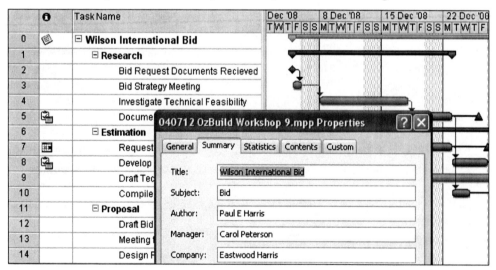

WORKSHOP 5

Entering Stages

Background
The summary tasks may be used to represent

The PRINCE2 Planning Process shows that you need to identify the following stages:
> Research
> Estimation
> Proposal

These will be added as Summary Tasks in this workshop.

Assignment

1. Go to the **View** tab in the **Tools, Options…** form and check the option to display the Project Summary Task, close the form and observe how the Project Summary Task is formatted
2. Remove the Project Summary Task as we will create an Outline Level for the Project Summary Task.
3. Create an Outline Level 1 for the whole project entitled "OzBuild Bid" and
4. Create an Outline Level 2 for each of the three Stages: Research, Estimation and Proposal. Try using the various methods for indenting and outdenting tasks.
5. Your schedule should look like this:

	🛈	Task Name	Duration	Start	Finish	1 Dec '08	8 Dec '08
						S S M T W T F S S M T W T F	
1		⊟ OzBuild Bid	9 days	1 Dec '08	11 Dec '08		
2		⊟ Research	8 days	1 Dec '08	10 Dec '08		
3		Bid Request Documents Received	0 days	1 Dec '08	1 Dec '08	◆ 1/12	
4		Bid Strategy	1 day	1 Dec '08	1 Dec '08		
5		Technical Feasibility Study	8 days	1 Dec '08	10 Dec '08		
6		⊟ Estimate	9 days	1 Dec '08	11 Dec '08		
7	📇	Installation Requirements	4 days	1 Dec '08	4 Dec '08		
8		Supplier Component Bids	3 days	1 Dec '08	3 Dec '08		
9	📇	Project Schedule	4 days	1 Dec '08	4 Dec '08		
10		Technical Specification	9 days	1 Dec '08	11 Dec '08		
11		Component Bids Costs	2 days	1 Dec '08	2 Dec '08		
12		⊟ Proposal	6 days	1 Dec '08	8 Dec '08		
13		Draft Bid Document	3 days	1 Dec '08	3 Dec '08		
14		Reviewed Draft Bid Document	1 day	1 Dec '08	1 Dec '08		
15		Design Validation	1 day	1 Dec '08	1 Dec '08		
16		Revised Bid Document	1 day	1 Dec '08	1 Dec '08		
17		Component Packages Negotiated	6 days	1 Dec '08	8 Dec '08		
18		Bid Document Final	1 day	1 Dec '08	1 Dec '08		
19		Bid Submitted	0 days	1 Dec '08	1 Dec '08	◆ 1/12	

6. Save your **OzBuild Bid** project.

Continued over…

7. The second level of the Outline Structure could have been used for the **Collective Groupings Products** and not Stages and would look like the example below:

	0	Task Name	Duration	Start	Finish
1		⊟ OzBuild Bid	9 days	4 Dec '06	14 Dec '06
2		Bid Request Documents Received	0 days	4 Dec '06	4 Dec '06
3		⊟ Commercial	3 days	4 Dec '06	6 Dec '06
4		Bid Strategy	1 day	4 Dec '06	4 Dec '06
5		Draft Bid Document	3 days	4 Dec '06	6 Dec '06
6		Reviewed Draft Bid Document	1 day	4 Dec '06	4 Dec '06
7		Revised Bid Document	1 day	4 Dec '06	4 Dec '06
8		Bid Document Final	1 day	4 Dec '06	4 Dec '06
9		Bid Submitted	0 days	4 Dec '06	4 Dec '06
10		⊟ Technical	9 days	4 Dec '06	14 Dec '06
11		Technical Feasibility Study	8 days	4 Dec '06	13 Dec '06
12	📋	Installation Requirements	4 days	4 Dec '06	7 Dec '06
13		Technical Details Schedule	9 days	4 Dec '06	14 Dec '06
14		Design Validation	1 day	4 Dec '06	4 Dec '06
15		⊟ Planning and Estimating	6 days	4 Dec '06	11 Dec '06
16	📋	Project Schedule	4 days	4 Dec '06	7 Dec '06
17		Component Bids	3 days	4 Dec '06	6 Dec '06
18		Component Bids Costs	2 days	4 Dec '06	5 Dec '06
19		Component Work Packages Negotiated	6 days	4 Dec '06	11 Dec '06

8   FORMATTING THE DISPLAY

This chapter covers the following topics, which are used to format the on-screen display and which are also reflected in print preview and printouts:

Topic	Menu Command
• **Table** – formatting the columns of data	<u>V</u>iew, Ta<u>b</u>le:Entry, <u>M</u>ore Tables…, or Select a column and right-click to insert, or Right-click on a column header and edit.
• **Formatting Columns**	Double-click on the column title.
• **Inserting Columns**	Highlight a column and strike the **Ins Key**, or Select **<u>I</u>nsert, <u>C</u>olumn…,** or Right-click and select **Insert <u>C</u>olumn….**
• **Deleting Columns**	Highlight a column and strike the **Delete** key, or Select **<u>E</u>dit, Hi<u>d</u>e Column,** or Right-click and select **Hide <u>C</u>olumn.**
• **Format Bars**	F<u>o</u>rmat, <u>B</u>ar Styles… or double-click on a bar. F<u>o</u>rmat, Gantt Chart <u>W</u>izard… F<u>o</u>rmat, <u>B</u>ar…
• **Row Height**	Drag with the mouse, or Edit the **Table.**
• **Format Text Font**	F<u>o</u>rmat, <u>F</u>ont… to format columns and F<u>o</u>rmat, <u>T</u>ext Styles… to format all other fonts.
• **Timescale**	F<u>o</u>rmat, Ti<u>m</u>escale…, or Double-click on the timescale.
• **Gridlines**	F<u>o</u>rmat, <u>G</u>ridlines….
• **Relationship Lines**	F<u>o</u>rmat, <u>L</u>ayout….

The formatting is applied to the current **View** and is automatically saved as part of the View when another View is selected. Views are covered in more detail in the **VIEWS, TABLE AND DETAILS** chapter.

Some formatting functions, such as dragging columns to a different location, are not available in earlier versions of Microsoft Project.

8.1   Formatting the Columns

There are two methods of formatting the columns:

- Using **Table Definition** form, this is where you set up the data columns in the way you want to see the information on the screen and in printouts. You may edit, create and delete **Tables** and select which one is used display the data.

- Inserting, editing and deleting columns of data using the **Column Definition** form.

8.1.1   Formatting Columns Using the Table Function

- Select **View**, **Table:Entry** and select from the list of predefined **Tables** the table you want to display:

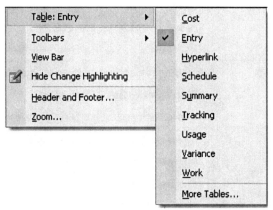

- Select **View**, **Table:**, **More Tables...** to open the **More Tables** form:

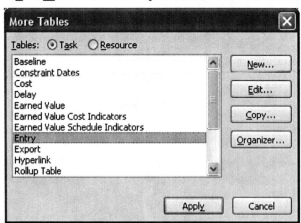

> **New...**   – To create a new Table.

> **Edit...**   – To edit the highlighted Table.

> **Copy...**   – To copy the highlighted Table.

> **Organizer...** – Opens the **Organizer** form which enables you to copy a Table from one opened project to another or to the Global Project.

> **Apply**   – Applies the selected Table making it visible on the screen.

- When you select [New...], [Edit...] or [Copy...] you will be presented with the **Table Definition** form:

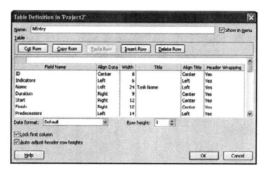

> ➤ Click on the **Show in menu** box to display the Table in the **View, Table:** menu.
> ➤ The columns of data will be displayed on screen from left to right in the same order as the rows in the form.
> ➤ Highlight a row and then you may use the [Copy Row], [Copy Row], [Paste Row], [Insert Row] or [Delete Row] buttons.
> ➤ The data to be displayed may be selected from the drop-down box in the **Field Name** column.
> ➤ **Align Data** and **Width** are used for formatting the data in the columns.
> ➤ The Microsoft Project **Field Name** may be replaced by typing your own title in the **Title** box.
> ➤ The **Date format:** drop-down box is used to change the format for this table only.
>
>   **(i)** This is a very useful function to ensure that other users of the project file see the intended date format and not their system default date format.

- **Row Height:** sets the default height of all the rows in this table. A row height may be changed by dragging the cell boundary line once a task has been created.

> ➤ **Lock first column** prevents the first column from scrolling and is useful when the first column contains the Task Name.
> ➤ **OK** takes you back to the **More Tables** form where you may click on the **Apply** button to commit the new or edited Table.

To save a table for use in all your new projects, copy the table to the **Global.mpt** template using **Tools, Organizer...** and select the **Tables** tab.

You may also copy a **Table** to another project or rename a **Table** using **Tools, Organizer...** and selecting the **Tables** tab.

8.1.2   Formatting Time Units

Select **Tools, Options...**, **Edit** and:

- The **View Options for time units in "Project"** always specifies the time units, for example **day, dy** or **d**.

- Check on the **Add space before label** check box to add a space between the value and label in date columns.

- Unchecking **Add space before label** and selecting **d** allows a narrower duration column.

8.1.3   Formatting Columns Using the Column Definition Form

When you use this function, you are editing the **Table** currently in use and your changes are permanent. Double-click on a column description to open the **Column Definition** form where you may edit the selected column in a similar way to the **Table Definition** form.

The IME Mode button, if displayed, allows the customization of the **Input Mode Editor** for some fields. This feature will only be displayed if it is installed with the Eastern Asian operating systems.

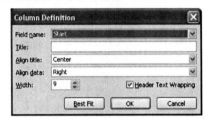

8.1.4   Deleting and Inserting Columns

Insert a column by clicking on the column title where you require the new column. This will highlight the column. To insert a new column:

- Select **Insert**, **Column…**, or
- Hit the **Ins** Key, or
- Right-click and select **Insert Column…**.

Delete a column by highlighting the column or by clicking on the title. Then:

- Select **Edit**, **Hide Column**, or
- Hit the **Delete** key, or
- Right-click and select **Hide Column**.

1. There will be no confirmation of deleting a column, but you are allowed to undo the deletion.
2. The term "hide" means "delete" and the column is removed from the Table in this project.

8.1.5   Adjusting the Width of Columns

You may adjust the width of the column either manually or automatically. For manual adjustment, move the mouse pointer to the nearest vertical line of the column. A ↔ icon will then appear and enable the column to be adjusted. For automatic adjustment, once again position the mouse pointer to the nearest vertical line of the column, and double right-click the mouse. The column width will automatically adjust to the best fit.

8.1.6   Moving Columns

Columns in a Table may be moved by clicking on the column header. The mouse pointer will change to a ✥ and the column may be dragged to a new location

8.2   Formatting the Bars

The bars in the Gantt Chart may be formatted to suit your requirements for display. Microsoft Project has the option to:

- Format all the Task Bars by using :
  - ➤ The **Bar Styles** form, or
  - ➤ The **Gantt Chart Wizard**, which is by far the easiest way to format bars, or
- Format one or more specific Task Bars using the **Format Bar** form.

8.2.1   Formatting Bars Using the Gantt Chart Wizard

There is a **Gantt Chart Wizard** available by clicking on the ⬛ icon or selecting **Format, Gantt Chart Wizard…**. This wizard will overwrite any formatting you may have created. This is a straightforward method of formatting your bars and often this is the best method of formatting bars. It is very simple to use but will not display the Negative Float and Free Float bars. These will have to be added manually using the **Bar Style** form as described next.

8.2.2   Formatting All Task Bars Using the Bar Styles Form

To format all the bars you must open the Bar Style form by selecting:

- **Format, Bar Styles…**, or

- Double-click anywhere in the Gantt Chart area, but not on an existing bar, as this will open the **Format Bar** form for formatting an individual bar.

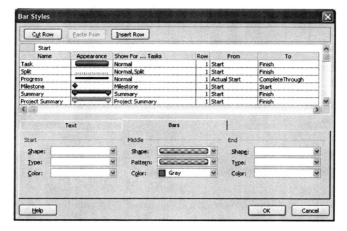

The following notes are the main points for using this function. Detailed information is available in the Help facility by searching for "Bar styles dialog box."

- Each bar listed in the table will be displayed on the bar chart.

- Bars may be deleted with the ⬚ Cut Row ⬚ button, pasted using ⬚ Paste Row ⬚ button and new bars inserted using the ⬚ Insert Row ⬚.

- The **Name** is the title assigned to the bar and is displayed in the printout legend. To hide the bar on the legend precede the **Name** with an *.

- The appearance of each bar is edited in the lower half of the form. The bar's start point, middle and end points may have their color, shape, pattern, etc. formatted.

- **Show For … Tasks** allows you to select which tasks are displayed. More than one task type may be displayed by separating each type with a ",". Bar types not required are prefixed with "**Not.**" For example, the ⌐Normal,Rolled Up,Split,Not Summary⌐ bar would not display a bar for a summary task. Should you leave this cell blank then all task types will be displayed in this format.

- The bars may be placed on one of four rows numbered from 1 to 4, top to bottom. If multiple bars are placed on the same row, the bar at the top of the list will be drawn first and the ones lower down the list will be drawn over the top.

- **From** and **To** allow you to establish where the bars start and finish. The picture below shows how to format **Total Float, Free Float** and **Negative Float**. Unlike other planning and scheduling software, the Negative Float is drawn from the Start Date of a task and not the Finish Date and therefore a separate bar is required for Negative and Positive Float.

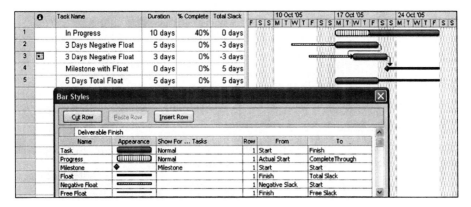

- The **Text** tab allows you to place text inside or around the bar:

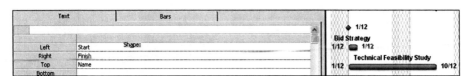

- It is not possible to format the font in this **Bar Styles** form. Select **Format, Text Styles…** to format the bar text font.

To show Critical and Non-critical tasks the bars should be formatted as shown below, with particular attention paid to the **Show For … Tasks** column. Non-critical Tasks are formatted as **Normal, Non-critical** and Critical Tasks as **Normal, Critical**.

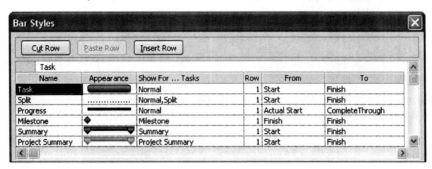

8.2.3   Format One or More Specific Task Bars

One or more individual bars may be formatted to make them look different from other bars.

To format one or more bars:
- Select:
  - ➤ One task bar by clicking on it, or
  - ➤ Multiple bars by Ctrl-clicking each bar or left-clicking and dragging with the mouse, then
- Open the **Format Bar** form by:
  - ➤ Selecting F**o**rmat, **B**ar..., or
  - ➤ Moving the mouse over a bar in the bar chart until the mouse changes to a ⊹ and double-clicking. When more than one bar has been selected you will need to hold the **Ctrl Key** down when double-clicking on a bar.
- Then select the required bar formatting options from the **Format Bar** form:

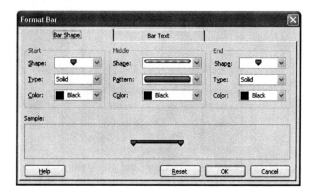

- The Reset is used to restore the default bar formatting to selected bars.

The bar shape may be formatted and text information added in the same way as formatting all the bars described earlier in this chapter.

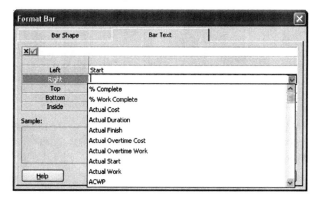

- Select F**o**rmat, **T**ext styles... to format the text font.
- A Tasks Bar may be hidden by checking the **Hide task b̲ar** option in the **Task Information** form.

8.2.4 Layout Form – Format Bars Options

Select **Format**, **Layout…** to open the **Layout** form. This form has some additional bar formatting options for users to customize the appearance of the Gantt Chart.

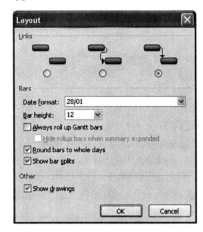

- **Date format:** sets the format for dates displayed on bars only. Dates are displayed on bars using **Format, Bar…** or **Format, Bar Styles…**.

- **Bar height:** sets the height of all the bars. Individual bars may be assigned different heights by selecting a bar shape in the styles form.

- **Always roll up Gantt bars** and **Hide rollup bars when summary expanded** works as follows:

  ➢ Tasks before roll up:

  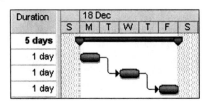

  ➢ With **Always roll up Gantt bars** checked and **Hide rollup bars when summary expanded** unchecked:

  ➢ With **Always roll up Gantt bars** and **Hide rollup bars when summary expanded** checked:

  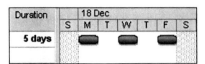

  ➢ An individual bar may be rolled up to a summary task using the **Roll up Gantt bar to summary** option in the **Task Information** form when **Always roll up Gantt bars** options are unchecked.

  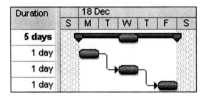

- **Round bars to whole days:**
  - ➢ When this option is unchecked, the length of the task will be shown in proportion to the total number of hours worked per day over the 24-hour time span. For example, an 8-hour working duration bar is shown below:

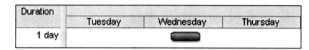

  - ➢ When this option is checked, the task bar will be displayed and spanned over the whole day irrespective of working time:

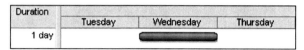

- **Splitting Tasks**
  - ➢ An un-started task may be split using the Split Task icon on the Task Bar, then highlighting the bar to be split and dragging the section of the bar with the mouse to the location where it is planned to conduct the work. The picture below shows Task 10 – Draft Technical Details Schedule – being split. Splits may be removed by dragging the bar back together again.

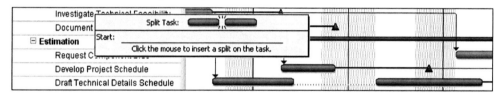

  - ➢ In-progress tasks may be split manually by dragging the incomplete portion to the right or a split may be created automatically by commencing a task before its predecessor is complete. Splitting in-progress tasks is covered in both the **TRACKING PROGRESS** and **OPTIONS** chapters. The two pictures below are of the same task, first with the option checked and then unchecked:

- **Show bars splits**
  - ➢ When checked, the activity bar will display splits:

  - ➢ When unchecked, the activity bar will <u>not</u> display splits:

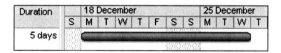

- **Bar Split Dates.** The start and finish dates of splits is not available through the user interface, only the start and finish of the task is available.

8.3   Row Height

Row heights may be adjusted to display text that would otherwise be truncated by a narrow column.

The row height may be set in the **Table Definition** form by selecting **View**, **Table:**, **More Tables....** From this view select the table you wish to edit the row height in and click on the Edit... button. Once the **Table Definition** form is open select the row height from the drop-down box next to **Row height:**.

The row height of one or more columns may also be adjusted in a similar way to adjusting row heights in Excel, by clicking on the row and dragging with the mouse:

- Highlight one or more rows that need adjusting by dragging or Ctrl-clicking. If all the rows are to be adjusted, then click on the **Select All** button above row number 1, to highlight all the tasks.

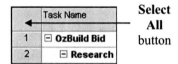 **Select All** button

- Then move the mouse pointer to the left-hand side of a horizontal row divider line. The pointer will change to a double-headed arrow ⬍. Click and hold with the left mouse button and drag the row or rows to the required height.

8.4   Format Fonts

8.4.1   Format Font Command

The **Format, Font...** function allows you to format any selected text in rows or columns:

- Select all the rows by clicking on the **Select All** button, this is the box above row number 1, or

- Select one or more rows, columns or cells by Ctrl-clicking or dragging, then

- Select **Format, Font...** to open the **Font** form:

- Select the **Font**, **Font style**, font **Size**, **Color** of the text, **Background Color** and **Background Pattern** from the **Font** dialog box.

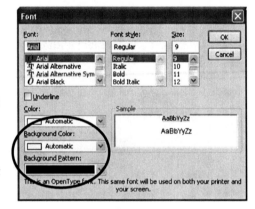

- The selected font style and type will be applied to the data column or task row in any table.

This function has been enhanced with Microsoft Project 2007 and now allows a **Background Color** and **Background Pattern** that was not available in earlier versions.

8.4.2   Format Text Style

The **Format, Text Styles...** command opens the **Text Styles** form and allows you to select a text type from the **Item to Change:** drop-down box and apply formatting to the selected text style. Microsoft Project 2007 added the **Background Color** and **Background Pattern** option:

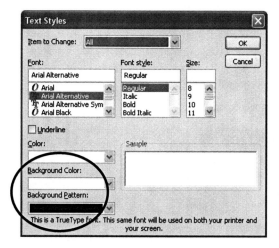

Text may formatted by using any of the styles listed below:

- **All**: This is all text including columns and rows,

- **Non-critical, Critical, Milestone, Summary, Project Summary, Marked, Highlighted** and **External tasks,**

- **Row** and **Column** titles,

- **Top, Middle** and **Bottom Timescale Tiers,** and

- **Bar Text** left, right, below, above and inside.

8.5   *Format Colors*

Colors are formatted in a number of forms and there is no single form for formatting all colors:

- **Nonworking time** colors in the Gantt Chart are formatted in the **Timescale** form, double-click on the timescale.

- **Text** colors are formatted in the **Text Styles** and **Font** forms, found under the **Format** command.

- **Gridline** colors are formatted in the **Gridlines** form, also found under the **Format** command.

- **Hyperlink** colors are formatted under **Tools, Options...,** **Edit.**

- **Timescale** colors are formatted with the system color scheme used in the **Start, Settings, Control Panel, Display** option.

- The **Logic Lines**, also known as **Dependencies, Relationships,** or **Links,** inherit their color from the predecessor's bar color in the Gantt Chart view and may be formatted in the Network Diagram view by selecting **Format, Layout....**

8.6   Format Timescale

8.6.1   Format Timescale Command

The **Timescale** form provides a number of options for timescale display, which is located above the Bar Chart, and the shading of **Nonworking** time. This function was enhanced with the release of Microsoft Project 2002; earlier versions had a Major and Minor scale only.

To open the **Timescale** form:

- Double-click on the timescale, or

- Select **Format, Timescale….**

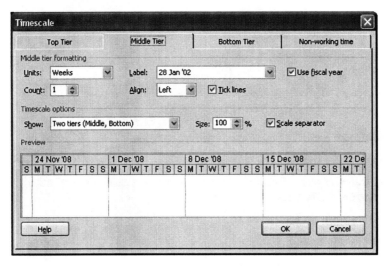

There are many options here, which are intuitive and will not be described in detail.

Top Tier, Middle Tier and Bottom Tier Tab

- These three timescales may have different scales. These are often set at "weeks and days" or "months and weeks." By default, the Top Tier timescale has been disabled. You may enable the three tiers together by selecting Three Tiers (Top, Middle, Bottom) from the **Timescale options, Show:.**

- The **Label** will affect how much space the timescale will occupy, so the selection of a long label will result in longer Task bars.

- **Tick lines** and **Scale separator** hide and display the lines between the text.

- **Size:** controls the horizontal scale of the timescale and in association with the **Label:** are the two main tools for scaling the horizontal axis in the Gantt Chart.

- Choose the **Use fiscal year** function to display the financial year and then select the **Tools, Options…, Calendar** tab to choose the month in which the fiscal year starts.

- Should you wish to number the time periods, for example, **Week 1**, **Week 2**, etc., there are a number of sequential numbering options available at the bottom of the label list.

Nonworking Time Tab
The **Nonworking time** tab allows you to format how the nonworking time is displayed. You may select only one calendar. The nonworking time may be presented as shading behind the bars, in front of the bars or hidden.

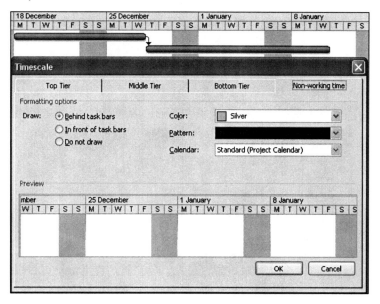

8.6.2 View Zoom

The **View**, **Zoom…** function, or clicking on the and ⊟ icons, is used to adjust the horizontal scale of the Gantt Chart only. It does not work like most other Windows products, which scale the whole work area.

i The **View**, **Zoom…** function is not a temporary change and overwrites any customized timescale settings.

8.6.3 Format Timescale Font

To format the Timescale font, select **Format**, **Text styles…** to open the **Text Styles** form:

The timescale fonts may be formatted separately by selecting the appropriate line item under **Item to Change:**.

A very tight timescale may be achieved by making the Bottom Timescale Tier a small font as displayed in the picture.

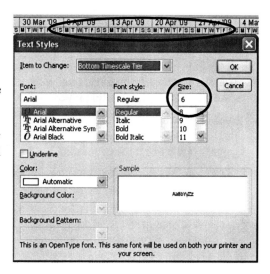

8.7 Format Gridlines

Gridlines are important to help divide the visual presentation of the Bar Chart. This example shows **Middle Tier Gridlines** every week and **Bottom Tier Gridlines** every day.

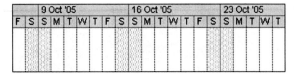

To format the Grid Line select **Format**, **Gridlines...** to open the Gridlines form:

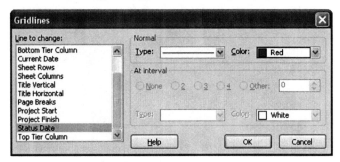

- Select the gridline from the drop-down box under **Line to change:**.

- Select color and type from under **Normal**.

- Date gridlines may be set to occur at intervals using the **At interval** option.

Some of the titles for the gridlines are not intuitive, so some interpretation is given below:

- For Data Column and Row dividing lines, use **Sheet Rows** and **Sheet Columns**.

- For Timescale and Column Titles, use **Title Horizontal** and **Title Vertical**.

- Gantt Chart area, including lines for **Project Start** and **Finish Date**, **Current** and **Status Date**, are clearly described.

- Page Breaks will only display manually-inserted breaks. A page will only break if the **Manual page breaks** check box in the **Print** form is checked.

Microsoft Project has two dates that may be used to identify the Status Date or Data Date, which is the date that the data has been collected for statusing a project schedule. These two dates are set in the **Project Information** form:

- By default Microsoft Project displays the **Current Date** as a gray dotted vertical line but this is reset to the computer's system date each time the project file is opened. It is suggested that this line be removed.

- The **Status Date** never changes once set and therefore it is suggested that this line should be displayed as per the picture above.

 Many laser printers will not print light gray lines clearly, so it is often better to use dark gray or black Sight Lines for better output.

8.8 Format Links, Dependencies, Relationships, or Logic Lines

The Links, also known as Dependencies, Relationships, or Logic Lines, may be displayed or hidden by using the **Layout** form.

- Select **Format, Layout...** to open the **Layout** form and click on one of the three radio buttons under **Links** to select the style you require:

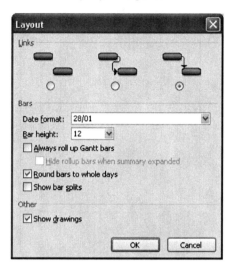

- ➢ The color of the **Link** is inherited from the color of the predecessor task.
- ➢ To display critical path on the relationship lines you will need to format the bars with a different color. This is often set to red.

The color of the successors' relationship lines is adopted from the task bar color. Therefore, re-formatting critical bars with the **Format Bar** form will also re-format the color of the successors' relationship lines and they will no longer display the Critical Path color on the Logic Lines. This will effectively mask the critical path and could provide misleading results.

Primavera products format the relationship separately from the bars and are able to identify the Critical, Driving and Non-Driving relationships, which is not possible with Microsoft Project.

WORKSHOP 6

Formatting the Bar Chart

Background
Management has received your draft report and requests some changes to the presentation.

Assignment
Format your schedule as follows:

1. Create a new **Table** titled **Review** by copying the **Entry** table. Select **View**, **Table**, **More Tables…**,

2. Add **Task Calendar** column between **Duration** and **Start** columns in the **Table Definition** form. Left Align this column,

3. Align Data for the Task Calendar on the left,

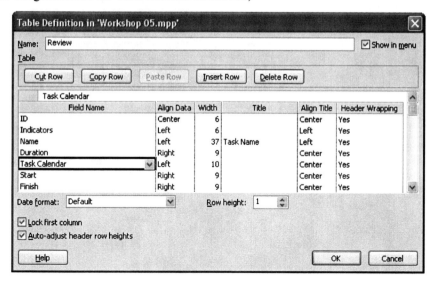

4. Check the **Show in menu** option.

5. Apply the Table.

6. To make the Duration Column narrower, select the **Tools**, **Options**, **Edit** tab. Under the View options select to display Days as "d" and uncheck **Add space before label**.

7. Double-click on the **Duration** column and rename the Title "Dur" and click Best Fit to produce a narrow column.

Continued Over….

WORKSHOP 6 CONTINUED

8. Double-click on the timescale and format the **Middle Tier Timescale (Major scale in MSP2000)** with **Units:** of **Months** with **Label:** of **Jan '02** and the **Bottom Tier Timescale (Minor scale in MSP2000)** with **Units:** of **Weeks** with **Label:** of **28,4,…** and **Size:** of 150%.

9. Select **Format**, **Gridlines…** and format the Gridlines with **Middle Tier Columns (Major Columns in MSP2000)** to solid black lines and **Bottom Tier Columns (Minor Columns in MSP2000)** to dotted black lines.

10. Double-click in the bar chart area to open the **Bar Styles** form and remove the date from the milestones. If you do not have dates by your milestones then add the dates to the right of the Milestones and then remove them.

11. From the **Bar Styles** form remove the **Resource** and add the task **Name** to the right of each **Task** bar. You will notice there is no name against the milestones, these have to be added separately against the Milestone line in the **Bar Styles** form.

12. Save your **OzBuild Bid** project.

13. Check your result with the example shown below.

	0	Task Name	Dur	Task Calendar	Start	Finish
1		⊟ OzBuild Bid	9d	None	1 Dec '08	11 Dec '08
2		⊟ Research	8d	None	1 Dec '08	10 Dec '08
3		Bid Request Documents Received	0d	None	1 Dec '08	1 Dec '08
4		Bid Strategy	1d	None	1 Dec '08	1 Dec '08
5		Technical Feasibility Study	8d	None	1 Dec '08	10 Dec '08
6		⊟ Estimate	9d	None	1 Dec '08	11 Dec '08
7		Installation Requirements	4d	6 Day Working Week	1 Dec '08	4 Dec '08
8		Supplier Component Bids	3d	None	1 Dec '08	3 Dec '08
9		Project Schedule	4d	6 Day Working Week	1 Dec '08	4 Dec '08
10		Technical Specification	9d	None	1 Dec '08	11 Dec '08
11		Component Bids Costs	2d	None	1 Dec '08	2 Dec '08
12		⊟ Proposal	6d	None	1 Dec '08	8 Dec '08
13		Draft Bid Document	3d	None	1 Dec '08	3 Dec '08
14		Reviewed Draft Bid Document	1d	None	1 Dec '08	1 Dec '08
15		Design Validation	1d	None	1 Dec '08	1 Dec '08
16		Revised Bid Document	1d	None	1 Dec '08	1 Dec '08
17		Component Packages Negotiated	6d	None	1 Dec '08	8 Dec '08
18		Bid Document Final	1d	None	1 Dec '08	1 Dec '08
19		Bid Submitted	0d	None	1 Dec '08	1 Dec '08

9   ADDING TASK DEPENDENCIES

The next phase of a schedule is to add logic to the tasks. There are two types of logic that you may use:

- **Dependencies (Relationships** or **Logic** or **Links**) between tasks, and

- Imposed **Constraints** to task start or finish dates. These are covered in the **CONSTRAINTS** chapter.

Microsoft Project's Help file and other text uses the terms "**Dependencies, Relationships** and **Links**" for Dependencies but does not use the term "**Logic**."

There are a number of methods of adding, editing and deleting task **Dependencies**. We will look at the following techniques in this chapter:

Topic	Notes for creating a Finish to Start Dependency
• Graphically in the Gantt, Calendar or Network Diagram Views	Drag the 4-headed mouse pointer ✛ from one task to another to create an FS dependency.
• With the **Link** and **Unlink** icon on the Standard toolbar	Select the tasks in the order they are to be linked and click on the Link 🔗 icon.
• By using the Menu command	Select the tasks in the order they are to be linked and select **Edit, Link Tasks**, or **Ctrl+F2**.
• By opening the **Task Information** form	Predecessor only may be added and deleted.
• Through the **Predecessor** and **Successor Details** forms	Open the bottom pane, **Windows, Split** and then select **Format, Details, Predecessors and Successors**.
• By editing or deleting a dependency using the **Task Dependency** form	Double-click on a task link (relationship line) in the **Bar Chart** or **Network Diagram** view.
• **Autolink** new inserted tasks and moved tasks	Select **Tools, Options…, Schedule** tab and check the **Autolink Inserted or Moved Tasks** box.
• By displaying the **Predecessor** or **Successor** column	Edit the relationships in the columns.

 Microsoft Project allows only one relationship between two tasks where as Primavera software allows two.

Dependencies

Generally, there are two types of dependencies that may be entered into the software:

- **Hard Logic,** also referred to as **Mandatory Logic,** are dependencies that may not be avoided. For example a footing would have to be excavated before it may be filled with concrete or a computer and software delivered before the software may be loaded onto the computer.

- **Soft Logic**, also referred to as **Sequencing Logic** or **Preferred Logic**, which often may be changed at a later date to reflect planning changes. An example would be determining the order in which a number of footings are dug or which computer is loaded with software first.

To create a **Closed Network** each task will require a Start predecessor and a Finish successor. Most schedules may be created using only Finish to Start relationships with positive or negative lags. This method ensures a Closed Network is created and the **Critical Path** flows through the activities and not just through the relationships. A delay to the completion of the first activity in the example on the left below will not delay subsequent task as the calculated critical path flows through the relationships and not the tasks, therefore a true critical path has not been created. The example on the right has created a true critical path because the driving path flows through the tasks and the relationships

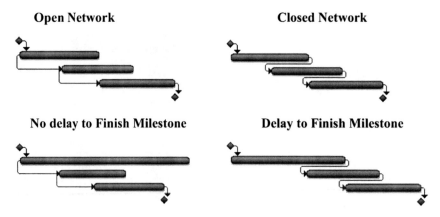

Open Network	Closed Network
No delay to Finish Milestone	**Delay to Finish Milestone**

There is no simple method of documenting which is hard and which is soft logic. A schedule with a large amount of soft logic has the potential of becoming very difficult to maintain when the plan is changed. You will also find that as a project progresses, soft logic converts to hard logic as commitments are made and tasks are started.

Constraints

Constraints are applied to Tasks when relationships do not provide the required result. Typical applications of a constraint are:

- The availability of a site to commence work.

- The supply of information by a client.

- The required finish date of a project.

Constraints are often entered to represent contract dates or **External Logic** and may be directly related to contract items. It is often useful to make notes about contract dates reflected in the schedule in either the Task Note area or one of the Text columns. Constraints are covered in detail in the **CONSTRAINTS** chapter.

9.1   Understanding Dependencies

Two other terms you must understand are:

- **Predecessor**, a task that controls the start or finish of another immediate subsequent task.

- **Successor**, a task whose start or finish depends on the start or finish of another immediately preceding task.

There are four types of dependencies available in Microsoft Project:

- Finish-to-Start (**FS**) (also known as conventional)

- Start-to-Start (**SS**)

- Start-to-Finish (**SF**)

- Finish-to-Finish (**FF**)

The following pictures show how the dependencies appear graphically in the **Gantt Chart** and **Network Diagram** (PERT) views.

The **FS** (or conventional) dependency looks like this:

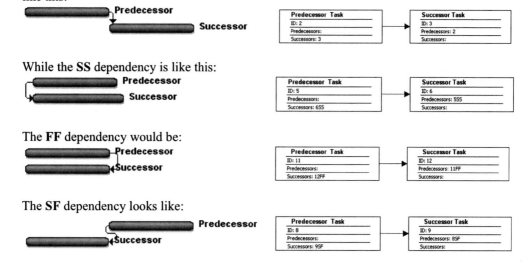

While the **SS** dependency is like this:

The **FF** dependency would be:

The **SF** dependency looks like:

9.2   Understanding Lags and Leads

A **Lag** is a duration that is applied to a dependency to make the successor start or finish earlier or later and may be applied to any relationship type.

- A successor task will start or finish later when a positive **Lag** is assigned. Therefore, a task requiring a 3-day delay between the finish of one task and start of another will require a positive lag of 3 days.

- Conversely, a lag may be negative (also called a **Lead)** when a new task can be started before the predecessor task is finished.

- **Leads** and **Lags** may be applied to any relationship type including Summary Task relationships.

An example of an **FS** with positive lag

An example of an **FS** with negative lag:

Here are some important points to understand about Lags.

- Lags are calculated on the **Successor Calendar** except with Microsoft Project 2000 which uses the **Project Calendar**, set in the **Project Information** form. Therefore files may calculate differently in 2000 and 2002 – 2007. (Primavera P3 and SureTrak software uses the predecessor's calendar and Primavera Enterprise has four options.)

- Lags may be assigned **Elapsed** durations, therefore they will be based on a 24-hour, 7-day per week. To enter an elapsed lag type an "e" before the unit, e.g., **5 ed**.

- Lags may be expressed in terms of % and in this situation the lag is a percentage of the predecessor's duration. The example below shows an FS dependency +250%; the predecessor is 1 day so the Lag is 2.5 days.

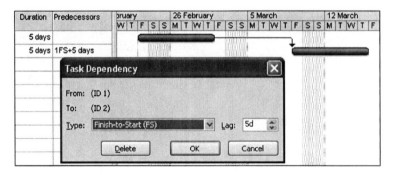

 You must be careful when using a lag to allow for delays such as curing concrete when the Successor Calendar is not a seven-day calendar. Since this type of activity lapses nonwork days, the activity could finish before Microsoft Project's calculated finish date. You may want to use elapsed durations in a lag in this situation.

9.3 Restrictions on Summary Task Dependencies

Dependencies may be made between Summary and Detailed tasks of a different Summary task. Consider the following points when using dependencies at Summary Task level:

- There is a built-in dependency between Summary and Detailed tasks. Detailed tasks may be considered as Start-to-Start successors and Finish-to-Finish predecessors of their Summary Task.

- Summary tasks may only have **FS** and **SS** dependencies; you will receive a warning message when you attempt to enter an illegal dependency.

 It is recommended that dependencies be maintained at the detail level. This is particularly important when moving tasks from one summary task to another since the dependencies will still be valid. Again, be aware that there is a function found under the **Tools**, **Options…**, **Schedule** tab which will Autolink moved tasks. This function should be turned off if you wish to move a task and keep the existing logic.

9.4 Displaying the Dependencies on the Gantt Chart

The dependencies may be displayed or hidden with the **Layout** form.

- Select **Format**, **Layout…** to open the **Layout** form and click on the radio button under the style you require:

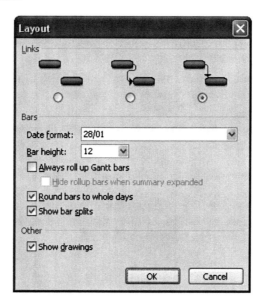

- The color of the dependency line is inherited from the color of the predecessor task.

- To display a critical path on the relationship lines you will need to format the bars as critical.

9.4.1   Graphically Adding a Dependency

You may graphically add a **Finish-to-Start** dependency only by:

- Selecting the **Gantt, Calendar** or **Network Diagram** views from the **View Bar** on the right-hand side of the screen or selecting **View, Gantt Chart, Calendar** or **Network Diagram**, then:

- Move the mouse pointer over a task until the mouse pointer changes to a ⊕, left-click and drag to the successor task. The cursor will change to a 🔗 shape during this operation.

9.4.2   Using the Link and Unlink Icon on the Standard Toolbar

The 🔗 **Link Tasks** icon on the toolbar may be used for linking tasks with a Start-to-Finish dependency:

- Highlight one or more tasks using Ctrl and left-click to select one task at a time and Shift and left-click to select a contiguous group of tasks.

- Then click the 🔗 **Link Tasks** icon on the toolbar and the tasks will be linked with Start-to-Finish dependencies in the order that they were selected.

To remove a dependency, select the tasks and click on the 🔗 **Unlink Tasks** icon.

9.4.3   Linking Using the Menu Command

The menu may be used for linking tasks with a Start-to-Finish dependency:

- Highlight one or more tasks using Ctrl-left-click to select one task at a time or Shift and left-click to select a group of tasks.

- Then select **Edit, Link Tasks,** or **Ctrl+F2** and the tasks will be linked with Start-to-Finish dependencies in the order that they were selected.

A maximum of 10 groups of tasks may be linked this way. A group of tasks is created by dragging over two or more tasks.

Dependencies may be removed with the menu using **Edit, Unlink Tasks.**

 Primavera P3 and SureTrak software links tasks that have been highlighted from top to bottom and not in the order they are selected. Microsoft Project links the tasks in the order they are highlighted.

9.4.4 Adding and Deleting Predecessors with the Task Information Form

The **Task Information** form may be used for adding and deleting predecessors only.

- Double-click on a task to open the **Task Information** form,

- Select the **Predecessors** tab,

- To select the predecessor, you may either:

  ➢ Type in the Predecessor Task ID in the first line under ID, or

  ➢ Use the drop-down box under task name:

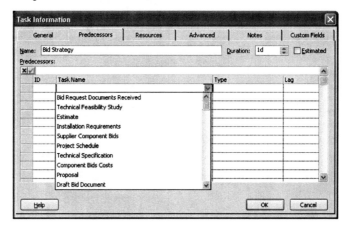

- Now enter the Relationship Type from the **Type** drop-down list and the lag, if required, from the **Lag** drop-down list.

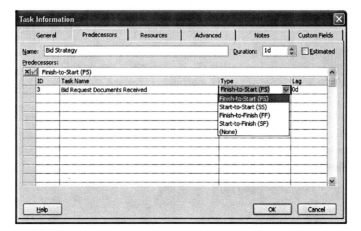

- To enter another relationship click on the next line.

- You are not able to scroll up or down to another task while the **Task Information** form is open.

To complete your operation, either:

- Press the **Enter Key** or click on the OK button to commit the changes, or

- Click on the **Esc Key** or click on the Cancel button to abort any changes.

9.4.5   Predecessor and Successor Details Forms

The Predecessor and Successor Details form may be displayed by:

- Opening the bottom pane by selecting **Window**, **Split**,

- Then make the lower pane active by clicking anywhere in the lower pane. The bar on the left-hand side of the lower pane will turn blue when it is active,

- Display the **Task Details Form**, **Task Entry** or **Task Form**,

- Then select **Format**, **Details**, **Predecessors and Successors** to display the **Predecessors and Successors Detail** form:

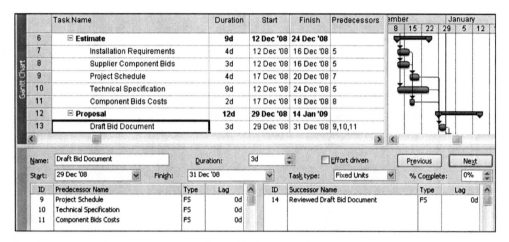

Predecessors and successors may be added using the same method as in the **Task Information** form.

 Double-clicking on a Predecessor or Successor in any of these forms will display the Predecessor or Successor **Task Information** form, allowing the dates, constraints, etc. of related activities to be examined.

9.4.6   Editing or Deleting Dependencies Using the Task Dependency Form

To use the **Task Dependency** form, a logic link between tasks must already exist. To open the **Task Dependency** form, double-click on a task link (relationship line) in the Bar Chart or Network Diagram.

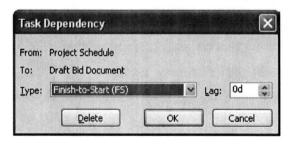

A Link may only be edited or deleted from this form.

9.4.7   Autolink New Inserted Tasks or Moved Tasks

This function automatically creates predecessors to tasks above it and successors below it when a task is moved or inserted. This option may be activated by selecting the **Tools**, **Options…**, **Schedule** tab and checking the **Autolink inserted or moved tasks** box. When activated you must ensure that:

- You have selected the whole task by clicking on the Task ID and therefore highlighting all the columns before you drag the task to a new location. Otherwise, you will only move the cell contents.

 When the task is moved, **Autolink New Tasks or Moved** tasks will change the existing predecessor and successor logic without warning. This function potentially makes substantial changes to your project logic and may affect the overall project duration. It is suggested that the option is **NEVER** switched on as dragging an activity to a new location may completely change the logic of a schedule.

9.4.8   Editing Relationships Using the Predecessor or Successor Columns

The **Predecessor** or **Successor** column may be displayed and edited following the example below.

	❶	Task Name	Successors	Predecessors	18 December S S M T W T F S S
1		Task 1	2SS+3 days,3		
2		Successor 1	3	1SS+3 days	
3		Successor 2		1,2	

9.4.9   Unique ID Predecessor or Unique ID Successor Columns

Each task is assigned a Unique ID when it is created and this number is not used again in the schedule, even if the task is deleted. There are two other columns that may be used to edit and display relationships using the Unique ID:

- The **Unique ID Predecessor**, and
- The **Unique ID Successor**.

 The unique Task **Unique ID** will allow users to identify easily which activities have been added or deleted when a revised schedule has been submitted. On the other hand if one wants to reset the unique ID, or hide the addition or deletion of tasks then a new schedule may be created, the calendars transferred with Organizer and all the tasks copied and pasted into the new schedule. There is also a unique **Resource ID** and a unique Resource Assignment **Unique ID**.

9.4.10   Editing Relationships Using WBS Predecessor or Successor Columns

There are two other columns that may be used only to display (and not edit) the **Predecessors** and **Successors**:

- The **WBS Predecessor**, and
- **WBS Successor**.

9.5   Scheduling the Project

Once you have your tasks and the logic in place, Microsoft Project calculates the tasks' dates/times. More specifically, Microsoft Project has **Scheduled** the project to calculate the **Early Dates**, **Late Dates** and the **Total Float**. This will allow you to review the **Critical Path** of the project. Microsoft Project uses the term **Slack** instead of the standard term **Float**. Both terms are used interchangeably throughout this book.

Sometimes it is preferable to prevent the **Automatic Calculation** of your project's start/end dates. To do this, select **Tools**, **Options…**, **Calculation** tab. Click on **Manual**.

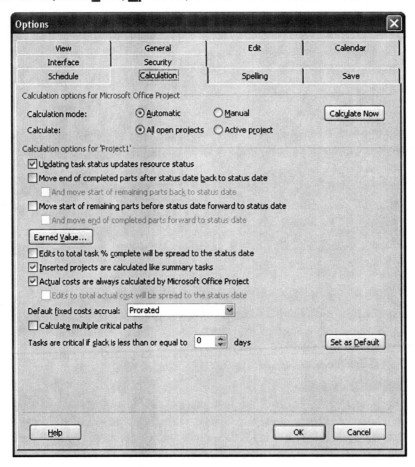

To calculate the schedule with the calculation mode set to manual:

- Press the **F9 Key**, or

- Click on the **Select All** button, top left-hand corner of the Gantt Chart view, right-click to open a menu and select **Calculate Project**.

9.6   Task Drivers

A task may not be on the Critical Path and may have more than one predecessor. A **Driving Relationship** is the predecessor that determines the Early Start of a task. Microsoft Project 2000 – 2003 does not identify the difference between **Driving** and **Non-driving Relationships**, which often makes analyzing a schedule difficult. In earlier versions of Microsoft Project often the simplest way to determine the driving relationship for tasks not on the critical path and with more than one predecessor was to delete the relationships until the task moved. Primavera products have always displayed the driving predecessors and successors in the Predecessor and Successors.

Microsoft Project 2007 introduced a **Task Drivers** form that indicates which is the driving predecessor and whether the schedule has been Resource Leveled. It will also display the effects of leveling.

Select the Task Drivers icon on the Standard Toolbar to open the **Task Drivers** pane:

- The picture below shows that task 10 is the driving predecessor of task 13.

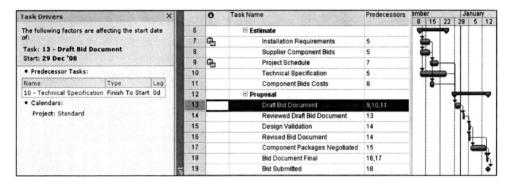

- The picture below shows that task 11 has been delayed by leveling:

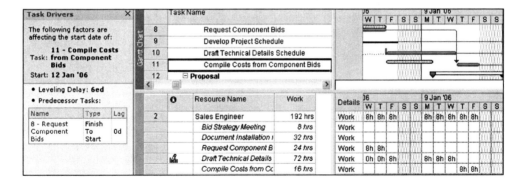

WORKSHOP 7

Adding the Relationships

Background

You have determined the logical sequence of tasks, so you may now create the relationships.

Assignment

1. Remove the text from the bars.

2. Apply the **Entry** table.

3. Input the logic below using several of the methods detailed in this chapter.

	Task Name	Predecessors
1	⊟ **OzBuild Bid**	
2	⊟ **Research**	
3	Bid Request Documents Received	
4	Bid Strategy	3
5	Technical Feasibility Study	4
6	⊟ **Estimate**	
7	Installation Requirements	5
8	Supplier Component Bids	5
9	Project Schedule	7
10	Technical Specification	5
11	Component Bids Costs	8
12	⊟ **Proposal**	
13	Draft Bid Document	9,10,11
14	Reviewed Draft Bid Document	13
15	Design Validation	14
16	Revised Bid Document	14
17	Component Packages Negotiated	15
18	Bid Document Final	16,17
19	Bid Submitted	18

4. Hide and display the Logic Links using **Format**, **Layout**…. (If your links are displayed by default, then hide and then display them again.)

5. Check your results against the diagram on the next page.

6. Save your **OzBuild Bid** project.

ANSWER TO WORKSHOP 7

	❶	Task Name	Duration	Start	Finish	Predecessors
1		⊟ OzBuild Bid	30d	1 Dec '08	14 Jan '09	
2		⊟ Research	9d	1 Dec '08	11 Dec '08	
3		Bid Request Documents Received	0d	1 Dec '08	1 Dec '08	
4		Bid Strategy	1d	1 Dec '08	1 Dec '08	3
5		Technical Feasibility Study	8d	2 Dec '08	11 Dec '08	4
6		⊟ Estimate	9d	12 Dec '08	24 Dec '08	
7	📇	Installation Requirements	4d	12 Dec '08	16 Dec '08	5
8		Supplier Component Bids	3d	12 Dec '08	16 Dec '08	5
9	📇	Project Schedule	4d	17 Dec '08	20 Dec '08	7
10		Technical Specification	9d	12 Dec '08	24 Dec '08	5
11		Component Bids Costs	2d	17 Dec '08	18 Dec '08	8
12		⊟ Proposal	12d	29 Dec '08	14 Jan '09	
13		Draft Bid Document	3d	29 Dec '08	31 Dec '08	9,10,11
14		Reviewed Draft Bid Document	1d	2 Jan '09	2 Jan '09	13
15		Design Validation	1d	5 Jan '09	5 Jan '09	14
16		Revised Bid Document	1d	5 Jan '09	5 Jan '09	14
17		Component Packages Negotiated	6d	6 Jan '09	13 Jan '09	15
18		Bid Document Final	1d	14 Jan '09	14 Jan '09	16,17
19		Bid Submitted	0d	14 Jan '09	14 Jan '09	18

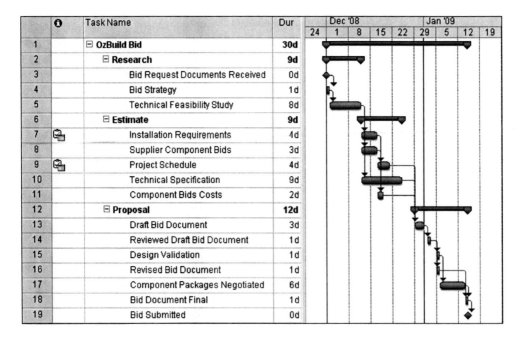

10 NETWORK DIAGRAM VIEW

The **Network Diagram View** is an enhancement of the earlier versions of Microsoft Project **Pert View** and displays tasks as boxes connected by the relationship lines. This chapter will not cover this subject in detail but will introduce the main features.

To view your project in the Networking View:

- Select **View**, **Networking Diagram**, or

- Click on the **Networking Diagram** icon ▨ on the **View Bar** on the left-hand side of the screen.

Many features available in the **Gantt Chart View** are also available in the **Network Diagram View**, including:

Topic	Menu Command
• Add new tasks	Click and drag into a blank area. This will add a new Task with a Finish-to-Start relationship, or Use the **Insert Key** or select **Insert, New Task**. These tasks are added after the highlighted task without a relationship.
• Delete Tasks	Select the task and press the **Delete** key.
• Display the **Task Information** form	Double-click on a Task Box, or Highlight a task and right-click on it and select **Task Information...** for the menu.
• Format Dependencies	Select **Format, Layout...**
• Display the **Task Dependency** form	Double-click on a relationship line.
• Display information in the lower pane	Select **Window, Split**, or Drag the dividing bar.
• Format Task Boxes	Select **Format, Box Styles...**, or Double-click on the outside edge of a box.
• Format an individual Task Box	Select **Format, Box...**
• Change the scale of the display	Select **View, Zoom...** which displays the **Zoom** form.

10.1 PRINCE2 Product Flow Diagram

The **Network Diagramming View** may be used to create and display the **PRINCE2 Product Flow Diagram** but the combination of the software functionality and the PRINCE2 requirements makes it difficult to use for this purpose:

- The formatting and presentation of the boxes around the Task Names are linked to scheduling functions; for example, Critical Activities may be assigned a specific box format. Thus it is not possible to automatically assign box formatting to External and Integration Products. It is possible to assign formatting to individual tasks, such as External Products, but this process is time consuming. It is also possible to make the formatting of all the box styles the same.

- Elliptical Boxes are not available for External Products and therefore these would have to be represented with, for example, boxes with round corners or a stretched octagon, as per the **Bid Request Documents Received** task in the picture below.

- A filter should be created to ensure that only tasks designated as Products are displayed. When a situation evolves where Products are a mixture of Detail and Summary tasks the filters become problematic because the filters have an option to show or not show Summary Tasks and the result will be some products hidden when they should be displayed. A text column could be considered to indicate which tasks are Products and a filter created to show only these tasks.

- The default boxes are designed to display scheduling data such as dates and float and are not ideal for the display of simple data such as descriptions.

Therefore to produce a Product Flow Diagram like the one below, which is covered in detail in **Chapter 13 VIEWS, TABLES & DETAILS**:

- The skill and experience of the operator in Microsoft Project needs to be high, and

- Different shapes specified by PRINCE2 for External and Integration Products will need to be abandoned.

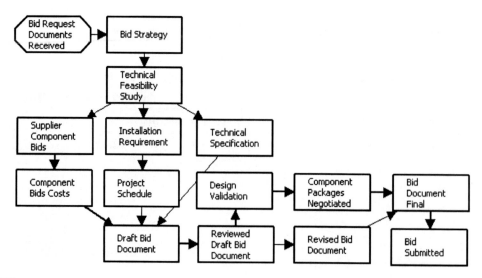

When more than one project requires the Product Flow Diagram to be displayed using Microsoft Project, then a template should be created to save time in formatting each project, or the **View** could be copied from one project to another using the **Organizer** function.

10.2   Understanding the Network Diagram View

The following list describes the main display features of the Network Diagram View:

- Summary Tasks, Detail Tasks and Milestones are normally formatted with a different shape. Typical shape examples are provided as follows:
  - ➢ Summary Tasks are Trapezoidal –
  - ➢ Detail Tasks are Rectangular –
  - ➢ The Milestone Task is an elongated diamond –

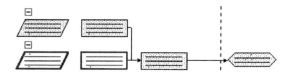

- Summary Tasks are positioned to the left and at the same level or above Detail Tasks.

- Summary Tasks may be rolled up by clicking on the ⊟ above the Task and expanded by clicking on the ⊞ above a rolled up summary task.

- All relationship lines are drawn as **Finish-to-Start** even when they are not linked as a **Finish-to-Start** relationship. The link type may be displayed on the arrow. See **Link style** later in this chapter.

- Critical Tasks may be formatted to have different borders and backgrounds.

- The contents of the Task Boxes and relationship lines may also be formatted.

10.3   Adding and Deleting Tasks in the Network Diagramming View

- A **New Task** may be created with a **Finish-to-Start** relationship by dragging from the center of a Task Box into a blank part of the screen.

- A **New Task** may be created without a relationship below the tasks position in the Gantt Chart by:
  - ➢ Using the **Insert Key**, or
  - ➢ Selecting **Insert, New Task**.

10.4   Adding, Editing and Deleting Dependencies

Dependencies may be added, deleted or edited using the following methods:

- Graphically add a relationship by clicking on the center of one task and dragging to the successor.

- Hold the **Ctrl Key** to select two or more tasks and then use the **Link** function.

- The **Unlink** removes dependencies between selected tasks.

- Open the **Task Information** form by double-clicking on a task and selecting the **Predecessors** tab.

- Double-click on a **Relationship line** to open the **Task Dependency** form and edit or delete a dependency.

- Create a split window by selecting **Window, Split.** Display the predecessors and successors in the lower pane by selecting **Format, Details, Predecessors and Successors**.

10.5   Formatting the Task Boxes

Task Boxes may be formatted from the **Box Styles** form, which is displayed by:

- Selecting **Format, Box Styles…,** or

- Double-clicking on the outside edge of a box.

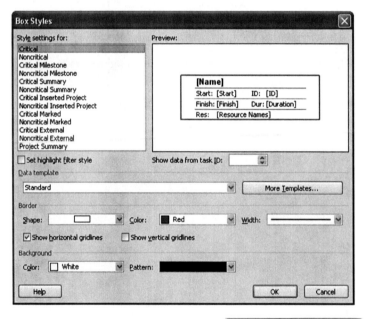

- A new template may be created by clicking on the ☐ More Templates… ☐ button which will open the **Data Templates** form.

10.6 Formatting Individual Boxes

One highlighted, **Task Box** may be formatted differently than all others by selecting **Format**, **Box...** to open the **Format Box** form.

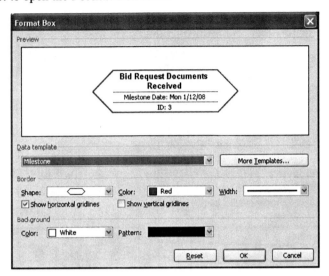

The [Reset] button is used to set the formatting back to default.

10.7 Formatting the Display and Relationship Lines

Most formatting, except formatting the boxes, is set within the **Layout** form. Select **Format**, **Layout...** to open the **Layout** form:

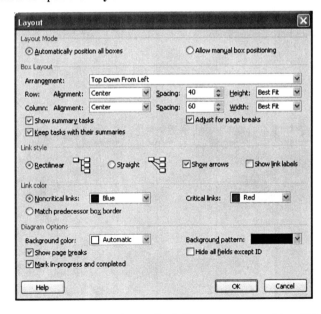

- The **Layout Mode** allows you to drag a Task Box to a new position. When **Allow manual box positioning** is selected, place the mouse over the Task Box. When it changes to a ✛, drag the box to the required location.

- **Box Layout** allows you to specify how the Task Boxes are arranged. This option will only work when **Layout Mode** is set to **Automatically position all boxes**. For example, when "Top Down by Week" is selected, all the Tasks that start in the first week will be placed in the first column. The other options under **Box Layout** should be self-explanatory.

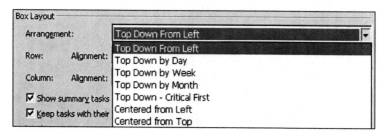

- **Link style** is an option to display relationships. Checking **Show link labels** will place the Relationship Type and Lag on the relationship line and is useful when all your relationships are not Finish-to-Start. See below.

- **Link color** allows you to specify the color of the critical links and other link types. Selecting the option **Match predecessor box border** sets the format of the relationship lines to the predecessor's box border format. The formatting of links is not available in the Gantt Chart view.

- **Diagram Options** are self-explanatory. The **Hide all fields except ID** will display the Task Boxes, as below. In the example, note that **Show link labels** has also been checked:

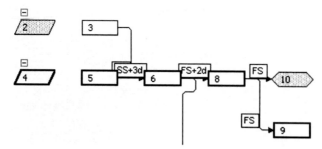

10.8 Early Date, Late Date and Float/Slack Calculations

To help understand the calculation of late and early dates, float and critical path, we will now manually work through an example. The boxes below represent tasks on a 7 day per week calendar..

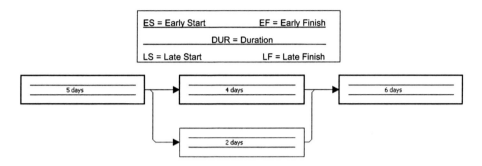

The forward pass calculates the early dates: $EF = ES + DUR - 1$

Start the calculation from the first task and work forward in time.

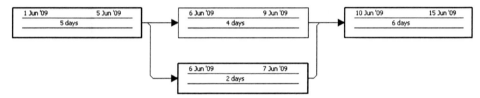

The backward pass calculates the late dates: $LS = LF - DUR + 1$

Start the calculation at the last task and work backward in time.

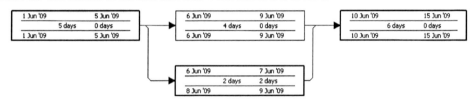

The **Critical Path** is the path where any delay causes a delay in the project and runs through the top row of tasks.

Total Float is the difference between either the **Late Finish** and the **Early Finish** or the difference between the **Late Start** and the **Early Start**. The 2 days' task has float of $10 - 8 = 2$ or $8 - 6 = 2$ days. None of the other tasks has float.

The example above would look like the picture below in the Gantt Chart view:

Duration	Early Start	Finish	Total Slack	1 Jun '09							8 Jun '09							15 Jun '09			
				S	M	T	W	T	F	S	S	M	T	W	T	F	S	S	M	T	W	T
5 days	1 Jun '09	5 Jun '09	0 days																			
4 days	6 Jun '09	9 Jun '09	0 days																			
6 days	10 Jun '09	15 Jun '09	0 days																			
2 days	6 Jun '09	7 Jun '09	2 days																			

WORKSHOP 8

Scheduling Calculations

Background

We want to practice calculating Early and Late dates with a simple manual exercise.

Assignment

Calculate the early and late dates for the following tasks, assuming a Monday to Friday working week and the first task starts on 1 Jun 09.

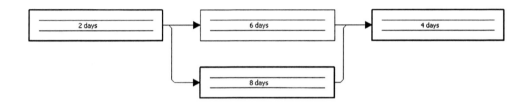

	June 2009					
M	T	W	Th	F	S	S
1	2	3	4	5	6	7
8	9	10	11	12	13	14
15	16	17	18	19	20	21
22	23	24	25	26	27	28
29	30					

ANSWER TO WORKSHOP 8

Early Start		Early Finish
	Duration	Float
Late Start		Late Finish

Forward Pass   EF = ES + DUR −1

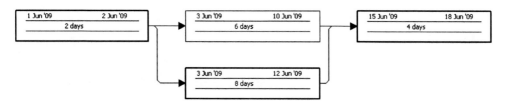

Backward Pass   LS = LF − DUR +1

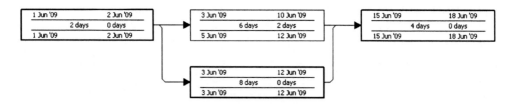

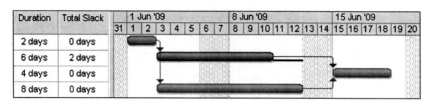

11 CONSTRAINTS

Constraints are used to impose logic on tasks that may not be realistically scheduled with logic links. Microsoft Project will only allow one constraint against a given task with the exception of a **Deadline Date**. This chapter will deal with the following constraints in detail which are the minimum number of constraints that are required to effectively schedule a project:

- **Start No Earlier Than**

- **Finish No Later Than**

These two constraints may be applied to summary and detailed tasks; all others may only be applied to detailed tasks.

- **Start No Earlier Than** (also known as an "Early Start" constraint) is used when the start date of a task has been set by a client or an external event. Microsoft Project will not schedule the task early start date prior to this date.

- **Finish No Later Than** (also known as a "Late Finish" constraint) is used when the latest finish date is stipulated. Microsoft Project will not show the task's Late Finish date after this date, but the Early Finish date will be able to exceed this date and Negative Float will be generated when the Late Date is earlier than the Early Date. This represents the amount of time to be "caught up" to finish the project on time.

The following chart summarizes the methods used to assign Constraints to Tasks:

Topic	Notes for Creating a Constraint
• Open the **Task Information** form.	Double-click on the Task and select the **Advanced** tab.
• Display the **Constraint Type** and **Constraint Date** columns.	Apply the **Constraint Table** or insert the columns in an existing table.
• Type a date into a date field of the **Task Information** form or the **Details** form or a column.	A date typed in an Early Start box will apply a **Start No Earlier Than** constraint of that date, without warning. A date typed in an Early Finish box will apply a **Finish No Later Than** constraint, without warning.
• Display a **Combination** view displaying the **Task Details** form in the lower pane.	Open the bottom pane, select **View**, **More Views…**, highlight the **Task Details** and click on Apply .

There is an option found under the **Tools**, **Options…**, **Schedule** tab titled **Tasks will always honor their constraint dates**. This function is described in detail in the **OPTIONS** chapter, **Schedule** section. When this option is checked, which is the default, constraints override a logic link. When unchecked, a logic link will override a constraint and a task may be delayed.

Only one constraint may be applied to an activity except when a **Deadline Date** is assigned to an activity. Primavera products allow two constraints per activity. This topic is discussed in this chapter.

A full list of **constraints** available in Microsoft Project:

- **As Soon As Possible**   This is the default for a new task. A task is scheduled to occur as soon as possible and does not have a Constraint Date.

- **As Late As Possible**   A Task will be scheduled to occur as late as possible and does not have any particular Constraint Date. The Early and Late dates have the same date. A task with this constraint has no Total Float and delays the start of all the successor activities.

- **Start No Earlier Than**   This constraint sets a date before which the task will not start.

- **Start No Later Than**   This constraint sets a date after which the task will not start.

- **Must Start On**   This constraint sets a date on which the task will start. Therefore the task has no float. The early start and the late start dates are set to be the same as the Constraint Date.

- **Must Finish On**   This constraint sets a date on which the task will finish and therefore has no float. The early finish and the late finish dates are set to be the same as the Constraint Date.

- **Finish No Earlier Than**   This sets a date before which the task will not finish.

- **Finish No Later Than**   This sets a date after which the task will not finish.

- **Deadline Date**   This is similar to applying a **Finish No Later Than** constraint. This offers the opportunity of putting a second constraint on a task.

Earlier Than constraints operate on the **Early Dates** and **Later Than** constraints operate on **Late Dates**. The picture below demonstrates how constraints calculate Total Float (Total Slack) of tasks (without predecessors or successors) against the first task of 10 days' duration:

	Duration	Constraint Date	Constraint Type	Total Slack	Late Start	Late Finish	15 Nov '09	22 Nov '09	29 Nov '09
1	10 days	NA	As Soon As Possible	0 days	17 Nov '09	30 Nov '09			
2	3 days	NA	As Late As Possible	0 days	28 Nov '09	30 Nov '09			
3	3 days	24 Nov '09	Start No Earlier Than	2 days	26 Nov '09	30 Nov '09			
4	3 days	25 Nov '09	Start No Later Than	6 days	25 Nov '09	27 Nov '09			
5	3 days	24 Nov '09	Must Start On	0 days	24 Nov '09	26 Nov '09			
6	3 days	21 Nov '09	Must Finish On	0 days	18 Nov '09	21 Nov '09			
7	3 days	25 Nov '09	Start No Earlier Than	1 day	26 Nov '09	30 Nov '09			
8	3 days	26 Nov '09	Finish No Later Than	5 days	24 Nov '09	26 Nov '09			

1. An **Expected Finish** is used in Primavera software to calculate the remaining duration of a task. There is no equivalent of this constraint in Microsoft Project 2003.

2. An activity assigned with an **As Late as Possible** constraint in Primavera software will schedule the activity so it absorbs only **Free Float** and will not delay the start of successor activities. In Microsoft Project, a task assigned with an **As Late as Possible** constraint will be delayed to absorb the Total Float and delay all its successor activities, not just the activity with the constraint. Therefore an **As Late as Possible** constraint must be used with care in Microsoft Project.

11.1   Assigning Constraints

11.1.1   Open the Task Information Form

To assign a constraint using the **Task Information** form:

- Double-click on a task to open the form,

- Select the **Advanced** tab,

- Select the **Constraint type:** from the drop-down box,

- Select the **Constraint date:** from the calendar, or type the date in the box, and

- Click on the [OK] button to accept the constraint.

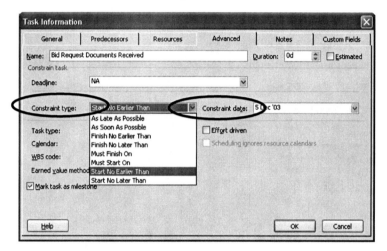

11.1.2   Displaying the Constraint Type and Constraint Date Column

To assign a constraint using the **Constraint Type** and **Constraint Date** columns:

- Either
  - ➢ Insert the **Constraint Type** and **Constraint Date** columns in your existing table by selecting **Insert, Column…**, or
  - ➢ Select the **Constraint Dates** table by selecting **View, Table:, More Tables….**

- Assign your **Constraint Type** and **Constraint Date** from the drop-down boxes in the columns.

	Task Name	Duration	Constraint Type
6	⊟ **Estimate**	**18d**	**As Soon As Possible**
7	Installation Requirements	4d	Start No Earlier Than
8	Supplier Component Bids	3d	As Late As Possible
9	Project Schedule	4d	As Soon As Possible
10	Technical Specification	9d	Finish No Earlier Than
11	Component Bids Costs	2d	Finish No Later Than
12	⊟ **Proposal**	**12d**	Must Finish On
13	Draft Bid Document	3d	Must Start On
			Start No Earlier Than
			Start No Later Than

11.1.3   Typing a Date into the Task Information or Details Form

You may assign some constraints from the **Task Information** or **Task Details** form:

- A **Start No Earlier** constraint is assigned by overtyping the Start date, and

- A **Finish No Earlier** constraint is assigned by overtyping the Finish date.

You may overtype or select a date from the drop-down box.

> This function provides no warning that a constraint has been set and new users need to be careful when they enter a date into a Start or Finish box.

11.1.4   Display a Combination View through the Task Details Form

There are a number of forms where constraints may be set, including the **Task Details** form, which is covered in detail in the **VIEWS, TABLES AND DETAILS** chapter. The **Task Details** form may be displayed by:

- Splitting the screen by selecting **Window**, **Split**,

- Making the bottom pane active by clicking in the bottom half anywhere, or

- Selecting **View**, **More Views…**, and the **Task Details** form from the drop-down list:

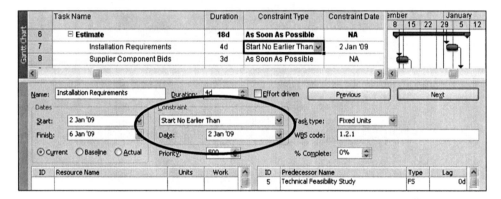

11.2   Deadline Date

Deadline Date was a new Microsoft Project 2000 feature, which allows the setting of a date that a task should be completed. A **Deadline Date** is similar to placing a **Finish No Later Than** constraint on a task and affects the calculation of the **Late Finish** date and float of the activity. A second constraint such as an Early Start constraint may also be assigned to a task with a Deadline Date.

The Deadline Date may be displayed as a column and the display on the bar chart may be formatted as such. This is covered in the **FORMATTING THE DISPLAY** chapter.

> An Indicator icon ◆ is placed in the Indicator column when the Deadline Date creates Negative Float.

11.3 Schedule From Project Finish Date

You are able to impose an absolute project finish date by setting the **Schedule from:** option to **Project Finish Date** in the **Project Information** form.

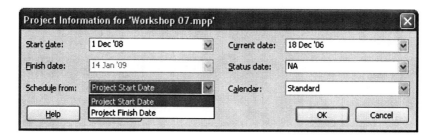

This option may be set after tasks have been added to the schedule. From the point in time that the project is set to schedule from the Project Finish date all new tasks will be assigned with an **As Late As Possible** (ALAP) constraint as they are created.

Any original tasks which may be set as **As Early As Possible** (AEAP) may either be:

- Reset as ALAP, and calculated with all new tasks as ALAP, or

- Left as AEAP.

When the original tasks are left as AEAP, the tasks will be scheduled as AEAP with a Start No Earlier constraint which is calculated either:

- With no float when their combined durations are greater than the ALAP tasks, and the Total Float extends beyond the Project Finish Date, identified by the vertical line in the pictures below:

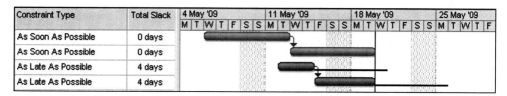

- Will not start earlier than the earliest Early Start of the ALAP tasks when their combined durations are greater than the ALAP tasks.

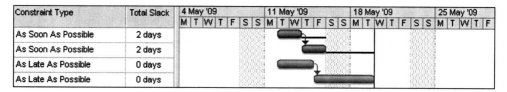

 Unlike Primavera software it is not possible in Microsoft Project to set both a start and finish date on a project. These dates are often called project constraints.

11.4 Task Notes

It is often important to note why constraints have been set. Microsoft Project has functions that enable you to note information associated with a task, including the reasons associated for establishing a constraint. Notes may also be used for recording Product Descriptions.

The **Task Information** form has a **Note** tab, which has some word processing-type formatting functions.

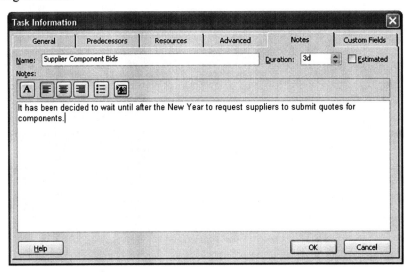

The notes may be displayed by:

- Inserting the **Notes** column. Now the Indicators column has a 📝 to indicate a note and a 🖻 to indicate a constraint:

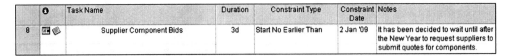

	ⓘ	Task Name	Duration	Constraint Type	Constraint Date	Notes
8	🖻📝	Supplier Component Bids	3d	Start No Earlier Than	2 Jan '09	It has been decided to wait until after the New Year to request suppliers to submit quotes for components.

- Displaying the note next to the task bar chart:

- There is an option for printing task notes in the **Page Setup...**, **View** form and this option prints the Task ID, Task Name and Note on a separate sheet:

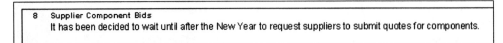

Other options for recording tasks notes are:

- Display and use one of the Text columns and the title may be renamed or customized.
- Insert a Text Box on the Gantt Chart using **Insert**, **Drawing** and clicking on the Text Box icon, 🖹, and placing a note in the Text Box.

WORKSHOP 9

Constraints

Background

Management has provided further input to your schedule.

Assignment

1. Insert the **Total Slack** (Float) column into the **Entry** table between the **Finish** and **Predecessor** column.

2. Run the **Gantt Chart Wizard** found under the **Format** command, and select **Custom Gantt** Chart. Display the Critical Path and Total Float (Slack) in the Gantt Chart, do not display resources and dates, and show the link lines between dependent tasks.

3. Create a **Negative Slack** (Float) bar by selecting **Format, Bar Styles...** and adding a bar as displayed below:

Name	Appearance	Show For ... Tasks	Row	From	To
Negative Float	▲————		1	Negative Slack	Start

4. Observe the calculated finish and the critical path of the project before applying any constraints.

5. The client has said that they require the submission on 22 Jan 09. Apply a **Finish No Later Than** constraint and assign a constraint date of 22 Jan 09 to task 19 **Bid Submitted** task review float. If you are presented with an error message, read the message carefully and then set the constraint. There should be no change in the Total Float.

6. Due to proximity to Christmas, management has requested we delay the **Supplier Component Bids** until first thing in the New Year, 02 Jan 09. Consensus is that a better response and sharper prices will be obtained after the Christmas rush. Record this in the task notes.

    ➢ To achieve this, set a **Start No Earlier Than** constraint and a constraint date of 02 Jan 09 on task 8, **Supplier Component Bids**. Should you be presented with an error message, allow scheduling conflict and set the constraint.

    ➢ Now observe the impact on the critical path and end dates.

7. After review, it is agreed that 2 days can be deducted from task 17 **Component Packages Negotiated**. Change the duration of this task to 4 days. Press **F9** to ensure the schedule is recalculated.

8. Save your **OzBuild Bid** project.

9. We will require a copy of this schedule later. Save the project as **OzBuild No Resources** and close it.

ANSWER TO WORKSHOP 9

Before delaying the **Supplier Component Bids** until 2 Jan 09:

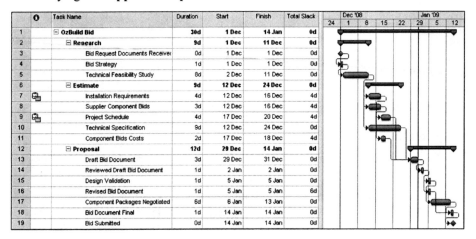

After delaying the **Supplier Component Bids** until 2 Jan 09:

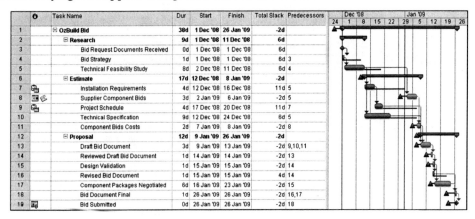

After trimming 2 days from **Component Packages Negotiated**:

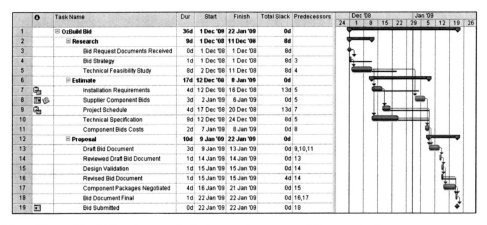

Note: If your Total Float is not calculating as above, press F9 to recalculate.

12 FILTERS

This chapter covers the use of **Filters** to select which activities are displayed on the screen and in printouts.

Filters could be created in a PRINCE2 project to display activities for Stage plans, Team plans or specific Products.

12.1 Understanding Filters

Microsoft Project has an ability to display tasks that meet specific criteria. You may want to see only the incomplete tasks, or the work scheduled for the next couple of months, or the tasks that are in-progress, assigned a specific resource, responsibility, phase, discipline, system or belong to a physical area of a project.

Microsoft Project defaults to displaying all tasks. It has a number of predefined filters available that you may use or edit and you may also create one or more of your own.

A filter may be applied to display or to highlight tasks that meet a criteria and operate on both the activities displayed on screen and in printouts.

There are **Task** filters that apply to **Task** views and **Resource** filters that apply to **Resource** views. Both types are created and applied in the same way.

There are two types of filters:

- The first is where you select a **Filter** which exists or has been created using the **Filters** form.

- The second is to create an **AutoFilter** which is very similar to the Excel **AutoFilter** (Drop-down filter) function.

Topic	Menu Command
• Apply a **Filter**	Select **Project**, **Filter for: All Tasks**, or With the **Formatting** toolbar displayed, select the filter from the **Filter** drop-down list.
• Create or modify a **Filter**	Select **Project**, **Filter for: All Tasks**, **More Filters...** to open the **More Filters...** form.
• Turn on **AutoFilter**	Select **Project**, **Filter for: All tasks**, **AutoFilter**, or Click on the **AutoFilter** ⧩ icon on the **Formatting** toolbar.
• Apply an **AutoFilter**	Click on the ⧩ icon in the column headers.

12.2   Applying an Existing Filter

Filters may be applied using several methods:

Method 1
Select **P̱roject, F̱ilter for: All Tasks,** and select the filter required from the menu.

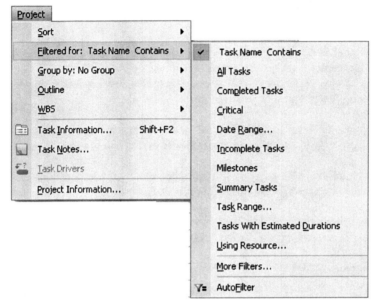

Only filters with the **Show in menu** check box checked in the **Filter Definition** form are displayed in the **Filtered for:** menu. The currently applied filter is always displayed after **Filtered for:** in the menu. See the picture above where the currently applied filter is the **Task Name Contains** filter.

This may not be a complete list of filters, as this list displays only filters selected to be displayed in the menu when they were created.

Method 2
Display the **Formatting** toolbar, and select the filter you require from the drop-down list:

Select **V̱iew, Ṯoolbars, Formatting** to display the formatting toolbar.

This may not be a complete list of filters, as this list displays only filters chosen to be displayed from the **Filter Definition** form in the menu when they were created or edited.

Method 3

Select **Project**, **Filter for: All Tasks**, **More Filters…** to open the **More Filters…** form:

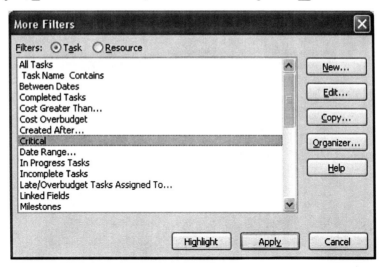

- The two radio buttons at the top of the form allow you to select filters that operate either on a **Task** criteria or on a **Resource** criteria.
  - ➢ **Task** criteria will operate on the criteria of most data such as dates, durations, text columns, number columns, outline and WBS.
  - ➢ **Resource** criteria will operate on a similar criteria as Tasks but will select the resource value and not the task value.
- Select the required filter from the drop-down list, and
- Select either:
  - ➢ Highlight to highlight the tasks that meet the criteria, or
  - ➢ Apply to display only the tasks that meet the criteria.

12.3 Creating and Modifying Filters

Select **Project**, **Filter for: All Tasks**, **More Filters...** to open the **More Filters** form where you may create or modify a filter:

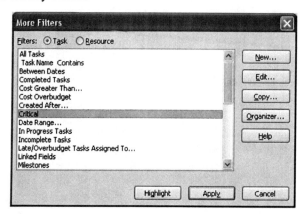

- Click on **Organizer...** to copy a filter to and from another open project.
- Click on:
  - ➤ **New...** to create a new filter, or
  - ➤ **Edit...** to edit an existing filter, or
  - ➤ **Copy...** to copy an existing filter.
- The **Filter Definition** form will be displayed. The one-line example below will only display critical tasks.

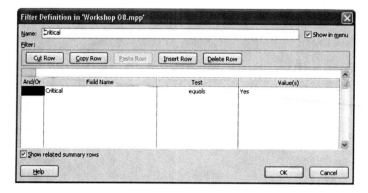

- The filter may be edited in the **Filter Definition** form to display or highlight the required tasks.
- Checking the **Show in menu** box will place the **filter** in the menu.
- Checking **Show related summary rows** will display any associated Summary Tasks.
- Select **OK** to return to the **More Filters** form.

> *i* It is useful to place a space at the start of the filter name when creating a new filter as this will place the filter at the top of the list, as per the **Task Name Contains** filter in the picture at the top of this page.

12.4 Defining Filter Criteria

The filter criteria is determined by four columns of information in the **Filter Definition** form:

- **And/Or** functions when you have two or more lines of data in the **Filter Definition** form to operate on.

- **Field Name** defines the data field you want to operate on.

- **Test** sets the criteria such as "Greater Than" or "Less Than" or "Equals."

- **Value(s)** is/are a date, number, Yes/No or text for the **Test** field to operate on. If more than one value is to be considered, for example when a **Test** is "Between," the two values are separated by a comma ",". The example below is a filter that will only display detail activities that will start between 1 Dec 08 and 30 Dec 08.

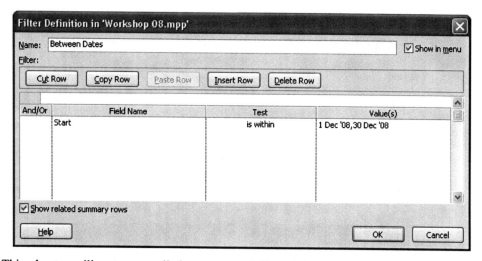

This chapter will not cover all the aspects of filter definitions but will cover the major principles, so you may experiment when you require a filter.

There are a number of predefined filters with a standard Microsoft Project installation. You should inspect these to gain an understanding of how filters are constructed and applied.

12.4.1 Simple Filters, Operator and Wild Cards

A simple **Filter** contains one line of data and therefore the **And/Or** function is not used. These are the most common filters and meet most common filtering requirements.

These filters are used for purposes such as displaying tasks which:

- Are not started, complete, or in-progress tasks.

- Have a Start or Finish before or after a particular date.

- Contain specific text.

- Are within a range of dates.

There are some operands you should be aware of:

- Some fields may have "**Yes**" or "**No**" entered in the **Value(s).** The task fields that may be filtered using a "**Yes**" or "**No**" include:
    - ➤ Summary, is the task a Summary or Detail task,
    - ➤ Critical, is the task identified as critical when the Total Slack is less than or equal to the value entered in the **Calculation** tab or the **Options** form,
    - ➤ Milestones,
    - ➤ Effort-Driven, and
    - ➤ Any other field that may be displayed in columns with a "**Yes**" or "**No**" option.

The filter below will select all tasks that are not Milestones:

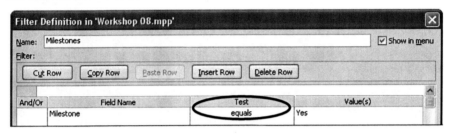

- The **Wildcard** functions are similar to the DOS Wildcard functions and are mainly used for filtering text:
    - ➤ You may replace a single character with a "?". Thus, a filter searching for a word containing "b?t" will display words like "bat", "bit" and "but."
    - ➤ You may replace a group of characters with an *. Thus, a filter searching for a word containing "b*t" will display words like "blot", "blight" and "but."

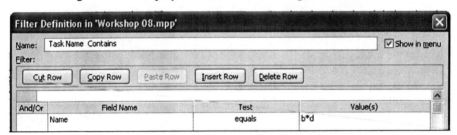

NOTE: For the Wildcard function to operate the **equals Test** must be used. This function does not work with other operands and in this mode works as a **contains** operand.

- **NA** allows the selection of a blank value. The filter below displays tasks without either a Baseline Start or Baseline Finish date:

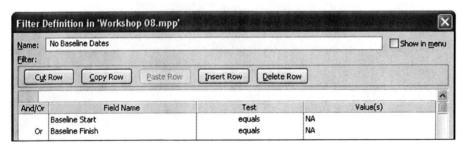

- A **Calculated Filter** compares one value with another. The **Value(s)** field is selected from the drop-down box. The example below will display those tasks that are scheduled to start later than the Baseline start:

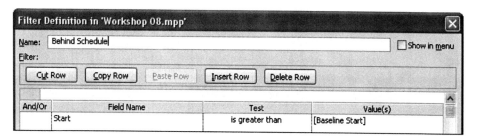

12.4.2   And/Or Filters

The **And/Or** function allows a search for tasks which meet more than one criteria by using the **And/Or** option:

- The filter below displays tasks with Slack less than 5 days **And** contain the word "Bid":

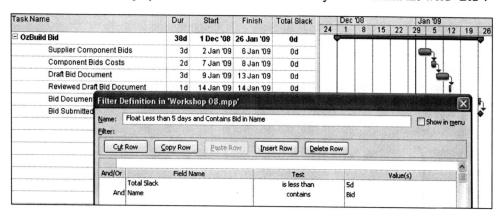

- The filter below is similar to the one above but displays tasks with Slack less than 5 days **Or** contain the word "Bid", It displays many more tasks:

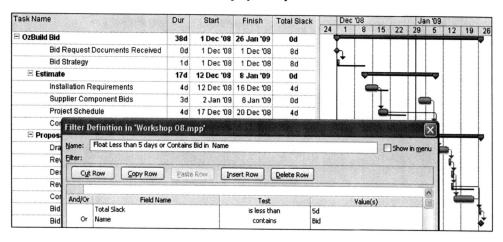

12.4.3 Multiple And/Or

Multiple **And/Or** statements are possible by placing a line with only an **And/Or** statement. The filter below selects tasks that have a Baseline Finish and are scheduled to finish late or are not completing their work quick enough, shown as the Budgeted Cost of Work Performed (Earned Value) is less than the Budgeted Cost of Work Scheduled (Planned Value):

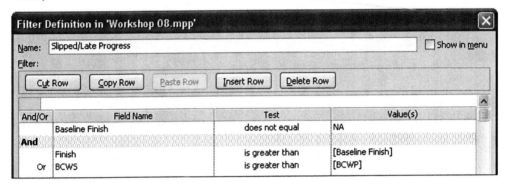

12.4.4 Interactive Filter

These filters allow you to enter the **Value(s)** of the filtered field after applying the filter. The filter is tailored each time it is applied via a user-prompt. The filter below will ask you to enter a word in the task name.

For this function to operate properly, the text in the **Value(s)** field must commence with a double quote " and end with a double quote and question mark "? :

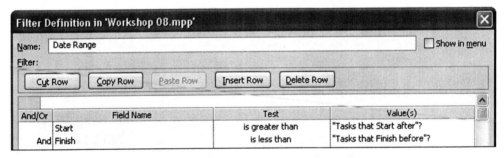

After the filter is applied, you will be presented with the **Interactive Filter** form to enter the required text:

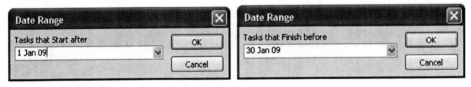

12.5 AutoFilters

Microsoft Project **AutoFilters** are similar to the Excel **AutoFilter** function and allow you to select the filter criteria from drop-down menus in the column headers.

To create an **AutoFilter** based on one parameter:

- Use one of the following methods to turn on the **AutoFilter** function:
    - ➤ **Project, Filter for: All tasks, AutoFilter**, or
    - ➤ Click on the **AutoFilter** [▼=] icon located on the **Formatting** toolbar.
- The column headers will display the [▼] icon in the column header. Click on this icon in one of the columns to display a drop-down box:

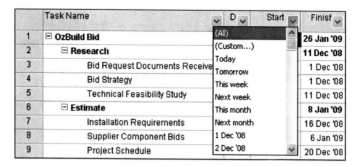

- Select the required criteria from the drop-down box. The period in the drop-down boxes refer to the Current Date, not the Status Date.

You may now select another column and create a filter based on a second parameter to further reduce the number of tasks displayed.

To create a **Custom AutoFilter**, which is based on two parameters:

- Click on the [▼] icon in the column headers.

- Select the **(Custom…)** option to open the **Custom AutoFilter** form:

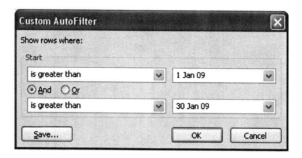

- Select the parameters you want to operate on from the four drop-down boxes and check the **And** or **Or** radio button.

- To save a drop-down filter as a normal filter, click on the [Save…] button, which opens the **Filter Definition** form.

 AutoFilters always select the associated Summary tasks of any selected detailed tasks.

12.6 PRINCE2 Product Activity Customized Field & Filter

Products may be represented in Microsoft Project in a number of ways:

- Single child tasks could be used to represent Products when a Project Plan has been created and each Product has been scheduled as a single task. This approach is similar to the workshops in this book.

- Summary tasks could represent a Product with child tasks representing activities that are required to deliver the product.

- When Outlining is not used to represent the PBS then a milestone may be used at the end of one or more chains of tasks that represent activities required to deliver the Product. A Custom Outline Code could be used to display the PBS in this situation.

A text column could be used to identify tasks that represent Products and a filter created to display only tasks that represent Products. Furthermore, a Text column may be renamed as **Products** and the Text column could be formatted so only a **Yes** or **No** may be entered and the default set as either **Yes** or **No**.

- Select **Tools**, **Customize**, **Fields….** To open the **Custom Fields** form,

- Select the **Type** of **Text** and use the [Rename…] button to rename **Text 1** to **Products**,

- Click on the [Lookup…] button to open the **Edit Lookup Table For Products** form,

- Enter the **Value** of **Yes** and **No**; a description is not required,

- Click on **No** and then click on [Set Default] to set **No** as the default for all new tasks.

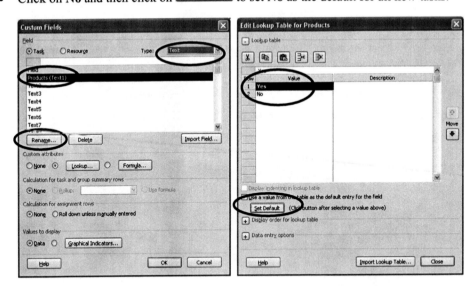

- Display and populate the Products column and a filter like the one below will only display activities that are Products.

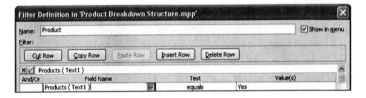

WORKSHOP 10

Filters

Background

Management has asked for reports on tasks to suit their requirements.

Assignment

Open the **OzBuild Bid** project to complete this exercise and ensure the **OzBuild No Resources** is closed.

1. They would like to see all the critical tasks.
   - ➤ Apply the **Critical** tasks filter. The Filter command is found under the **Project** menu item.

   You will see only tasks that are on the critical path and their associated summary tasks.

2. They would like to see all the tasks with float less than 5 days:
   - ➤ Create a new filter titled **Float Less Than 5 Days,**
   - ➤ Create the condition to display a **Total Slack** of less than 5 days,
   - ➤ Show Summary tasks,
   - ➤ Show the filter in the menu, and
   - ➤ Apply the filter.

   You should find that one extra task is now shown.

3. They would like to see all the tasks with float less than 5 days or contain the word "Bid."
   - ➤ Copy the **Float Less Than 5 Days** filter,
   - ➤ Assign a title to the filter: **Float Less Than 5 Days or Contains "Bid",**
   - ➤ Add the condition: **Or** Name (Task Name) contains **Bid,**
   - ➤ Show in the menu, and
   - ➤ Apply the filter.

   You should find that one extra task is now shown.

4. We now wish to create an **AutoFilter** that displays all the activities containing the word "Component".
   - ➤ Apply the **All Tasks** Filter,
   - ➤ Click on the [icon] icon to activate the Auto Filters, and
   - ➤ Create a Custom Auto filter to select tasks containing the word "component."

5. Now apply the **All Tasks** Filter, remove the **AutoFilter** and save your **OzBuild Bid** project.

ANSWERS TO WORKSHOP 10

After applying the Critical Filter:

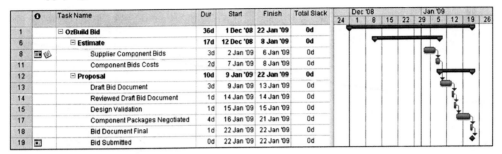

Creating the **Float Less Than 5 Days** Filter:

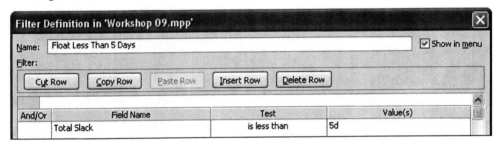

After applying the **Float Less Than 5 Days or Contains "Bid"** Filter:

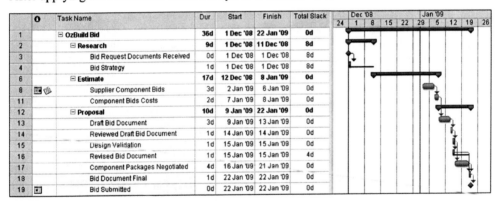

Creating an AutoFilter that displays Task Names containing **component**:

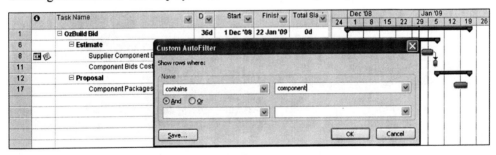

13 VIEWS, TABLES AND DETAILS

A **View** is a function where the formatting such as the **Table**, **Details** and **Bar** formatting are saved and reapplied later. A filter is saved as part of a **View**.

In a PRINCE2 project a **View** could be created for each type of report and for displaying Team Plan or Stage Plan activities. It is highly recommended that a View be produced for each frequently-created report.

The views displayed in the menu and on the **View Bar** with a standard load of Microsoft Project are listed below. There are more views available from the **More Views** form, which will not be covered in detail in this book.

View Name	Notes on the View
• Calendar	This may be applied to the top window only and displays the tasks overlaid on a calendar.
• Gantt	Displays a Table on the left of the screen and Gantt Chart on the right.
• Network Diagram	This view is a PERT-style display and is covered in the **NETWORK DIAGRAM VIEW** chapter.
• Task Usage*	Similar to Resources Usage, displays a Table with Tasks with associated Resources on the left and the Resources usage data apportioned over time on the right.
• Tracking Gantt	Similar to the **Gantt** view.
• Resource Graph*	A split table displaying the Resource name on the left-hand side and resource usage in bar chart format on the right-hand side.
• Resource Sheet*	A single table displaying Resource information such as costs and calendars.
• Resource Usage*	Similar to the Task usage, displays a Table with Resources with associated Tasks on the left and the Resources usage data apportioned over time on the right.

* The Views containing resource information are covered in more detail in the **STATUSING PROJECTS WITH RESOURCES** chapter.

The **Calendar** view is not covered in detail in this book and **Network** views are covered in the **NETWORK DIAGRAM VIEW** chapter.

13.1 Understanding Views

There are two types of Views:

- A **Single View** is normally applied to the top pane only; when the pane is split, the **Details** form is displayed in the bottom pane.

- A **Combination View** is comprised of two **Single Views**, one displayed in the top pane and one in the bottom pane.

All **Single Views** may be applied to the top pane and when the window is split, most may be applied to the bottom pane. When a **Single View** is applied to the bottom pane, it will only display the information attributed to the task that is highlighted in the top pane.

When a **Single View** is applied to the top or bottom pane, the other pane is left with the contents of the previous **Combination View**.

A **View** is based on a **Screen** when it is created. The **Screen** may not be changed after the **View** is created. There are 14 **Screens**:

- Calendar
- Network Diagram
- Resource Form
- Resource Name Form
- Resource Usage
- Task Form
- Task Sheet

- Gantt Chart
- Relationship Diagram
- Resource Graph
- Resource Sheet
- Task Details Form
- Task Name Form
- Task Usage

The Table in **APPENDIX 1 – SCREENS USED TO CREATE VIEWS** lists the Screens and provides further detail about formatting the screens. A few important points to consider are:

- The **Calendar** screen may only be displayed in the top pane.

- The **Gantt Chart**, **Network Diagram** and **Relationship Diagram** screens are often best displayed in the top pane and have limited use when displayed in the bottom pane.

- The **Forms** are best displayed in the bottom pane and convey **Task** or **Resource** information about a task that is highlighted in the top pane. **Forms** may be further formatted by selecting **Format, Details**.

- The **Task Sheet** is similar to the **Gantt Chart** but does not display bars and is best displayed in the top pane.

- The **Resource** and **Task Usage** screens display resource information and are further discussed in the **RESOURCE HISTOGRAMS AND TABLES** chapter.

13.2 Applying a View

Some Views will be available from the **View** menu and **View Bar** and others will only be available from the **More Views** form. To display a View in the **View** menu and the **View Bar**, the View should be edited and the **Show in menu** box checked in the **View Definition** form.

- Select **View** from the menu and then select the required View from the list above **More Views…**:

- Display the **View Bar** and click on the icon of the required View. To display or hide the **View Bar**, select **View**, **View Bar**. The **View Bar** will be displayed on the left-hand side of the screen, and will display the same list of Views as those in the menu.

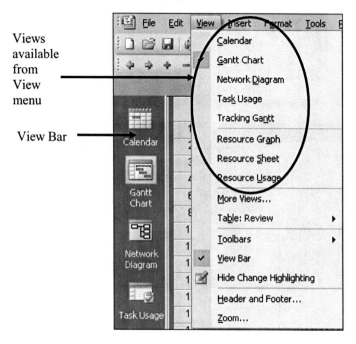

- Select **View**, **More Views…** to open the **More Views** form and select the required View from the drop-down list.

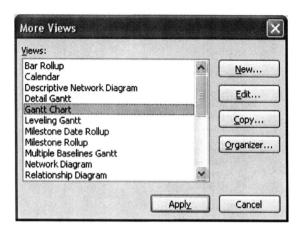

13.3   Creating a New View

A new View may be created by copying and editing an existing View, or creating a new View.

13.3.1   Creating a New Single View

To create a new Single View:

- Select **View**, **More Views…** to open the **More Views** form,

- Click on the [New…] button to open the **Define New View** form:

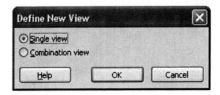

- Click on the **Single view** radio button to open the **View Definition** form:

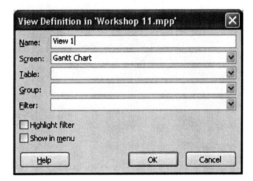

- You may now enter:
  - ➤ The new View name in the **Name:** box by overtyping the "**View 1**" name assigned by Microsoft Project,
  - ➤ Select the **Screen:** View, see **APPENDIX 1** for more information on the screens. A list of available screens is displayed below:

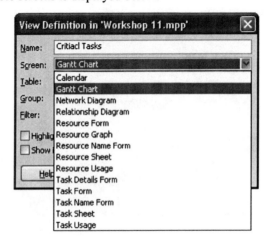

> ➤ Select the **Table:** you want to apply with the view.
> ➤ You may not want to display your tasks using the Outline display mode. The **Group:** function allows you to group your tasks by other data items such as a **Text Column** or **Constraint Type** and is covered in the **GROUPING, OUTLINE CODES AND WBS** chapter.
> ➤ You may also select a filter to apply with the layout from the **Filter:** drop-down box.
> ➤ Click the **Highlight filter** box to highlight the tasks that meet the filter specification as opposed to applying the filter.
> ➤ Click on the **Show in menu** box to display the View in the **View** menu.

- Click on the ⬛ OK ⬛ button to create the new **View**.

- From the **More Views** form click on the ⬛ Apply ⬛ button to apply the new **View**.

 Inserting a space before the filter name will put the filter to the top of the list making it simpler to identify those filters that you have created or edited.

13.3.2 Creating a Combination View

Before creating a new Combination View the two Views that are to be displayed in the top and bottom Pane must have been created:

- Select **View**, **More Views…** to open the **More Views** form,

- Click on the ⬛ New… ⬛ button to open the **Define New View** form:

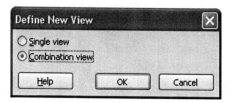

- Select **Combination view** and click ⬛ OK ⬛; this will open the **View Definition** form:

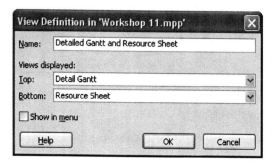

- Enter your View name and select the Views you want to display in the top and bottom pane,

- Click on **Show in menu** to display the View in the menu and on the **View Bar**, and

- Click on the ⬛ OK ⬛ button to create the new **View**.

 A useful technique is to create a View, and associated Table and Filter, with the same name and keep them together as a set. For example, a Layout created to show critical tasks could have a View, with Table and Filter all titled "Critical."

13.3.3   Copying and Editing a View

To copy an existing View:

- Select **View**, **More Views…** to open the **More Views** form:

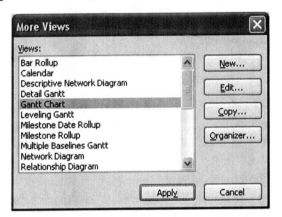

- Select the View you want to copy from the drop-down list and click on the ⟨Copy…⟩ button to open the **View Definition** form. This form is different for Single and Combination Views. The example below is a **Single View** created from the **Gantt Chart** Screen:

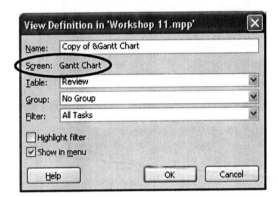

- The **Screen:** may not be changed in an existing or copied view and the screen option is shown as gray. See picture above.

- Change the name and any other parameters and then click on ⟨OK⟩ to create the **View**.

13.3.4   Copying a View to and from Another Project

Views may be copied from one project to another with the **Organizer** function. This may be accessed by selecting:

- ⟨Organizer…⟩ from the **More Views** form, or

- **Tools**, **Organizer…**, and selecting the **Views** tab.

13.4   Tables

A table selects and formats the columns of data to be displayed in a view. The formatting of tables is covered in the **FORMATTING THE DISPLAY** chapter.

- A table may be applied to **Views** that display data in tables, such as the Gantt, Chart, Resource Sheet, Resource Usage, Task Sheet and Task Usage.

- There are two types of tables, **Task** tables that are applied to **Task Views** and **Resource** tables that are applied to **Resource Views**.

- When the view is active and you assign it a different table, the View is permanently changed and the table permanently associated with the Table. Unlike Primavera software, the user does not have the option to save changes to a view when another is selected.

A table may be applied by:

- Assigning a different table to the active View using **View**, **Table:** , or

- By editing the **View**.

 Formatting a table by adding or removing columns, etc., is editing the current table on a permanent basis. These changes will appear when the table is next applied and this will affect any View the table is associated with. It is therefore strongly recommended that each View be paired with a unique table of the same name. Consider carefully when adding or deleting columns from a table as the changes are permanent.

13.4.1   Applying a Table to a View

A **Table** may be applied by:

- Selecting **View**, **Table:** and selecting from the list in the menu, or

- Clicking the **Select All** button, the box above the row 1 number, then right-clicking the mouse to display a sub-menu with the table options, or

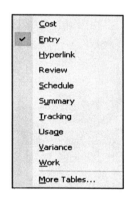

- Selecting **View**, **Table:**, **More Tables...** and selecting a table from the list which displays all existing Tables and clicking on Apply.

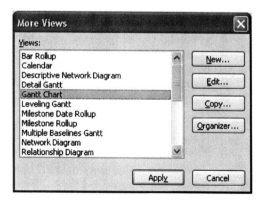

13.4.2   Creating and Editing a Table

A **Table** may be created or edited by:

- Selecting **View**, **Table:**, **More Tables…** to open the **More Tables** form:

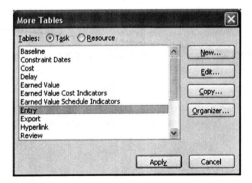

- Clicking on [New…] to create a new table, [Edit…] to edit an existing table or [Copy…] to create a copy of an existing table. All these buttons open the **Table Definition** form shown below:

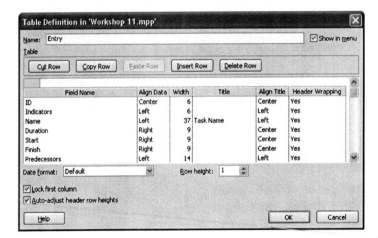

- The functions in this form are similar to those in many other forms. The functions that are unique to this form are listed below:

  - ➢ **Date format:** – Changes the format of the dates in this project and table only.
  - ➢ **Row height:** – Allows you to specify the row height for this table.
  - ➢ **Lock first column** – Ensures the first column is always displayed when scrolling to the right.
  - ➢ **Auto-adjust header row heights** – Automatically adjusts the header height when the width of the column is adjusted so the column text wraps.

- [Organizer…] – Allows a table to be copied from one schedule to another.

- [Apply] – Applies the table to a view.

> *i* The date format selected in the **Tools**, **Options**, **View** tab is overridden by a date format selected in a Table. Therefore, if you have a project that requires a unique date format then the option of selecting a date format in a Table overrides the default on any computer for anyone who opens the project file.

13.5   Details Form

Details forms are the third level of formatting that may be assigned in some views. An extensive list of the Details forms is outlined in **APPENDIX 1 – SCREENS USED TO CREATE VIEWS.**

Each view has a number of Details options, which tends to make this aspect of Microsoft Project difficult for all levels of users.

The **Details** forms may be selected by:

- Selecting **Format**, **Details**, or

- Right-clicking in the active pane to open a menu.

Example of Details forms:

- Task Form with Resource Costs Details form:

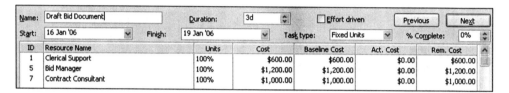

- Task Details with Predecessors and Successors Details form:

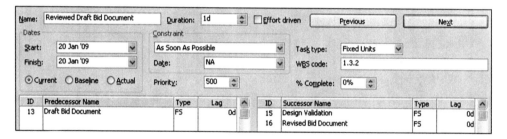

13.6 PRINCE2 Product Flow Diagram View

A View could be created to show a close representation of a **PRINCE2 Product Flow Diagram** consisting of:

- Network Diagram screen edited to display only the task Name, and

- Filter designed and a Custom Field tailored to show only the **PRINCE2 Products**.

This view could be incorporated into a template for other people in your organization to use.

The following process could be used to create a **Product Flow Diagram** View.

- Display the **Network Diagram** view by selecting **View, Network Diagram**,

- Select **Format, Box Styles...** to open the **Box Styles** form,

- Click on the More Templates... button to open the **Data Templates** form,

- Click on New... to open the **Data Template Definition** form,

- Enter a **Template name** of **Product**,

- Use the Cell Layout... button to open the **Cell Layout** form and set the **Number of rows** and **Number of columns** to 1,

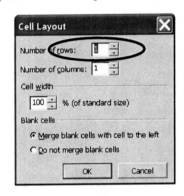

- Click OK to return to the **Data Template Definition** form,

- From the **Data Template Definition** form select task **Name** as the data to be displayed in the one cell available,

- **Limit the cell text** to 3 lines to provide a reasonable amount of description to be displayed,

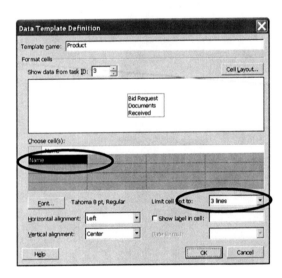

- Click on the OK button to go back to the **Data Templates** form,

- Click on the Close button to return to the **Box Styles** form,

- From the **Box Styles** form select all the **Style Settings** by dragging and editing the form as per below; this will make all the styles identical.

- Select **Product** from the **Data template** drop-down list,

- Under **Border** select the Rectangle for the **Shape:**, **Color:** Black and select a **Width:**.

- Under **Background** select White as **Color:**

- **Pattern:** as the blank option at the top of the list.

- Click on the OK button to apply the same style to all the tasks.

- At this point you will need to filter out all the tasks you do not require and format the Layout.

- The example on the next page was developed by opening the **Layout** form by selecting **Format, Layout...** and un-selecting **Show summary tasks** and changing a number of settings as shown below:

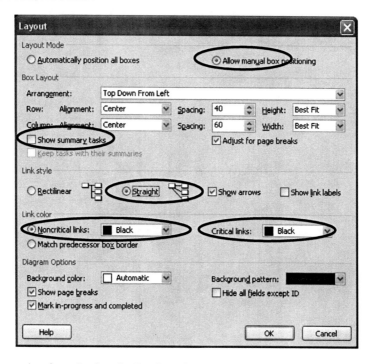

- Another option for selecting the Products is to use a Text column to indicate which tasks are Products. Create a filter to select only the tasks that represent Products. This was outlined in detail in the **FILTERS** chapter.

- The use the Zoom function to scale the screen,

- Drag the boxes to the required position.

- The **Bid Request Documents Received** task below was reformatted to an octagonal shape by selecting and clicking on it, then selecting **Format, Box…** to open the **Format Box** form, then choosing a different shape:

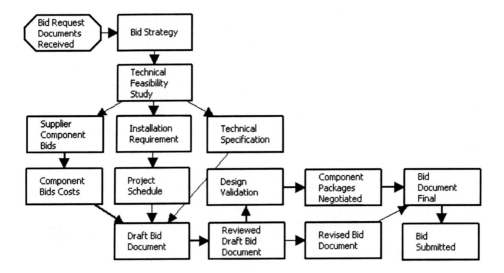

- This Network Diagram View may be renamed or copied to another project using the **Tools, Organiser…** function.

WORKSHOP 11

Organizing Your Data

Background

Having completed the schedule you may report the information with different views.

Assignment

Display your project in the following formats, noting the different ways you may represent the same data. Open your **OzBuild Bid** project from the previous workshop to complete the following exercise.

1. Display the **Calendar** view and scroll through a few months and see the holidays. This view only displays the Standard calendar. Right-click and view the menu options.
2. Display the **Network Diagram** view and zoom to 50%, then scroll around the schedule and then roll up the summary tasks.
3. Display the **Gantt Chart** view and split the screen.
4. Display the **Relationship Diagram** view in the bottom pane and scroll around the schedule by double-clicking on tasks in the top and bottom panes.
5. Apply the **Task Details Form** view in the bottom screen.
6. Apply each one of the following **Details** forms to the **Task Details** view in the bottom screen.

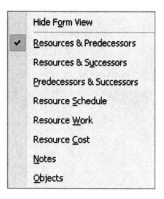

7. Apply the following Tables to the **Gantt Chart** view in the top pane:
   ➢ Schedule, then
   ➢ Entry, then
   ➢ Tracking.
8. Close the split.

Continued Over...

9. We now will create a Combination View to show only Critical Tasks in the Upper Pane with the Task Details form in the Lower Pane.

> Copy the **Entry** table and create a **Critical** table with the following columns: ID, Indicators, Name, Start, Finish, Total Slack and do not show in the menu.

> Create a Single Pane Gantt Chart View titled Critical Top Pane by selecting **View, More Views....**

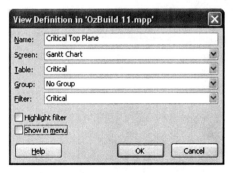

> Create a Single Pane View titled Critical Bottom Pane using the Task Details form and All Tasks filter.

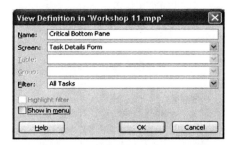

> Create a Combination View titled Critical and apply it.

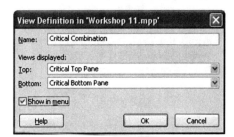

> Apply the Critical View and save your project:

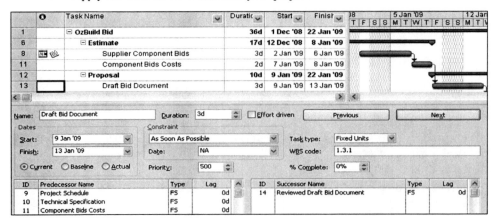

10. Now create the Product Flow Diagram from para 13.6.

14 PRINTING AND REPORTS

You are now at the stage to print the schedule so the project team may review and comment on it. This chapter will examine one of the many options for printing your project schedule.

There are two tools available to output your schedule to a printer:

- The **Printing** function prints the data displayed in the current Active View.

- The **Reporting** function prints reports, which are independent of the current View. Microsoft Project supplies a number of predefined reports that may be tailored to suit your own requirements. Reports will not be covered in detail in this book. In Microsoft Project the menu for Reports was moved from the **View** menu to the **Report** menu.

 It is recommended that you consider using a product such as Adobe Acrobat to output your schedule in pdf format. You then will be able to email high quality outputs that recipients may print or review on screen without needing a copy of Microsoft Project.

14.1 Printing

Only the active View may be printed when a screen is split. The active view normally has a blue bar down the left-hand side of the screen. Views created from **Forms** (for example, the Task Form) may not be printed, so the printing options will be shown in gray when the forms are active.

Print settings are applied to the individual Views and the settings are saved with the currently displayed View.

There are three commands used when printing:

- **File**, **Page Setup…**
- **File**, **Print Preview**
- **File**, **Print…** or **Ctrl+P**

Each of these functions will be discussed only for printing the Gantt Chart. Printing all other Views is a similar process.

Some Views will have additional options and others reduced functionality. These other options should be easily mastered once the basics covered in this chapter are understood.

Microsoft Project sometimes makes it difficult to print a Gantt Chart on one page. In the author's experience, adjusting the timescale so the whole project fits into half the screen before selecting **Print Preview** make this process simpler.

 Each time you report to the client or management, it is recommended that you save a complete copy of your project and change the name slightly (perhaps by appending a date to the file name or using a revision or version number) or create a subdirectory for this version of the project. This allows you to reproduce these reports at any time in the future and an electronic copy is available for dispute resolution purposes.

14.2   Print Preview

To preview the printout, use Microsoft Project's **Print Preview** option:

- Select **File**, **Print Preview**, or

- Click the Print Preview 🔍 icon on the toolbar to view the printout in the window, or

- Click on the [Preview] button from the **Print** form. The **Print** form is covered later in this chapter, or

- Click on the [Print Preview...] button in the **Page** tab of the **Page Setup** form.

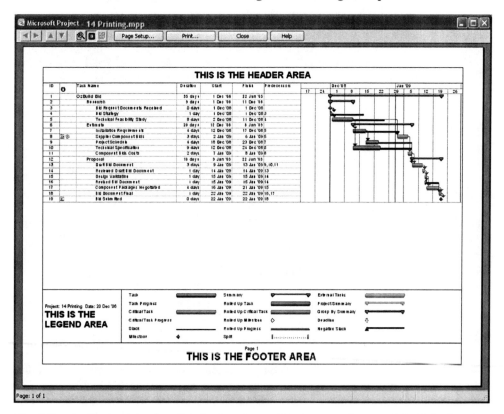

The following paragraphs describe the functions of the icons at the top of the Print Preview screen from left to right:

- The first four icons on the left, ◄ ► ▲ ▼, allow scrolling when a printout has more than one page.

- The magnifying glass 🔍 zooms in only. You will need to click on the preview screen to zoom out again. You may also click on the preview screen to zoom in.

- The next two icons, ▣ and ▦, display one or all pages, respectively.

- The next four are self-explanatory buttons labeled [Page Setup...], [Print...], [Close] and [Help].

14.3 Page Set-up

To open the **Page Setup** form:

- Click the [Page Setup...] button on the **Print Preview** toolbar, or

- Select **File**, **Page Setup...** to display the **Page Setup** form:

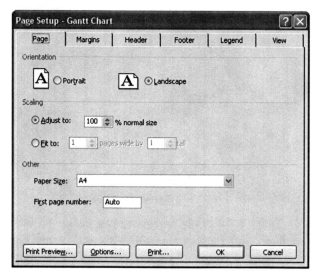

The **Page Setup** form contains the following tabs:

- Page

- Margins

- Header

- Footer

- Legend

- View

Depending on the View being printed, some options in the **Print Setup** form will be unavailable and shown in gray.

The [Options...] button opens the printer setup/options form.

14.3.1   Page Tab

The Microsoft Project options in the **Page** tab are:

- **Scaling** allows you to adjust the number of pages the printout will fit onto:
  - ➤ **Adjust to:** – Allows you to choose the scale of the printout that both the bars and column text are scaled to. Microsoft Project will calculate the number of pages across and down for the printout.
  - ➤ **Fit to:** – Allows you to choose the number of pages across and down and Microsoft Project will scale the printout to fit.
- The **First page number:** – Allows you to choose the first page number of the printout. This is useful when enclosing the printout as an attachment or an appendage to another document.
- Pages are numbered down first and then across:

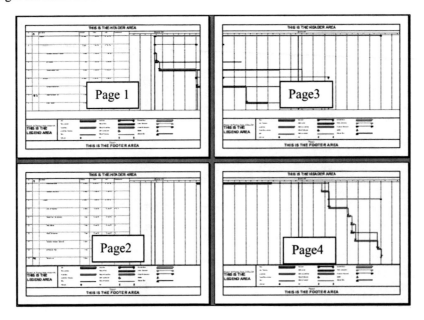

14.3.2   Margins Tab

With this option you may choose the margins around the edge of the printout.

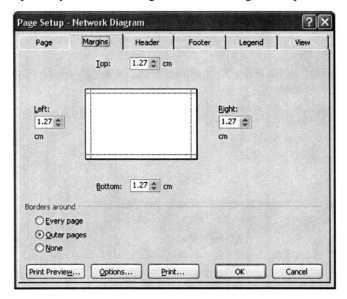

- Type in the margin size around the page. It is best to allow a wider margin for an edge that is to be bound or hole-punched; 1" or 2.5 cm is usually sufficient. The units of measurement, in. or cm, are adopted from the operating system **Control Panel**, **Regional and Language Option** settings.

- Microsoft Project will print a border around the Gantt Chart bars and Columns. **Borders around** places a border line around the outside of all text in the Headers and Footers. There are three options:

  ➢ **Every page** – This places a border around every page.

  ➢ **Outer pages** – This capability is only available with a **Network Diagramming** View. It allows you to join all the pages into one large printout with a border only on the outside edge of all the pages once they are joined up.

  ➢ **None** – Does not place a border on any sheets of the printout.

14.3.3   Header and Footer Tabs

Headers appear at the top of the screen above all schedule information and footers are located at the bottom, below the **Legend** if it has been selected to be displayed. Both the headers and footers are formatted in the same way. We will discuss the setting up of footers in this chapter.

Click on the **Footer** tab from the **Page Setup** form. This will display the settings of the default footers and headers.

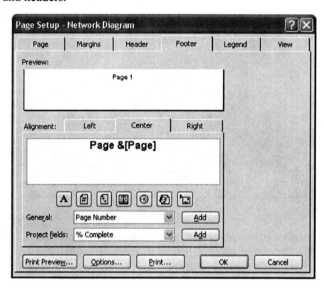

- **Preview:** – The box at the top of the form shows how your Footer will be displayed.

- Text may be placed in all three positions in the Footer and Header – on the Left, Center and Right. Click on the required tab to the right of **Alignment:** to select the alignment position and insert new text or remove existing text in the box below.

- Text may be added by using a number of methods:
  - ➢ Freeform text may be typed into the footer box below the **Alignment:** box,
  - ➢ Add data in the footer by clicking one of these icons, ⊞ **Page Number**, ⊞ **Total Page Count**, ⊞ **Current Date**, ⊗ **Current Time**, ☑ **File Name** or ☑ **Insert Picture** (for example a corporate logo),
  - ➢ To insert Microsoft Project field-type information to your footer, click on ⬚ **Add** to insert the field into the footer. You may select from the drop-down box to the right of **General:** or **Project fields:**,
  - ➢ To format the text you must first highlight the text and then click on the **Format Text Font** icon ⒶA to open the **Font** form.
  - ➢ **Print Preview…** – Returns you to the **Print Preview** form.
  - ➢ **Options…** – Opens the **Printer Properties** form.
  - ➢ **Print…** – Opens the **Print** form.
  - ➢ **OK** – Accepts the changes.
  - ➢ **Cancel** – Cancels any recent changes that have not yet been saved.

14.3.4   Legend Tab

The **Legend Text** is printed to the left of the **Legend**:

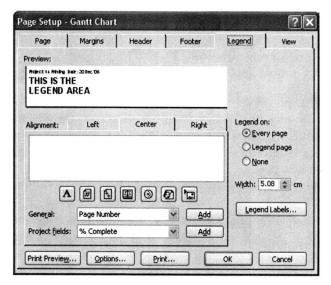

The **Legend Text** is formatted in the same way as the **Header** and **Footer**.

The **Legend** has three additional options not available in the **Header** and **Footer**.

- Click on the radio button below **Legend on:**
  - ➤ **Every page** will print the legend at the bottom of every page.
  - ➤ **Legend page** will print the legend on a separate page with no detailed schedule data, bars, or columns.
  - ➤ **None** will not print a legend.
- **Width:** sets the width of the **Legend Text**.
- **Legend Labels...** Opens the **Font** form for formatting the font of the text in the legend next to each of the bars and milestones.
- To hide a bar type in the Legend, type an * in front of the description in the **Bar Styles** form. This bar will still be displayed but will not be displayed in the Legend:

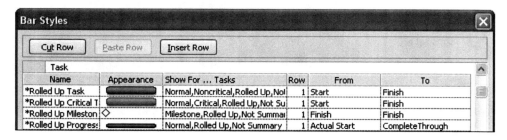

14.3.5   View Tab

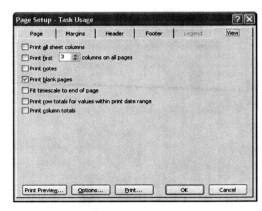

The View tab has five options:

- **Print all sheet columns:** – This option applies to the left-most horizontal pages only when there is more than one page across a printout.
  - ➤ When checked, this option will print all the sheet columns displayed by the current table in the Gantt Chart, even if the columns are hidden by the vertical divider in the normal view.
  - ➤ When unchecked, this option will only print the completely visible columns.
- **Print first … columns on all pages** – Applies to all pages. The greater of the number of columns between this option and the options above will be printed on the first page.
  - ➤ **When checked**, this will allow repetitiously printing the selected number of columns on all pages.
  - ➤ **When unchecked**, this will not print any columns on the second and subsequent pages.
- **Print notes** will allow the printing of any **Notes** such as **Task Notes** on a separate page.
- **Print blank pages** will prevent the printing of all pages in the Gantt Chart, when there are no bars.
- **Fit timescale to end of page** will extend the timescale and associated bars so they fit to the end of a page:

  - ➤ Option is unchecked, the bars stop in the middle of a page:

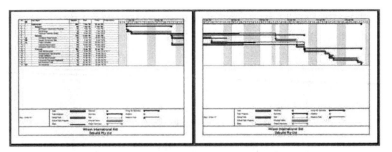

  - ➤ Option is checked, bars and timescale extend to the end of a page:

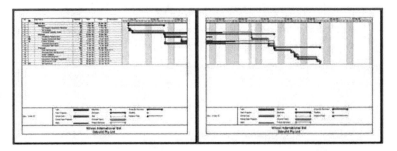

- **Print row totals for values within date range** and **Print column totals** options become available when tabular data is selected for printing such as a Resource Sheet view.

14.4   Print Form and Manual Page Breaks

The **Print** form may be opened by:

- Selecting **File**, **Print…**, or

- Executing the keystrokes **Ctrl+P**, or

- Clicking on the 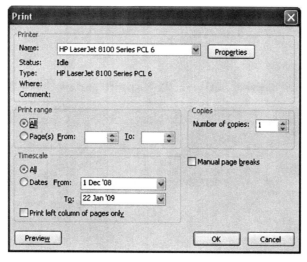 print icon normally found on the Standard toolbar. This choice will automatically print out the document.

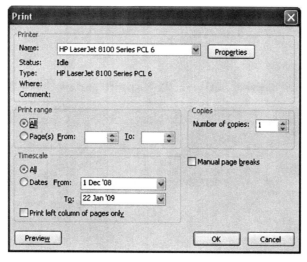

The following options are available:

- The **Printer** options are only available when this form is accessed from the main menu and are shown in gray when accessed from **Print Preview**.

- **Print range** allows you to choose the pages to be printed.

- **Copies** specifies the number of copies to be printed.

- **Timescale** allows specifying a Gantt Chart date range that will be printed. It does not filter out tasks. It is used to reduce the range of the Gantt Chart that will be printed. Unlike earlier versions of Microsoft Project, this setting is saved with a **View** when the project is saved.

- **Print left column of pages only** will print only the left pages of a printout that are more than one page wide.

- **Manual page breaks:**
  - ➢ Manual page breaks are inserted by highlighting the row above where a page break is required. Then, select **Insert**, **Page Break**. A dotted line will indicate the location of the manual page break.
  - ➢ To remove a manual page break, highlight the row above where there is a page break and select **Insert**, **Remove Page Break**.
  - ➢ The **Manual page breaks** check box in the **Print** form must be checked to acknowledge manual page breaks in the printout.

14.5   Reports

There have been some menu changes in Microsoft Project 2007 and there is a new **Report** menu item, which includes the following options:

- **Visual Reports….** – These are a new set of graphical reports in Microsoft Project 2007 which allow reports to be exported to Excel or Visio.

- **Copy Picture…** – This function has been moved from the **Edit** menu but the functionality has not been changed.

- **Reports…** – This menu item has been moved from the **View** to **Reports** menu item in Microsoft Project 2007.

14.5.1   Visual Reports

Select **Report**, **Visual Reports….** to open the **Visual Reports – Create Report** form.

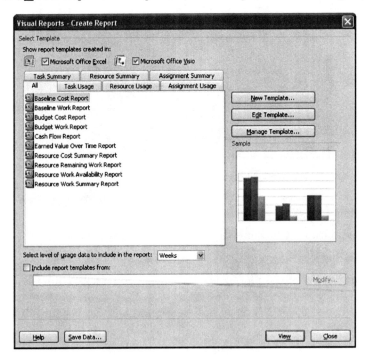

Visual Reports allow:

- The creation of reports, such as Histograms and Cash Flows, are generated from templates to be exported and displayed in Excel or Visio.

- The templates may be modified and new ones created.

- Report data may also be saved as an Access database.

14.5.2 Reports

Select **Report, Reports…** in Microsoft Project 2007 and **View, Reports…** in Microsoft Project 2000 – 2003 to open the **Reports** form which displays six icons.

- Select a Report option by:
  - ➢ Double-clicking on any one of the icons, or
  - ➢ Clicking on an icon and clicking on the [Select] button.
- This will open up a menu of reports under the chosen heading. The picture below displays the **Current Activities…** menu. The remaining five headings are done similarly and therefore are not explained in detail:

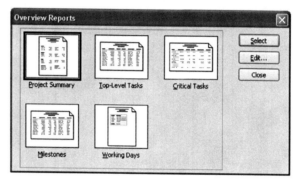

Double-click on any report and it will be sent to **Print Preview.** Here the print settings may be edited prior to printing.

Some of the report parameters may be further edited; for example, select the **Critical Tasks** report and click on the [Edit…] button to open the **Task Report** form.

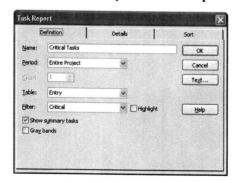

The following reports are available:

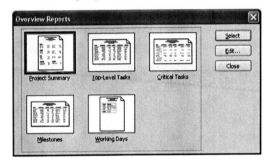

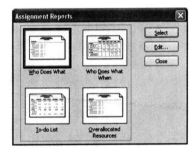

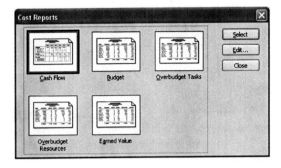

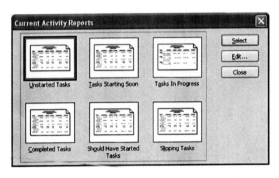

WORKSHOP 12

Reports

Background

We want to issue a report for comment by management.

Assignment

Open your **OzBuild Bid** project from the previous workshop to complete the following steps:

1. Apply the **Gantt Chart** view.
2. Select the top pane and apply the Entry Table.
3. Display the Task ID, Indicators, Name, Duration, Start Date, Finish Date and Predecessors columns.
4. Adjust the columns to the best fit.
5. We wish to fit all the activities on one A4 or letter-size landscape page by:
   - Adjusting the middle tier unit of timescale to **Months** with **Label** of **Jan '02** and bottom tier to **Weeks** with **Label** of **27,3...** and **Size** of **150%**.
   - Selecting Print Preview and showing all data columns.
   - Setting the page size to fit to 1 page wide by 1 page tall.
6. Hide all the Rolled Up Tasks Bars by placing a * in front of the Bar Name in the Bar Styles form.
7. Place only the Company Name and Project Title in the center of the Footer with a font of Arial Bold 14.
8. Place only the date in the Legend at Arial 8.
9. Remove any text from the Header.
10. Compare your result with the picture on the next page.

ANSWERS TO WORKSHOP 12

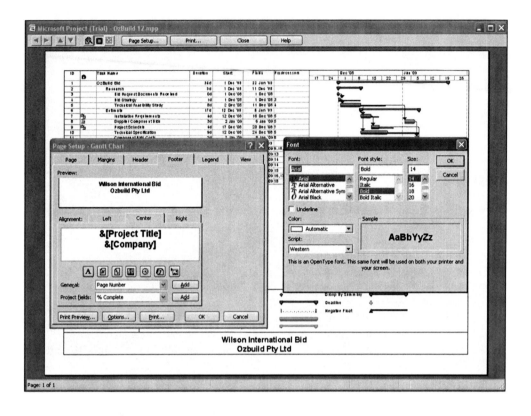

15 TRACKING PROGRESS

The process of tracking progress is used after the plan has been completed, the Baseline set and the project is underway. Now the important phase of regular monitoring begins. Monitoring is important to help catch problems as early as possible, and thus minimize the impact of problems on the successful completion of the project.

The main steps for monitoring progress are:

- Set the **Baseline Dates**, also known as **Target Dates**. These are the dates against which progress is compared.

- Approve the work to commence in accordance with the plan.

- Record or mark-up progress as of a specific date, often titled the **Data Date**, **Status Date**, **Current Date** and **As-of-Date**.

- **Update** or **Status** the schedule with **Actual Start** and **Actual Finish** dates where applicable, and adjust the task durations and percent complete.

- Compare and **Report** actual progress against planned progress and revise the schedule, if required.

In a PRINCE2 project the Baseline for a Project Plan would be set against the tasks (which could represent Products) after the Project Plan has been approved in **DP2 – Authorising a Project**. The Stage or Exception Plans are developed by adding the activities required to create the Products as tasks under the Products. The Stage or Exception Plan Baseline would be set after each Plan has been approved in **DP3- Authorising a Stage or Exception Plan**.

You should have a schedule that compares your original plan with the current plan, showing where the project is ahead or behind and if the PRINCE2 **Tolerances** have been broken. If you are behind, you should be able to use this schedule to plan appropriate remedial measures to bring the project back on target and if necessary produce an **Exception Plan**.

This chapter will cover the following topics:

Topic	Menu Command
• Setting the **Baseline**	Select **T**ools, Trac**k**ing, **S**ave Baseline…
• Recording Progress	Guidelines on how to record progress.
• **Current Date** and **Status Date**	May be edited from the **P**roject, **P**roject **I**nformation… form.
• Updating the Schedule	Select **T**ools, Trac**k**ing, Update **P**roject…
• Move the **Incomplete Work** of an **in-progress** task into the future	Select **T**ools, Trac**k**ing, Update **P**roject…
• Updating the Tasks	Select **T**ools, Trac**k**ing, Update **T**asks…

15.1   Setting the Baseline

Setting the Baseline copies the following information into Baseline fields in the existing file:

- **Early Start** and **Finish** dates into fields titled **Baseline Start** and **Baseline Finish**.

- **Original Duration** into the **Baseline Duration**.

- Each resource's **Costs** and **Work** into **Baseline Costs** and **Baseline Work** (work is typically the number of hours) when resources are assigned to tasks.

Once the Baseline is set you will be able to compare your progress with your original plan. You will be able to see if you are ahead or behind schedule and by how much.

Some important points you should understand before setting the Baseline:

- The Baseline Dates should be established before you status the schedule for the first time.

- The Baseline Dates and Duration fields are not calculated fields and may be edited in columns and forms. Caution should be used before changing a Baseline Date or Duration, since it is the basis for all project deviation measurements.

- Summary tasks scheduled Start, Finish, Duration, Costs and Work are recalculated as Detailed tasks are added or deleted. Setting the Baseline copies these values and the Baseline values are **NOT** recalculated when new tasks are created or existing tasks are moved to a different Summary task.

- Setting the Baseline Date does not store the logic, float/slack times, or constraints.

- A Baseline is normally applied to all tasks irrespective of their Outline levels.

15.1.1   Setting Baseline Dates

To set the Baseline select in Microsoft Project 2007 select <u>T</u>ools, Trac<u>k</u>ing, <u>S</u>et Baseline... and in Microsoft Project 2000 – 2003 <u>T</u>ools, Trac<u>k</u>ing, <u>S</u>ave Baseline... to display the **Save Baseline** form.

- The <u>S</u>ave baseline option copies the **Early Start** and **Finish** dates into the **Baseline Start** and **Finish** date fields respectively.

- You may highlight some tasks before opening the **Save Baseline** form and clicking on the **Selected tasks** radio button to set the Baseline for the specified tasks only.

This operation will overwrite any previous Baseline settings.

The **Set/Save Baseline** form default settings selects **All Tasks** and the **Early dates** which are titled **Start/Finish**. This is the normal method of setting the Baseline.

After establishing the Baseline, you can input the progress data without fear of losing the original dates. This will also enable you to compare the progress with the original plan.

15.1.2   Setting an Interim Baseline

It may be necessary to save an interim baseline. This may occur when the scope of a project has changed and a new baseline is required to measure progress against, but at the same time you may also want to keep a copy of the original baseline. This process may also be used to display the effect of scope changes on an original project plan by comparing one baseline with another. This feature was new to Microsoft Project 2002.

There are two types of data fields to save interim baselines:

- Using one of the 10 additional baselines titled **Baselines 1** to **10**. These Baselines will save start date, finish date, work and cost information.

- Using one of the 10 sets of **Start Date**, **Finish Date** and **Duration** fields. This function will only save the start and finish date information. This is termed an **Interim Plan** by Microsoft Project.

To set the Interim Baseline or Interim Plan, select **Tools, Tracking, Set/Save Baseline...** To display the **Save Baseline** form, select either:

- **Set/Save baseline** to save the current schedule to one of the 11 Baselines, or

- **Set/Save interim plan** then:
  - ➢ Select the dates you want to copy from using the **Copy:** drop-down box, and then
  - ➢ Select where you want to copy the dates to using the **Into:** drop-down box.

The **Baseline** data may be reviewed in some Views such as the **Task Details Form** and in columns. You will be able to display the **Baseline 1** to **10** and **Interim Plan** dates and durations in columns and as a bar on the Gantt Chart but not in the forms. Therefore, it is recommended that the current baseline be saved as **Baseline** since the data is more accessible that way. Previous baselines should be copied to **Baselines 1** to **10**.

Custom Date fields may be renamed with the **Customize Fields** form. Select **Tools, Customize, Fields...** to open this form. This may be useful to record the reason why a baseline has been saved.

In a PRINCE2 project, a Stage schedule is developed and approved by the Project Board prior to starting the Stage. The Stage schedule may be created by adding more activities to an existing project schedule and developing a more detailed Stage schedule in a single project file. The Baseline for each Stage may be saved using Baselines 1 to 10, allowing the original Baseline to be recorded and not lost when tasks are re-baselined.

15.1.3 Clearing and Resetting the Baseline

You may clear some or all of the Baseline fields using the **Clear Baseline** form. This is opened by selecting **Tools**, **Tracking**, **Clear Baseline…**:

15.1.4 Resetting the Baseline Using "Roll Up Baselines"

This is a new function to Microsoft Project 2002. When a Detailed task is moved from one Summary task to another, the Baseline dates are moved with the Detailed task. The Summary task Baseline dates are not recalculated and may not be valid. Likewise, the original Summary Baseline dates are not recalculated when new tasks are added to a schedule and may not be valid.

When a task has costs or work assigned to it, then any movement of a detailed task from one summary task to another summary task should result in a change to the baseline value of the summary tasks, but these new values are not automatically recalculated by Microsoft Project. Costs and Work Baseline calculations are covered in the **STATUSING PROJECT WITH RESOURCES** chapter.

In the pictures below, the task Detailed 2.3 was moved from below Parent 2 to below Parent 1 and the baseline of tasks Parent 1 and Parent 2 (the lower bar on each task) are no longer an accurate summary of the detailed task Baseline dates.

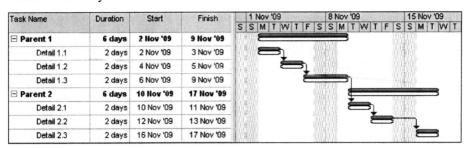

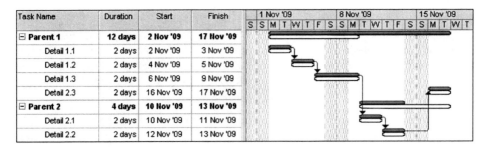

 In the example above, when the task was moved the option **Autolink inserted or moved tasks** found under the **Tools. Options…**, Schedule tab is unchecked, otherwise the logic would have been changed.

The **Roll up baselines** option in the **Set/Save Baseline** form will recalculate the Summary Task Baseline data when a Detailed task is moved to a different Summary task or a new task is added to the schedule. There are three options when **Selected tasks: - Roll up Baselines:** is selected:

> Check only **To all summary tasks,**
> Check only **From subtasks to selected summary task(s)**, or
> Check both of the above options.

The options function differently when a summary task or when a detail task is selected. These options are difficult to understand and the author prefers to reset Baselines of summary tasks manually.

In the example below two new activities have been added, thus the old Baseline is no longer valid. In addition the start date has been delayed:

	Task Name	Duration	Start	Finish
1	⊟ **Project Task**	**12 days**	**3 Nov '09**	**18 Nov '09**
2	⊟ **Parent 1**	**6 days**	**3 Nov '09**	**10 Nov '09**
3	Detail 1.1	2 days	3 Nov '09	4 Nov '09
4	Detail 1.2	2 days	5 Nov '09	6 Nov '09
5	New Detailed 1.3	2 days	9 Nov '09	10 Nov '09
6	⊟ **Parent 2**	**6 days**	**11 Nov '09**	**18 Nov '09**
7	Detail 2.1	2 days	11 Nov '09	12 Nov '09
8	Detail 2.2	2 days	13 Nov '09	16 Nov '09
9	New Detailed 2.3	2 days	17 Nov '09	18 Nov '09

To all summary tasks

- When the **To all summary tasks** option is checked and only a **Detailed task** is selected, such as the New Detailed 2.3 task below, then in this option:
  > The selected detailed task has its Baseline set based on the current schedule, see New Detailed Task 2.3, and
  > Related summary tasks have their baselines set based on the new child task Baseline, see Parent Task and Parent 2.

- When the **To all summary tasks** option is checked and a **Detailed task** and a **Summary task** is selected, such as the Parent 2 and New Detailed 2.3 task below, then:
  - ➤ The selected Detailed task and Summary Task have their Baseline set based on the Current dates, not the Baseline dates, see New Detailed Task 2.3 and Parent 2,
  - ➤ Related summary tasks have their baselines set based on the new Baseline dates, see Project Task:

	Task Name	Duration	Start	Finish
1	⊟ Project Task	12 days	3 Nov '09	18 Nov '09
2	⊟ Parent 1	6 days	3 Nov '09	10 Nov '09
3	Detail 1.1	2 days	3 Nov '09	4 Nov '09
4	Detail 1.2	2 days	5 Nov '09	6 Nov '09
5	New Detailed 1.3	2 days	9 Nov '09	10 Nov '09
6	⊟ Parent 2	6 days	11 Nov '09	18 Nov '09
7	Detail 2.1	2 days	11 Nov '09	12 Nov '09
8	Detail 2.2	2 days	13 Nov '09	16 Nov '09
9	New Detailed 2.3	2 days	17 Nov '09	18 Nov '09

Resetting Baseline dates of the Summary task may not be intended and in the example above the Parent 2 Baseline dates are no longer summarized on the child Baseline dates. So when using the **To all summary tasks** option it is recommended that no summary tasks should be selected.

From subtasks to selected summary task(s)

- When the **From subtasks to selected summary task(s)** option is checked and both Summary and Detailed Tasks are selected, such as Parent 2 and New Detailed 2.3 task below:
  - ➤ The selected Detailed tasks have their Baseline reset based on the current schedule,
  - ➤ Selected Summary tasks have their Baseline dates set based on the Baseline dates of their child tasks,
  - ➤ The unselected Summary tasks do not have their baselines reset, see task Parent 1 and Parent Task below.

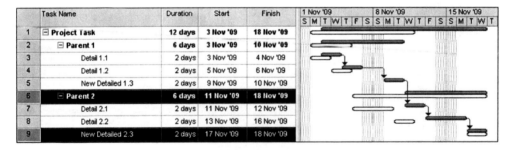

From subtasks to selected summary task(s) and To all summary tasks option selected

- When the **From subtasks to selected summary task(s)** option and the **To all summary tasks** option is checked then:
    - ➢ Any selected Detail task has the Baseline set or reset, and
    - ➢ All associated Summary tasks have their Baselines reset based on the associated Baseline dates.

 It is recommended to set a revised baseline when a new detailed activity has been added. The new activity and the associated Parent tasks should be highlighted and the option **From subtasks to selected summary task(s)** applied.

15.1.5 Displaying the Baseline Data

The Baseline dates data may be displayed by:

- Displaying the Baseline columns where the data may be edited, or

- Displaying the dates in a form such as the Resources Details Form. This will only display the **Baseline** data and not for **Baseline 1** to **10**, or

- Show a baseline bar on the Bar Chart.

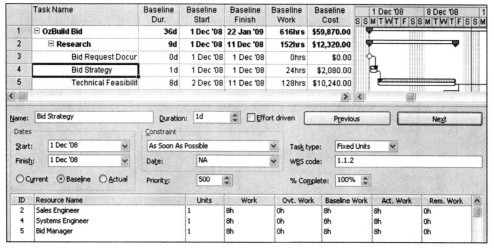

 The Baseline Start Dates, Finish Dates and Durations may be edited and are not linked by logic. Therefore, a change to a Baseline Duration will not affect either the Baseline Start Date or the Baseline Finish date.

15.2 Practical Methods of Recording Progress

Normally a project is statused once a week, bi-weekly, or monthly. Very short projects could be statused daily or even by the shift or hour. As a guide, a project would typically be statused between 12 and 20 times in a project life cycle. Progress is recorded on or near the **Data Date** and the scheduler updates the schedule upon the receipt of the information.

The following information is typically recorded for each task when statusing a project:

- The task start date and time if required,

- The number of days/hour the **Task** has to go or when the task is expected to finish,

- The percentage complete, and

- If complete, the task finish date and time, if required.

A marked-up copy recording the progress of the current schedule is often produced prior to updating the data in Microsoft Project. Ideally, the mark-up should be prepared by a physical inspection of the work or by a person who intimately knows the work. It is good practice to keep this marked-up record for your own reference at later date. Ensure that you note the date of the mark-up (i.e., the data date) and, if relevant, the time. It is important to ensure that each Actual Start and Actual Finish date be tied to independent evidence such as daily reports or photographs when a project is likely to be subject to dispute resolution.

Often a Statusing Report or mark-up sheet, such as the one below, is distributed to the people responsible for marking up the project progress. The marked-up sheets are returned to the scheduler for data entry into the software system.

A View, such as the one below, could be created for recording progress:

- It may have a filter applied to display only tasks that are in-progress or due to start in the next few weeks.

- A manual page break could be placed at each responsible person's band, and when the schedule is printed each person would have a personal listing of their tasks that are either in-progress or due to commence. This is particularly useful for large projects.

Task Name	Duration	% Comp	Start	Actual or Expected Start	Finish	Actual or Expected Finish
⊟ **Reponsibility: Angela Lowe - Purchasing**	**14 days**	**0%**	**2 Jan '09**	**NA**	**21 Jan '09**	**NA**
8 Supplier Component Bids	3 days	0%	2 Jan '09	NA	6 Jan '09	NA
11 Component Bids Costs	2 days	0%	7 Jan '09	NA	8 Jan '09	NA
17 Component Packages Negotiated	4 days	0%	16 Jan '09	NA	21 Jan '09	NA
⊟ **Reponsibility: Carol Peterson - Bid Manager**	**39 days**	**0%**	**1 Dec '08**	**NA**	**22 Jan '09**	**NA**
4 Bid Strategy	1 day	0%	1 Dec '08	NA	1 Dec '08	NA
9 Project Schedule	4 days	0%	18 Dec '08	NA	23 Dec '08	NA
14 Reviewed Draft Bid Document	1 day	0%	14 Jan '09	NA	14 Jan '09	NA
16 Revised Bid Document	1 day	0%	15 Jan '09	NA	15 Jan '09	NA
18 Bid Document Final	1 day	0%	22 Jan '09	NA	22 Jan '09	NA
⊟ **Reponsibility: David Williams - Account Manager**	**39 days**	**0%**	**1 Dec '08**	**NA**	**22 Jan '09**	**NA**
3 Bid Request Documents Received	0 days	0%	1 Dec '08	NA	1 Dec '08	NA
13 Draft Bid Document	3 days	0%	9 Jan '09	NA	13 Jan '09	NA
19 Bid Submitted	0 days	0%	22 Jan '09	NA	22 Jan '09	NA

Other electronic methods, discussed next, may be employed to collect the data, but irrespective of the method used, the same data needs to be collected.

The above View has been created by:

- Entering the responsible person in Text 1,
- Renaming Text 1 as Responsibility using **Tools**, **Customize**, **Fiel_d_s...**, and
- Grouping by Text 1, which has been renamed **Responsibility**.

There are several methods of collecting the project status:

- By sending a sheet of paper to each responsible person to mark up and return to the scheduler.
- By cutting and pasting the data from Microsoft Project into another document, such as Excel, and emailing the data to each responsible person as an attachment.
- By giving the responsible party direct access to the schedule software to update it. This approach is not recommended, however, unless the project is broken into sub-projects. By using the sub-project method, only one person updates each part of the schedule.
- Microsoft Server, a companion Microsoft Project product that allows collaborative scheduling, could be implemented. This topic is beyond the scope of this book.
- By using a task based timesheet system which would also collect the hours expended on each task.

Some projects involve a number of people. In such cases, it is important that procedures be written to ensure that the status information is collected:

- In a timely manner,
- Consistently,
- In a complete manner, and
- In a usable format.

It is important for a scheduler to be aware that some people have great difficulty in comprehending a schedule. When there are a number of people with different skill levels in an organization, it will be necessary to provide more than one method of updating the data. You even may find that you have to sit down with some people to obtain the correct data, yet others are willing and comfortable to email you the information.

15.3 Understanding Tracking Progress Concepts

There are some terms and concepts used in Microsoft Project that must be understood before we update a project schedule:

15.3.1 Task Lifecycle

There are three stages of a task's lifecycle:

- **Not Started** – The **Early Start** and **Early Finish** dates are calculated from the logic, **Calendars**, **Constraints** and the **Task Duration**.

- **In-Progress** – The task has an **Actual Start** but is not complete.

- **Complete** – The task is in the past, the **Actual Start** and **Actual Finish** dates have been entered into Microsoft Project, and they override the logic and constraints.

15.3.2 Actual Start Date Assignment of an In-Progress Task

This section will explain how Microsoft Project assigns the **Early Start** of an **In-Progress** task.

- A task **Duration** is the duration from the **Early Start** or **Actual Start** to the **Early Finish** or **Actual Finish** and is calculated over the **Task Calendar**.

- When an **Actual Start** is entered into the **Actual Start** field, this date overrides the **Early Start date**. The predecessor logic and start date constraints are ignored.

- For an un-started task, **Actual Start date** is set to equal the **Early Start** date when:
  - ➢ A **% Complete** between 1% and 99% is entered, or
  - ➢ An **Actual Duration** is entered, or
  - ➢ An **Actual Finish** is entered, or
  - ➢ When a % Complete of 100% is entered, then an Actual Start date is set equal to the Early Start and an Actual Finish date equal to the Early Finish date are both set.

15.3.3 Calculation of Actual & Remaining Durations of an In-Progress Task

- The **Actual Duration** is normally the worked duration of a task and **Remaining Duration** is the un-worked duration of a task.

- **Duration** = **Actual Duration** + **Remaining Duration**. Before a task is commenced the **Actual Duration** is zero and the **Remaining Duration** equals the **Duration** assigned to the task.

- There is an in-built proportional link between **Duration**, **Actual Duration**, **Remaining Duration** and **% Complete**. It is not possible to unlink these fields (as in other scheduling software) and therefore not possible to enter the **Remaining Duration** independently of the **% Complete**.
  - ➢ Change the **Duration**: the **Actual Duration** remains constant and the **% Complete** and the **Remaining Duration** changes proportionally.
  - ➢ Change the **% Complete**: the **Duration** remains constant and the **Actual Duration** and the **Remaining Duration** change proportionally.
  - ➢ Change the **Actual Duration**: the **Duration** remains constant and the **% Complete** and the **Remaining Duration** changes proportionally.
  - ➢ Change the **Remaining Duration**: the **Actual Duration** remains constant and the **% Complete** and the **Duration** changes proportionally.

- When a **% Complete** is assigned, then the **Actual Start** date is set to be equal to the **Early Start** date and durations are recalculated as per the above rules.

- When the **% Complete** is set to 100 or the **Remaining Duration** is set to zero, the **Actual Finish** date is set to the **Early Finish date** and the **Actual Duration is** set to the **Duration**.

- An **Actual Finish** date overrides an **Early Finish** date, and finish date constraints are ignored.

The example below shows three tasks, the first un-started, the second in-progress and the third complete. You should observe:

- The relationship between the **Duration, Actual Duration, Remaining Duration** and **% Complete** in each of the tasks, and

- How the **Actual Start** and **Actual Finish** are set.

	Start	Act. Start	Finish	Act. Finish	% Comp.	Duration	Act. Dur.	Rem. Dur.	2 Nov '09 S M T W T F S	9 Nov '09 S M T W T F S
1	2 Nov '09	NA	13 Nov '09	NA	0%	10 days	0 days	10 days		
2	2 Nov '09	2 Nov '09	13 Nov '09	NA	25%	10 days	2.5 days	7.5 days		
3	2 Nov '09	2 Nov '09	13 Nov '09	13 Nov '09	100%	10 days	10 days	0 days		

 Unlike in Primavera software, it is not possible in Microsoft Project to unlink the **Remaining Duration** and **% Complete**. This will prove frustrating to some schedulers, as you will not be able use the **% Complete** column to represent the amount of work complete when the task is not progressing at a linear rate. Furthermore, Microsoft Project calculates the Finish Date of a task from the Actual Start plus the Duration. It ignores the Remaining Duration, the Current Date and Status Date when calculating the Finish Date of a task. Primavera users will find this a difficult concept but these concepts must be understood to use Microsoft Project effectively.

15.3.4 Calculating the Early Finish Date of an In-Progress Task

Retained Logic and Progress Override are not terms used by Microsoft Project documentation. These terms are used by other Primavera software and are used here to help clarify how Microsoft Project performs its calculations. In the example below, there are two tasks with a Finish-to-Start relationship:

	Act. Start	Act. Finish	% Comp.	2 Nov '09 S M T W T F S	9 Nov '09 S M T W T F S	16 Nov '09 S M T W T F S
1	NA	NA	0%			
2	NA	NA	0%			

There are two options for calculating the finish date of the successor when the successor task starts before the predecessor task is finished:

- **Retained Logic**. In the example below, the logic relationship is maintained between the predecessor and successor for the un-worked portion of the Task, the Remaining Duration, and continues after the predecessor has finished.

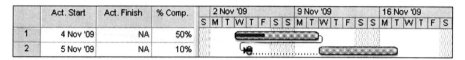

	Act. Start	Act. Finish	% Comp.	2 Nov '09	9 Nov '09	16 Nov '09
1	4 Nov '09	NA	50%			
2	5 Nov '09	NA	10%			

This option will operate when the following conditions are met:
➢ The Project Option **Split in-progress tasks** is checked, and
➢ There is an **Actual Start**, and
➢ A **% Complete** between 1% and 99% is assigned to the successor task.

- **Progress Override**. In the example below, the Finish-to-Start relationship between the predecessor and successor is disregarded, and the un-worked portion of the Task, the Remaining Duration, continues before the predecessor has finished:

	Act. Start	Act. Finish	% Comp.	2 Nov '09	9 Nov '09	16 Nov '09
1	4 Nov '09	NA	50%			
2	5 Nov '09	NA	10%			

Progress Override option will operate when:
➢ The Project Option **Split in-progress tasks IS NOT** checked,
or
➢ The task has an **Actual Start** and 0% Complete and Project Option **Split in-progress tasks IS** checked.

This function may result in some problems in reporting a schedule when the **Split in-progress tasks** option is used in combination with some Tasks set to 0% Complete and other tasks set between 1% and 99% Complete. The two examples below are from the same schedule, both with the **Split in-progress tasks** option checked, one with 0% and one with 1%. You will notice the task assigned 0% has an earlier Finish Date than the task assigned 1% Complete, which has split.

	Act. Start	Act. Finish	% Comp.	2 Nov '09	9 Nov '09	16 Nov '09
1	4 Nov '09	NA	50%			
2	4 Nov '09	NA	0%			

	Act. Start	Act. Finish	% Comp.	2 Nov '09	9 Nov '09	16 Nov '09
1	4 Nov '09	NA	50%			
2	4 Nov '09	NA	1%			

You therefore need to pay careful attention to any warning messages Microsoft Project presents.

15.3.5   Summary Bars Progress Calculation

Summary bars are not normally statused by entering the **Actual Start** date, **Actual Finish** date, or **% Complete** against them. This is possible in Microsoft Project and is covered later in this chapter in the section titled **Marking Up Summary Tasks**.

This status information is usually entered against the detailed tasks, and the summary tasks inherit the status data from the detailed tasks.

- An **Actual Start** is assigned against a Summary Task when any Child Task has an **Actual Start**.

- A Summary Task's **% Complete** is calculated from the total of all the child tasks' **Actual Durations** divided by the total of all the child tasks' **Durations**.

- A Summary Task's **Actual** and **Remaining Durations** are calculated from the **Duration** and **% Complete**.

- An **Actual Finish** is assigned against a Summary task when all Detail tasks have an **Actual Finish**.

15.3.6   Understanding the Current Date, Status Date & Update Project Date

Microsoft Project has two project data date fields that may be displayed as vertical lines on the schedule, and these dates may be edited from the **Project, Project Information...** form:

- **Current Date** – This date is set to the computer's date each time a project file is opened. It is used for calculating **Earned Value** data when a **Status Date** has not been set.

- **Status Date** – This field is blank by default with a value of **NA**. When this date is set, it will not change when the project is saved and reopened at a later date. When set, this date overrides the **Current Date** for calculating **Earned Value** data.

It is recommended that the **Status Date** be set and displayed as a vertical line on a progressed schedule and that the **Current Date** not be displayed, as the **Current Date** represents the date today and does not normally represent any scheduling significance.

The **Update Project Date** may also influence how Microsoft Project calculates the end date of some activities. This date may not be displayed as a vertical line on the screen but may be used in conjunction with the **Reschedule Uncompleted Work To Start After** function covered later in this chapter.

NEITHER the **Current Date** nor the **Status Date** is used to calculate the **Early Finish** of an **In-Progress** task of a schedule using **F9** or **Automatic Scheduling**, unless one of the following two functions is used:

- The **Tools, Tracking, Update Project...**, **Reschedule incomplete to start after: Current Date**, or

- The **Status Date** may be used to move the start of incomplete and the finish of completed parts of a task back or forward to the **Status Date** with the function **Status Date Calculation Options** (new to Microsoft Project 2002). This option will be discussed at the end of this chapter. It also has restrictions that could make the function difficult to use on a project.

Ideally, scheduling software has one **Data Date** and its function is to:

- Separate the completed parts of tasks from incomplete parts of tasks,

- Calculate or record all costs and hours to date before the data date, and to forecast costs and hours to go after the data date.

- Calculate the **Finish Date** of an in-progress task from the **Data Date** plus the **Remaining Duration** over the **Task Calendar**.

Therefore, it is relatively simple in Microsoft Project to be in a situation where you have complete or in-progress tasks with start dates later than the data date, and/or incomplete or un-started tasks with a finish date earlier than the data date. This is an unrealistic situation, which is more difficult to achieve in other scheduling software packages. Care should be taken to avoid this situation.

15.4   Updating the Schedule

The next stage is to update the schedule by entering the mark-up information against each task.

When dealing with large schedules it is normal to create a look-ahead schedule with a filter to display incomplete and un-started tasks commencing in the near future only.

Microsoft Project provides several methods of statusing the schedule:

- **Update Project** – This is an automated process that assumes all tasks have progressed as planned. After updating a project, you may adjust the dates and percent complete to the recorded progress.

- **Update Tasks** – This function is used to status tasks one at a time.

- Update tasks using the **Task** or **Task Details** form.

- Update tasks by displaying the appropriate tracking columns by:
  - ➢ Selecting the **Tracking** table, or
  - ➢ Creating your own table, or
  - ➢ Inserting the required columns in an existing table.

Each of these four methods is discussed in the following sections. Then we will discuss the following two functions which are designed to assist you in moving tasks to their logical places in relation to the **Status Date**:

- **Move Incomplete Work into the Future**, and

- **Status Date Calculation Options**.

15.4.1 Using Update Project

Microsoft Project has a facility titled **Update Progress** for updating a project as if it had progressed according to plan. This function sets **Actual Start** and **Actual Finish** dates, **% Complete** and **Renaming Durations** in proportion to a user-assigned date.

Select **Tools, Tracking, Update Project…** to open the **Update Project** form:

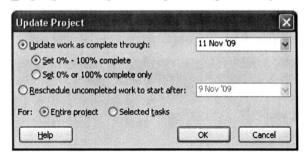

There are two options under **Update work as complete through:** which apply to in-progress tasks only.

- **Set 0% – 100 % Complete**:
  - ➢ This option sets the **Actual Start** to the **Early Start**, and
  - ➢ Sets the **% Complete** and **Actual Duration** in proportion to the amount of time worked for any in-progress tasks.
  - ➢ Sets the **Status Date** to the date you have nominated as the update date, the vertical line in the Gantt chart below:

- **Set 0% or 100 % Complete only**. This option sets:
  - ➢ The **Actual Start** to the **Early Start** but leaves the **% Complete** and **Actual Duration** at zero.
  - ➢ The **% Complete** is set to 100% only when the task is complete.
  - ➢ Does not set the **Status Date** (or reset if it has been set in a previous update) to the date you have nominated as the update date. There is no vertical line representing the **Status Date** in the picture below:

You may use the **Selected tasks** option when you highlight the tasks to be progressed before opening the **Update Project** form. Unselected tasks will not be progressed, but these tasks may be scheduled to occur after the **Status Date** by using the **Reschedule uncompleted work to start after:** function. This is covered later in this section.

You may not reverse progress with this option as one is able to do with SureTrak.

15.4.2   Update Tasks

Microsoft Project has a function that may be used for updating tasks one at a time or may be used for updating selected tasks with the same information. For example, there may be several tasks with the same Actual Start or % Complete.

- Select one or more tasks that you want to update with the same information such as the same Actual Start date.

- Select **Tools**, **Tracking**, **Update Tasks…** to open the **Update Tasks** form:

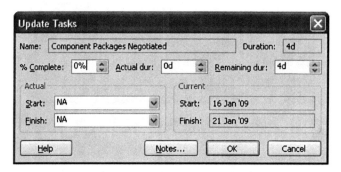

- Enter the required data and click on the [OK] button to close the form.

 Using the **Update Tasks** or the **Task Information** forms are a cumbersome method for updating a large number of individual tasks since the form has to be closed after each task has been updated, the cursor moved to the next task and the form reopened. If you have a large number of tasks to be updated, it is quicker to use columns or a **Detailed** form in the lower pane.

15.4.3   Updating Tasks Using the Task Information Form

You may use the **Task Information** form to update progress:

- Open the **Task** form by double-clicking on a task:

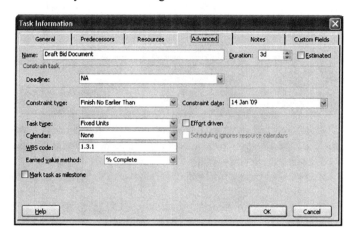

Using the **Task Information** form function is a cumbersome method for updating a large number of tasks, since the form has to be closed after each task has been updated, the cursor moved to the next task and the form reopened. If you have a large number of tasks to be updated, it is quicker to use columns or a **Detailed** form in the lower pane.

15.4.4   Updating Tasks Using the Task Details Form

- To open the **Task Details** form, open the dual-pane view by either:
  - ➢ Selecting **Window**, **Split**,
  - ➢ Dragging the divider line with the mouse, or
  - ➢ Selecting a **View** with a dual pane or right-click.
  - ➢ Then, click in the bottom pane to make it active. There will be a blue bar down the left-hand side when the bottom pane is active.

  Now select **View**, **More Views…**, **Task Details Form** if an acceptable view is not available:

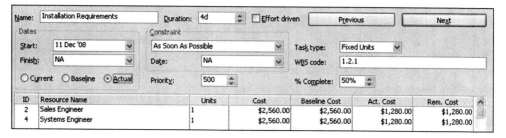

- Updating a task:
  - ➢ Click on the **Actual** radio button.
  - ➢ Enter a **% Complete**. An **Actual Start** date will be set by Microsoft Project and may be edited from the **Start:** drop-down box.
  - ➢ The **Duration** may be edited in order to calculate a new finish date. You will note that the % Complete will change when the duration is edited.
  - ➢ When a date is typed into the **Finish:** drop-down box, a **Finish Constraint** may be set without warning when the task is not 100% complete. These may be edited from the **Task Information** form's **Advanced** tab.

15.4.5   Updating Tasks Using Columns

An efficient method of updating tasks is by displaying the data in columns. This may be achieved by:

- Applying the **Tracking Table**, or

- Creating your own table, or

- Inserting the required columns.

To apply the tracking table, select **View**, **Table:**, **Tracking** table. This table may not exist if you are working on a schedule that has had this table deleted or if you have a non-standard load of Microsoft Project in which this table has been deleted from the Global.mpt. If you do not use the tracking table, be sure to add the following columns: **Actual Start**, **Actual Finish**, **% Complete**, **Actual Duration**, and **Remaining Duration**.

The status data may now be entered directly into the columns.

15.4.6   Marking Up Summary Tasks

It is not normal to mark up Summary Tasks, and Actual Dates may not be entered against Summary tasks. % Complete may be entered against a Summary Task and all the subordinate tasks will be auto-statused to match the summary % Complete.

When a **% Complete** is entered against a Summary task, all subordinate tasks, both Summary and Detailed, inherit a value depending upon the setting of the **Updating task status updates resource status** option found in **Tools**, **Options…**, **Calculation** tab.

To explain this concept further, see the following two examples. Both schedules pictured below had 60% entered against Task 2, the Research Phase of the OzBuild Bid task. All other Actual dates and % Completes were calculated by Microsoft Project.

- With the **Updating task status updates resource status CHECKED** the activities are statused as if they were completed according to plan:

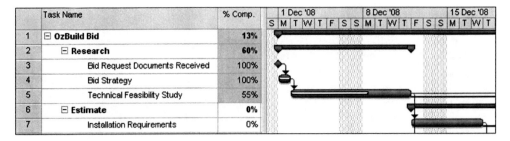

- With the **Updating task status updates resource status UNCHECKED** all activities are assigned to 60% complete, which is not the logical progression of the project:

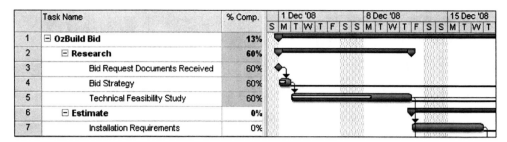

15.4.7 Reschedule Uncompleted Work To Start After

There is a feature available in the **Update Project** form titled **Reschedule uncompleted work to start after:** which will schedule the **Incomplete Work** of an **In-Progress** task to start on a specific date in the future.

- If you want to apply this operation to some tasks, then these should be selected first.

- Select **Tools**, **Options…**, **Schedule** tab and ensure the **Split in-progress tasks** option is checked. If this option is not checked, then this function will not operate.

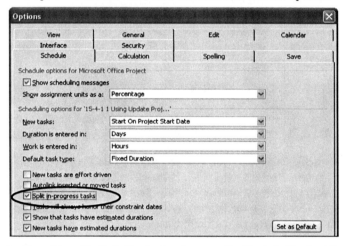

- Select **Tools, Tracking, Update Project…** to open the **Update Project** form.

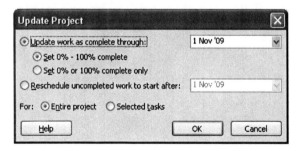

- Click on the **Reschedule uncompleted work to start after:** radio button.

- In the drop-down box to the right, specify the date after which incomplete work should commence. Then click on the [OK] button.

A task may be split without the split being displayed in the Gantt Chart by un-checking the **Show bar splits** in the **Layout** form. In the examples below, the **Incomplete Work** has been moved after 12 November:

- The task has been split in the picture below and the splits displayed:

	Act. Start	Act. Finish	% Comp.
1	3 Nov '09	NA	20%

- The task has been split in the picture below and the splits **NOT** displayed; select **Format, Layout** to hide splits:

	Act. Start	Act. Finish	% Comp.
1	3 Nov '09	NA	20%

Un-started tasks will have a **Start No Earlier Constraint** set to the **Update Project** date. This constraint will have to be removed from tasks if it is required to move the **Update Date** back in time. Also, task splits will have to be manually dragged back in time.

When a project is updated using the **Update Project** function, the **Status Date DOES NOT** change to equal the **Project Update Date**. You may end up with two dates that represent the **Data Date**—the **Update Project** date and the **Status Date**, which may both reflect different dates. The picture below shows the Status Date in the black vertical line at 11 Nov 09 and the **Update Project** date set at 17 Nov 09, which has split the last activity. In this situation the Status Date should be set manually.

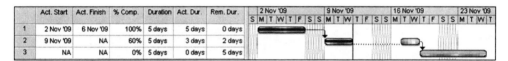

	Act. Start	Act. Finish	% Comp.	Duration	Act. Dur.	Rem. Dur.
1	2 Nov '09	6 Nov '09	100%	5 days	5 days	0 days
2	9 Nov '09	NA	60%	5 days	3 days	2 days
3	NA	NA	0%	5 days	0 days	5 days

For tasks that are behind schedule, you may use the **Update Project** function to reschedule them after the **Update Project** date. This date will effectively become the **Data Date**. However, it is not possible to show the **Update Project** date as a vertical line on the bar chart. You may set and display the **Status Date** at the same date so incomplete work is all scheduled after a line displayed on the Gantt Chart.

It is recommended when you use the **Update Project** function that you should open the **Project Information** form and set the **Status Date** to the same date as the **Update Project** date. This enables you to display a **Data Date** in the bar chart in the correct place.

15.4.8   Status Date Calculation Options - New Tasks

New functions were introduced in Microsoft Project 2002 intended to assist schedulers to place the new tasks as they are added to the schedule in a logical position with respect to the **Status Date**. If the **Status Date** has not been set then the **Current Date** is used. In the example below the vertical black line is the **Status Date**:

- Task 1 has complete work in the future which is not logical,

- Task 2 would normally be considered in the logical position with respect to the **Status Date**, and

- Task 3 has incomplete work in the past, which is also not logical.

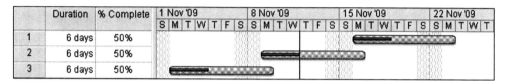

Select **Tools**, **Options**, **Calculation** tab and these options are found under the **Calculation options for 'Project 1'**:

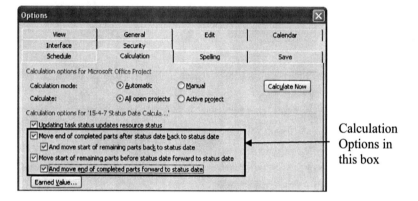

Calculation Options in this box

For all these options to operate all four of the following parameters must be met:

- The **Split in-progress tasks** option in the **Schedule** tab must be checked, and

- The required option on the **Calculation** tab under **Calculation** tab must be checked before the task is added or edited, and

- The **Updating task status updates resource status** option on the **Calculation** tab must be checked.

- The Task **MUST NOT BE** assigned **Task Duration Type** of **Fixed Duration**.

 The documentation found in the earlier Microsoft Project Help files is not precise and does not make it clear to the user that these options may NOT be turned on and off to recalculate all tasks. The options only work on new tasks when they are added to a schedule or when a task is updated by changing the % Complete.

The following four options are available:

- Check only **Move end of completed parts after status date back to status date** and this is the effect on task 1 in the picture on the previous page when the % Complete is increased to 60%:

	Duration	% Complete	1 Nov '09	8 Nov '09	15 Nov '09	22 Nov '09
			S M T W T F S	S M T W T F S	S M T W T F S	S M T W
1	6 days	60%				

- The **And move start of remaining parts back to status date** option is only available after the option above is checked:

	Duration	% Complete	1 Nov '09	8 Nov '09	15 Nov '09	22 Nov '09
			S M T W T F S	S M T W T F S	S M T W T F S	S M T W
1	6 days	70%				

- The **Move start of remaining parts before status date forward to status date** may be checked at any time. The picture below shows the effect on task 3 in the picture on the previous page when the % Complete is changed to 60%:

	Duration	% Complete	1 Nov '09	8 Nov '09	15 Nov '09	22 Nov '09
			S M T W T F S	S M T W T F S	S M T W T F S	S M T W
3	6 days	60%				

- The **And move end of completed parts forward to status date** may be checked after the option above is checked:

	Duration	% Complete	1 Nov '09	8 Nov '09	15 Nov '09	22 Nov '09
			S M T W T F S	S M T W T F S	S M T W T F S	S M T W
3	6 days	60%				

This function will ignore constraints even when the Schedule Option **Tasks will always honor their constraint date** has been set.

 Experimentation by the author indicates that the activities will adopt the rules that are set in the options form when the task is added or when a task Percentage Complete is changed. Therefore this function may not be applied to existing schedules, but only to new tasks if the options are set before the tasks are added or when a task Percentage is updated.

This function in its current form has some restrictions that schedulers may find unacceptable:

- Existing schedules may not be opened and the function applied.

- When the **Move start of remaining parts before status date forward to status date** is used, it overrides any **Actual Start** date that you have entered prior to entering a % Complete.

This option should be used with caution and users should ensure they fully understand how this function operates by statusing a simple schedule multiple times.

15.4.9 Status Date Calculation Options - When Statusing a Schedule

The Status Date Calculation Options also operates when a schedule is statused by changing the Percent Completes of Tasks. The example below shows a task with the Status Date, the dark vertical line, set to the next period:

	Duration	% Complete	1 Nov '09	8 Nov '09	15 Nov '09	22 Nov '09
			S M T W T F S	S M T W T F S	S M T W T F S	S M T W
1	6 days	0%				

When all the **Status Date Calculation Option** options are checked and the percent complete is changed from 0% to 50% the task is aligned to the new Status Date:

	Duration	% Complete	1 Nov '09	8 Nov '09	15 Nov '09	22 Nov '09
			S M T W T F S	S M T W T F S	S M T W T F S	S M T W
1	6 days	40%				

Now the status date has been moved to the next week and the tasks have not moved in respect to the Status Date and will not move when the project is recalculated:

	Duration	% Complete	1 Nov '09	8 Nov '09	15 Nov '09	22 Nov '09
			S M T W T F S	S M T W T F S	S M T W T F S	S M T W
1	6 days	40%				

After percent complete changed to 60%, the task splits and the un-worked portion of the task is set to be completed after the new Status Date:

	Duration	% Complete	1 Nov '09	8 Nov '09	15 Nov '09	22 Nov '09
			S M T W T F S	S M T W T F S	S M T W T F S	S M T W
1	6 days	50%				

15.4.10 Tracking Toolbar

The tracking toolbar may be displayed by selecting **View**, **Toolbars** and selecting the **Tracking** toolbar. This toolbar has some useful functions for auto statusing one task at a time. The **Update Project** option allows updating all or selected tasks. It is simple to use and should be experimented with. It is usually better to set the Status Date first and then use the toolbar. The functions available are:

- Displays the **Project Statistics** form,

- **Update as Scheduled** updates the task as if it has proceeded exactly as it was scheduled. An in-progress or completed task could be dragged to where it actually happened and then the button clicked to progress the task.

- **Reschedule Work** will split a task that is behind schedule and place the incomplete portion after the Status Date. This will only work if **Split in Progress** is checked in the **Tools, Options, Schedule** tab.

- **Add Progress Line** will add a progress line displaying if tasks are ahead or behind schedule. **Tools, Tracking, Progress Lines...** opens the **Progress Lines** form where the lines are formatted. A Baseline should be set to provide a comparison to the original plan. Multiple Progress lines may be recorded.

- **Percent Complete** buttons set the percent complete as indicated by the button and may be used in conjunction with the **Reschedule Work** button.

- **Update Tasks** opens the Update Tasks form:

15.5 Simple Procedure for Statusing a Schedule

For those people who require just one simple method of statusing a schedule the following process should be considered, but may not suit all situations especially when a project is way off plan:

- Set the Baseline by selecting **Tools**, **Tracking**, **Save Baseline…**.

- Display the Baseline bars by selecting **Format**, **Gantt Chart Wizard…**.

- Display the Status Date Gridline, select **Format**, **Gridlines**…, select Status Date.

- Select **Tools**, **Tracking**, **Update Project…** to open the **Update Project** form and select **Set 0% – 100 % Complete**, set the date in the form to the new **Status Date**.

- The project should be statused as if it has progressed exactly as planned and the Status Date should now be displayed in the bar chart.

- Displaying the **Tracking Table** may assist here.

- Now adjust the task dates by dragging the bars or entering the dates in the appropriate column, the order that the actions take place is important:
  - ➢ **Complete** tasks should have the Actual Start and then the Actual Finish dates adjusted to when the task actually started and actually finished.
  - ➢ **In-Progress tasks** should have the Actual Start adjusted first, then the task bar dragged so the finish date is where it is expected to finish and finally the % Complete adjusted.
  - ➢ **Unstarted** tasks should have their logic and durations revised.
  - ➢ Consider using the **Tracking Toolbar** at this point.

- Add any scope changes to the schedule.

- Save the project with a new filename and save for future reference.

15.5.1 Comparing Progress with Baseline

There will normally be changes to the schedule dates and more often than not these are delays. The full extent of the change is not apparent without having a Baseline bar to compare with the statused schedule.

- To display the **Baseline Bar** in the **Bar Chart** you may use either the **Format**, **Bar Styles…** function covered in the **FORMATTING THE DISPLAY** chapter, or

- You may use the **Gantt Chart Wizard** as follows:
  - ➢ Select **Format**, **Gantt Chart Wizard…** to open the Gantt Chart Wizard.
  - ➢ Select the **Baseline** or **Custom Gantt Chart** option. This will display both the current schedule and the baseline.

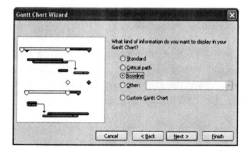

> ➤ Hit the [Next >] button and follow the remainder of the instructions to complete the formatting. You will be given options for applying text and relationships in the Gantt Chart.

This wizard will overwrite any customized formatting you have made using the **Format, Bar Styles...** option.

The Start and Finish Date variances are available by displaying the **Start Variance** and **Finish Variance** columns. These variance columns use the **Baseline** data and variance columns and are not available for **Baseline 1** to **10**.

Some users like to display **Progress Lines** which are usually displayed as zigzag lines on the Gantt chart showing how far ahead or behind the project tasks are. Select **Tools, Tracking, Progress Lines...** to open the **Progress line** form where the progress lines may be formatted:

	Task Name	Finish Variance	Dec '08					Jan '09				
			24	1	8	15	22	29	5	12	19	26
1	⊟ OzBuild Bid	0d										
2	⊟ Research	2d										
3	Bid Request Documents Received	0d										
4	Bid Strategy	2d										
5	Technical Feasibility Study	2d										

15.5.2   Corrective Action

There are two courses of action available with date slippage:

- The first is to accept the slippage. This is rarely acceptable, but it is the easiest answer.

- The second is to examine the schedule and evaluate how you could improve the end date.

Solutions to return the project to its original completion date must be cleared with the person responsible for the project, since they can have the most impact on the work.

Suggested techniques to bring the project back on track include:

- Reducing the durations of tasks on, or almost on, the critical path. When tasks have resources, increasing the number of resources working on the tasks may reduce duration. Changing longer tasks is often more achievable than changing the length of short duration tasks.

- Changing calendars, say from a five-day to a six-day calendar, so that tasks are being worked on for more days per week.

- Reducing the project scope and deleting tasks.

- Changing task relationships so tasks take place concurrently. This may be achieved by introducing negative lags to Finish to Start relationships which maintains a Closed Network.

- Introducing Start-to-Start relationships which has the potential of creating an open network. Should maintaining the critical path be important then this option should be avoided.

- Changing the logic or sequencing of tasks to reduce the overall length of the critical path. This may take a lot of work and reviews.

- Change the method of execution, for example moving work off site.

15.5.3   In-progress Schedule Check List

The following check list may be used to check an in-progress schedule.

Complete Activities

- Have all activities an Actual Start and an Actual Finish in the past.

In-Progress Activities

- Actual Start Dates should all be in the past and Early Finish dates in the future.

- Check activities with Constraints, are the constraints still valid?

- Do all activities have Finish successors?

- Are there any activities with progress greater than planned and require the duration shortened?

- Are there any activities that have progress slower than planned and require the duration lengthened or split and delayed using the **Reschedule uncompleted work to start** (after date) function.

Not Started Activities

- Check all the constraints on these activities are still valid.

- Do activities have Finish successors?

Open Ends & Total Float

- Confirm all activities have successors and review float. Activities with excessive float should be assigned dummy successors or delayed if they are not scheduled in a realistic timeframe with sequencing logic or Early Start constraints.

Critical And Near Critical Path

- Check the Critical Path, is the scheduled critical path realistic and aligned with what project personnel consider critical?

Baseline Comparison

- Review the Baseline dates with the current schedule and confirm that any delays are legitimate.

- Have there been many changes and delays and therefore should the schedule be re-baselined?

WORKSHOP 13

Statusing the Schedule and Baseline Comparison

Background

At the end of the first week you have to update the schedule and report progress and slippage.

Assignment

Open your **OzBuild Bid** project file and complete the following steps:

1. Set the Baseline for all the tasks on your project using the **Tools**, **Tracking** command.
2. Use the **Format**, **Gantt Chart Wizard** and the **Custom Gantt Chart** to display the Critical Path, Baseline Bars, and Relationships. Do not display dates or resources.
3. Set the timescale as per the pictures below.

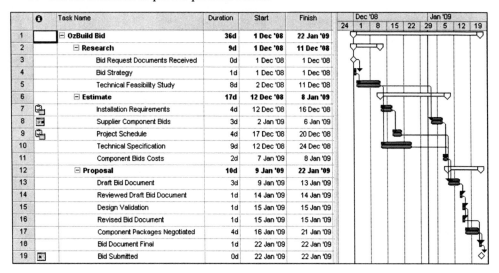

	❶	Task Name	Duration	Start	Finish
1		⊟ OzBuild Bid	36d	1 Dec '08	22 Jan '09
2		⊟ Research	9d	1 Dec '08	11 Dec '08
3		Bid Request Documents Received	0d	1 Dec '08	1 Dec '08
4		Bid Strategy	1d	1 Dec '08	1 Dec '08
5		Technical Feasibility Study	8d	2 Dec '08	11 Dec '08
6		⊟ Estimate	17d	12 Dec '08	8 Jan '09
7		Installation Requirements	4d	12 Dec '08	16 Dec '08
8		Supplier Component Bids	3d	2 Jan '09	6 Jan '09
9		Project Schedule	4d	17 Dec '08	20 Dec '08
10		Technical Specification	9d	12 Dec '08	24 Dec '08
11		Component Bids Costs	2d	7 Jan '09	8 Jan '09
12		⊟ Proposal	10d	9 Jan '09	22 Jan '09
13		Draft Bid Document	3d	9 Jan '09	13 Jan '09
14		Reviewed Draft Bid Document	1d	14 Jan '09	14 Jan '09
15		Design Validation	1d	15 Jan '09	15 Jan '09
16		Revised Bid Document	1d	15 Jan '09	15 Jan '09
17		Component Packages Negotiated	4d	16 Jan '09	21 Jan '09
18		Bid Document Final	1d	22 Jan '09	22 Jan '09
19		Bid Submitted	0d	22 Jan '09	22 Jan '09

4. It is a Prince2 requirement to create a Stage Plan for the first Stage before it has begun. Granulate the **Technical Feasibility Study** into the following Tasks, which are each 2 days long using **Insert**, **New Task**:
   ➢ Research Available Documents
   ➢ Conduct Technical Study
   ➢ Draft Technical Feasibility Study
   ➢ Publish Technical Feasibility Study
5. Connect up logic as per the first picture on the next page, with no logic from or to Parent tasks.

6. Set the Baseline for the new tasks only:

	Task Name	Duration	Start	Finish	Predecessors	Successors	Dec '08 24	1	8	15	22	29	Jan '09 5	
1	⊟ OzBuild Bid	36d	1 Dec '08	22 Jan '09										
2	⊟ Research	9d	1 Dec '08	11 Dec '08										
3	Bid Request Documents Received	0d	1 Dec '08	1 Dec '08		4								
4	Bid Strategy	1d	1 Dec '08	1 Dec '08	3	6								
5	⊟ Technical Feasibility Study	8d	2 Dec '08	11 Dec '08										
6	Research Available Documen	2d	2 Dec '08	3 Dec '08	4	7								
7	Conduct Technical Study	2d	4 Dec '08	5 Dec '08	6	8								
8	Draft Technical Feasibility Stu	2d	8 Dec '08	9 Dec '08	7	9								
9	Publish Technical Feasibility S	2d	10 Dec '08	11 Dec '08	8	11,14								
10	⊟ Estimate	17d	12 Dec '08	8 Jan '09										
11	Installation Requirements	4d	12 Dec '08	16 Dec '08	9	13,12								
12	Supplier Component Bids	3d	2 Jan '09	6 Jan '09	11	15								
13	Project Schedule	4d	17 Dec '08	20 Dec '08	11	17								
14	Technical Specification	9d	12 Dec '08	24 Dec '08	9	17								
15	Component Bids Costs	2d	7 Jan '09	8 Jan '09	12	17								

7. Apply the **Gantt Chart** view and the **Tracking** table.
8. Hide the **Physical %**, **Actual Cost** and **Actual Work** columns.
9. Select **Format, Gridlines…** and set the **Status Date** as a solid red line.
10. Use **Tools, Tracking, Update Project…** to update progress to 8 Dec 08.
11. Check the **Status date** in the **Project Information** form; it should be 8 Dec 08.

	Task Name	Act. Start	Act. Finish	% Comp.	Act. Dur.	Rem. Dur.	Dec '08 24	1	8
2	⊟ Research	1 Dec '08	NA	67%	6d	3d			
3	Bid Request Documents Received	1 Dec '08	1 Dec '08	100%	0d	0d			
4	Bid Strategy	1 Dec '08	1 Dec '08	100%	1d	0d			
5	⊟ Technical Feasibility Study	2 Dec '08	NA	63%	5d	3d			
6	Research Available Documents	2 Dec '08	3 Dec '08	100%	2d	0d			
7	Conduct Technical Study	4 Dec '08	5 Dec '08	100%	2d	0d			
8	Draft Technical Feasibility Study	8 Dec '08	NA	50%	1d	1d			
9	Publish Technical Feasibility Study	NA	NA	0%	0d	2d			

12. Update the following tasks using the table below and note there is no change in the end date of project as there is sufficient Float to absorb the delay:

Task Name	Act. Start	Act. Finish	% Comp.
Research Available Documents	2 Dec '08	5 Dec '08	100%
Conduct Technical Study	3 Dec '08	NA	50%
Draft Technical Feasibility Study	4 Dec '08	NA	25%

13. Now use the **Reschedule uncompleted work to start after:** to schedule the **Incomplete Work** of an **In-Progress** task to start after 8 Dec 08. The tasks will only split if the **Split in-progress** option is checked.

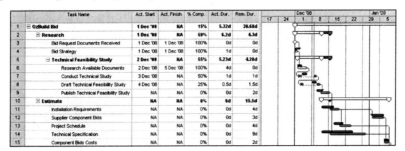

14. Save your **OzBuild Bid** project.

16   GROUPING, OUTLINE CODES AND WBS

Outlining was discussed earlier as a method of organizing detailed tasks under summary tasks. There are alternative data fields and functions available in Microsoft Project for recording, organizing, grouping and displaying task information:

- Custom Fields and Grouping

- Custom Outline Codes

- User Defined WBS (Work Breakdown Structure)

These functions are addressed in this book but are not examined in detail. These functions enable the presentation of the tasks under other project breakdown structures.

16.1   Understanding a Project Breakdown Structure

A Project Breakdown Structure often represents a hierarchical breakdown of a project into logical functional elements. Some organizations have highly organized and disciplined structures with "rules" for creating and coding the elements of the structure. Some clients also impose a WBS code on a contractor for reporting and/or claiming payments. The following are examples of such structures:

- PBS   **Product Breakdown Structure**, the method used by the **PRINCE2 Product Based Planning Technique.**

- WBS   **Work Breakdown Structure**, breaking down the project into the elements of work required to complete a project.

- OBS   **Organization Breakdown Structure**, showing the hierarchical management structure of a project.

- CBS   **Contract Breakdown Structure**, showing the breakdown of contracts.

- SBS   **System Breakdown Structure**, showing the elements of a complex system.

We will discuss the following functions available in Microsoft Project to represent these structures in your schedule.

Topic	Menu Command
• Customize Fields	Select **Tools, Customize Fields…** to open the **Customize Fields** form.
• Grouping	Select **Project, Group by:**
• Custom Outline Codes	Select **Tools, Customize, Fields…** and select the **Custom Outline Codes** tab to create a Custom Outline Code, Assign the codes by displaying a column, or Select **Project, Group by:, More Groups…** option to create a grouping to display the tasks under the Custom Outline Code.
• Outline Codes	Display the **Outline Code** column or the **Outline Code** with the **Task Name** by selecting **Tools, Options…, View** tab and checking the **Show outline number**.
• User defined WBS	Select **Project, WBS, Define Code…**

16.2   Customize Fields

Select **Tools**, **Customize Fields...** to open the **Customize Fields** form. This function includes a number of predefined fields for both Task and Resources. Task fields may be used for recording additional information about Tasks (such as responsibility, location, floor, system) Resource fields may record information such as telephone number, address, office and skills. Formulas may be created to populate the fields with calculated data.

The form has two tabs in Microsoft 2000 – 2003 but has a slightly changed format in 2007, which is shown below:

These predefined fields fall into the following categories:

- Cost

- Date

- Duration

- Finish (date)

- Flag

- Number

- Outline Code (this option is on a separate Tab in Microsoft Project 2000 – 2003)

- Start (date)

- Text

Both the title and content of these fields may be edited with options including:

- Rename... allows the renaming of the filed name.
  - ➢ This new name is then available when inserting columns and is displayed in the column header.
  - ➢ After Custom Field is renamed the new name will be displayed in the **Custom Fields** tab of the **Task** or **Resource Information** form and the appropriate information may then be entered in this form.

- Import Field... allows importing from other fields or project files.

- **Custom Attributes**:
  - ➢ **None** allows data to be entered into the field without any restrictions.
  - ➢ Lookup... opens the **Edit Lookup Table** where a table of values and descriptions may be entered. The Value is displayed in columns and Description in bands when the tasks are grouped by this field.
  - ➢ Formula... allows the assigning of formulae for the calculation of field value from other task and project fields.

- **Calculation for task and group summary rows** specifies how summary tasks calculate their value, such as Maximum, Minimum, Sum, None and Average. For example, the following options may be used:
  - ➢ A Start Date would select Minimum,
  - ➢ A Finish Date would select Maximum,
  - ➢ Cost would use Sum.
- **Calculation for assignment rows** determines if the field value is displayed only against the resource in Task Usage and Resource Usage fields or against the resource and assignment. This is only available in Microsoft Project 2007.

Resource Only   Resource and Assignment

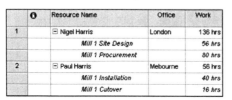

	❶	Resource Name	Office	Work
1		⊟ Nigel Harris	London	136 hrs
		Mill 1 Site Design		56 hrs
		Mill 1 Procurement		80 hrs
2		⊟ Paul Harris	Mebourne	56 hrs
		Mill 1 Installation		40 hrs
		Mill 1 Cutover		16 hrs

	❶	Resource Name	Office	Work
1		⊟ Nigel Harris	London	136 hrs
		Mill 1 Site Design	London	56 hrs
		Mill 1 Procurement	London	80 hrs
2		⊟ Paul Harris	Mebourne	56 hrs
		Mill 1 Installation	Mebourne	40 hrs
		Mill 1 Cutover	Mebourne	16 hrs

- **Value to display** allows the options of displaying the value in the cell or generating graphical indicators such as traffic lights. A very simple example is displayed below when the Number 1 Custom Field has been renamed Risk and three values entered and three different images displayed:

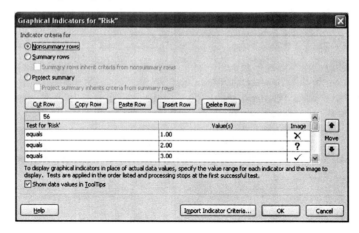

Outline Codes will be covered in more detail later in this chapter.

Primavera software users will find the formatting options available when using Value and Description restrictive, because the description may not be displayed in columns and the value not displayed when Grouping.

16.3 Grouping

Grouping allows grouping of tasks under data items such as Customized fields, Durations, Constraints, etc. This function is particularly useful with schedules with a number of tasks and there is a requirement to work with a related group of tasks throughout a project. The picture below displays a simple project where the relationship between each Task is difficult to check by inspection of the Gantt Chart organized with Outlining by Phase:

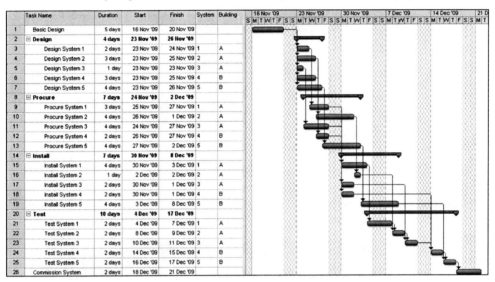

With the Grouping function it is possible to Group on a text field to reorganize the data. In this example, the schedule has been reorganized by the Text 1-System and Text 2- Building fields, which have been renamed using the **Tools**, **Customize**, **Field...** to System and Building. You may now clearly see the logic between the Items:

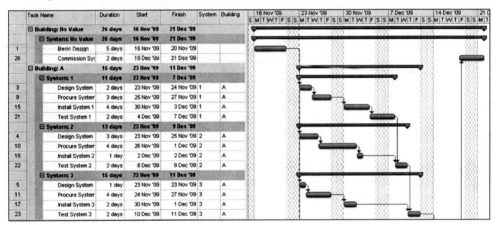

 The first few characters of the field determine the sort order when tasks are grouped by a Text Field. To order items differently to the fields' text values, place a number or letter at the start of the description, or create a **Custom Outline Codes** which will take a little more effort but provide a more satisfactory result.

16.3.1 Customize Group

The **Customize Group** option allows you to create a temporary Group where the settings are not saved. Select **Project**, **Group by:** and there will be a predefined list of Groups for you to choose from:

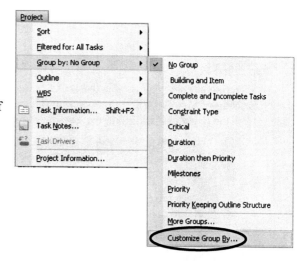

Click on **Customize Group By...** to open the **Customize Group By** form:

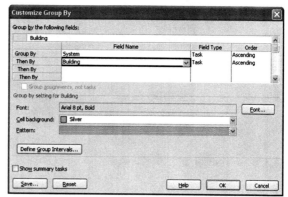

A hierarchical multiple grouping is available by selecting how you require the Tasks to be Grouped. The form above produces the result below:

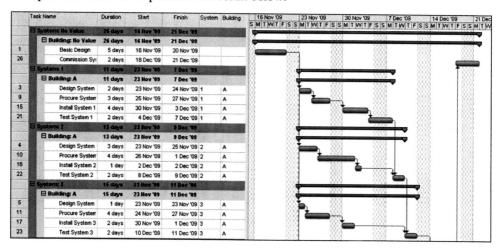

16.3.2   Using a Predefined Group

The Grouping function works in a similar way to Filters and Tables. A predefined Group may be assigned by:

- Selecting **Project**, **Group by:**

- Then either:
  - ➤ Selecting a grouping from the list, or
  - ➤ Selecting **More Groups…** to open the **More Groups** form and then selecting one from the list after clicking on the **Task** or **Resource** radio button.

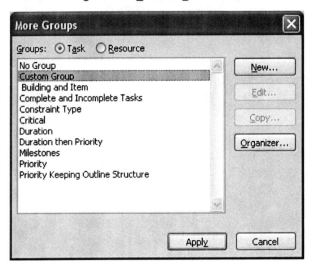

16.3.3   Creating a New Group

Create a new Group by:

- Selecting **Project**, **Group by:**, **More Groups…** to open the **More Groups** form,

- Click on the ⬚ **New…** ⬚ button to open the **Group Definition** form,

- Now create a "Grouping" which may be reapplied at a later date or copy to another project using **Organizer**.

- The **Define Group Interval** form is available with many **Group By** options, such as Start or Finish, and allows further formatting options by defining the intervals of the banding.

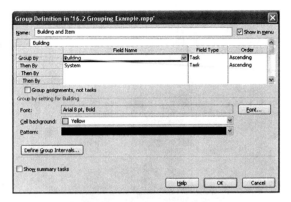

Grouping is similar to the Primavera P3 and SureTrak organize function. It is possible to mimic this Primavera function using the text columns as Activity Code dictionaries. Projects converted from Primavera P3 or SureTrak using the mpx format often translate Primavera's Activity Codes to Microsoft Project's Text 1 through Text 6 fields. After conversion, the project may be **Grouped** by Text 1–6. **Custom Outline Codes** may produce a better result as bands may be ordered with this function.

16.3.4 Grouping Resources in the Resource Sheet

Resources may be created in the **Resource Sheet**. Then the resources may be grouped by a number of attributes. The standard options are shown below:

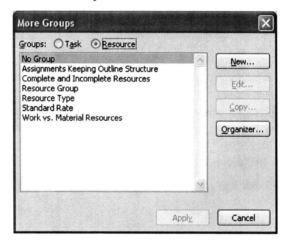

Resources are covered in more detail in the **RESOURCES** chapters.

There are many uses for Grouping Resources, which may be used in conjunction with Customized Fields:

- In a PRINCE2 project a hierarchical organizational structure may be created using this function and resources displayed, for example, under their manager or department.

- Resources details such as address, office, department and telephone number may be recorded in Customized Fields and the resources grouped by department or office location.

16.4   Custom Outline Codes

There are ten Task Custom Outline Codes and ten Resource Outline Codes that may be renamed to suit the project requirements.

- Task Custom Outline Codes may be used for any hierarchical project breakdown structure, such as a PRINCE2 Product Breakdown Structure or Contract Breakdown Structure, and

- Resource Custom Outline Codes may be used for organizational breakdown structures such as the hierarchy of authority, locations and departments.

The process to use this function has three steps:

- Define the new Custom Outline Code structure,

- Assign the codes to the tasks, and

- Create a Group to organize the tasks under the new Custom Outline Code structure.

There are now two forms that need to be accessed and the method of accessing them is different between Microsoft Project 2007 and Microsoft Project 2000 – 2003. The two forms are:

- The **Outline Code Definition** form where the code structure is defined, and

- The **Edit Lookup Table** form where the number of characters and character separators are defined.

16.4.1   Define a Custom Outline Code Structure, Microsoft Project 2007

Select **Tools**, **Customize**, **Fields…** to open the form:

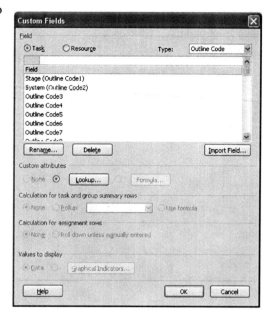

- An Outline Code may be created for either Task or Resource data by clicking on the appropriate radio button under the title **Field**.

- The **Import Field…** function allows you to copy a code structure from another project in a similar method to Organizer.

- The **Rename…** button opens a form to edit the name of the Outline Code. Two codes in the picture have been renamed Stage and System.

- The [Lookup...] in Microsoft Project 2007 opens **Edit Look Up Table** form for the selected Outline Code.

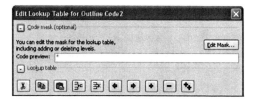

- Before codes are entered the **Mask** or code structure should be defined by clicking on the [Edit Mask...] button at the top right-hand side. This will open the **Outline Code Definition** form where the code structure is defined.

  ➤ As each **Level** is created it is assigned a number.
  ➤ The **Sequence** defines the type of text that may be entered for the code: Numbers, Upper Case, Lower Case or Characters (text).
  ➤ The **Length** specifies how many characters the Code Level may have: any, or a number between 1 and 10.
  ➤ The **Separator** defines the character that separates each level in the structure.

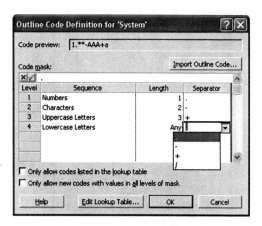

- Click the [OK] button to return to the **Edit Lookup Table** form where the Code Values and Descriptions are entered:

  ➤ The picture shows two "Units" at level 1 and each Unit's Subsystem at level 2.
  ➤ The icons along the top of the form have a similar function to their use in Outlining and may be used to indent and outdent codes and copy and paste code groups.
  ➤ The other options in the form are self-explanatory.

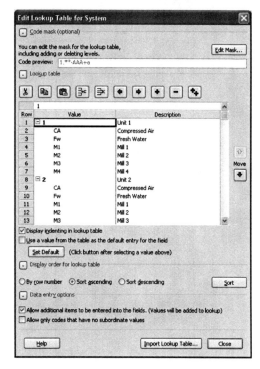

16.4.2 Define a Custom Outline Code Structure, Microsoft Project 2000 – 2003

Select **Tools**, **Customize**, **Fields…** and select the **Custom Outline Codes** tab to open the form:

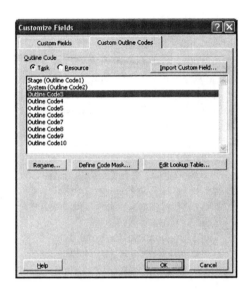

- An Outline Code may be created for either Task or Resource data by clicking on the appropriate radio button under the title **Outline Code**.

- The **Import Custom Field…** function allows you to copy a code structure from another project in a similar method to Organizer.

- The **Rename…** button opens a form to edit the name of the Outline Code. Two codes in the picture have been renamed Stage and System.

- The **Define Code Mask…** button opens the **Outline Code Definition** form where the code structure is defined.

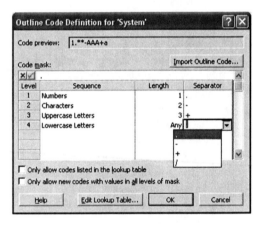

  - ➢ As each **Level** is created it is assigned a number.
  - ➢ The **Sequence** defines the type of text that may be entered for the code: Numbers, Upper Case, Lower Case or Characters (text).
  - ➢ The **Length** specifies how many characters the Code Level may have: any, or a number between 1 and 10.
  - ➢ The **Separator** defines the character that separates each level in the structure.

- The [Edit Lookup Table...] opens a form to enter the codes and descriptions for the Outline Code.

  ➤ The picture shows two "Units" at level 1 and each Unit's Subsystem at level 2.

  ➤ The icons along the top of the form have a similar function to their use in Outlining and may be used to indent and outdent codes and copy and paste code groups.

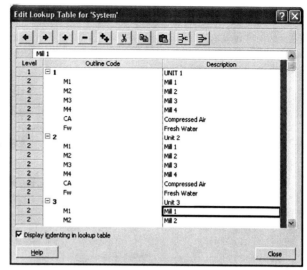

16.4.3 Assigning Custom Codes to Tasks

The codes are assigned by:

- Displaying the appropriate column:

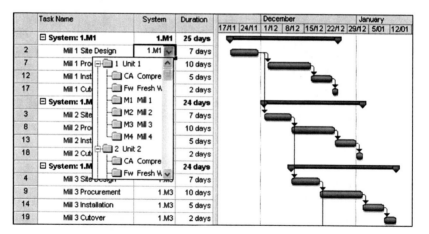

- Or by opening the **Task Information** or **Resource Information** form:

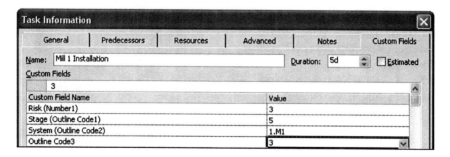

16.4.4 Organize Tasks Under a Custom Outline Code Structure

Select the **Project**, **Group by:**, **More Groups…** option to create a grouping to display the tasks under the Custom Outline Code. The same process is used as outlined in the previous section to create a grouping:

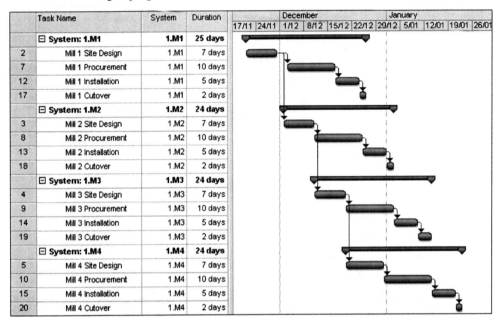

The Summary Tasks are virtual tasks and may **NOT** have resources and costs assigned to them.

 There are some restrictions with the use of Custom Outline Codes as the code **Value** is only shown in columns and the code **Description** only in the banding.

16.5 Outline Codes

The Microsoft Project **Outlining** function may be used to identify the Project Breakdown Structure with summary tasks. It is possible to display the Outline Code against each task in the schedule by:

- Displaying the **Outline Code** column, or

- Displaying the **Outline Code** with the **Task Name** by selecting the **Tools**, **Options…**, **View** tab and checking the **Show outline number**.

An **Outline Level** displays how many levels down in the Outline Code structure the Task lies.

	Outline Number	Outline Level	Task Name
1	1	1	⊟ 1 OzBuild Bid
2	1.1	2	⊟ 1.1 Research
3	1.1.1	3	1.1.1 Bid Request Documents Received
4	1.1.2	3	1.1.2 Bid Strategy Meeting
5	1.1.3	3	1.1.3 Investigate Technical Feasibility
6	1.1.4	3	1.1.4 Document Installation Requirements
7	1.2	2	⊟ 1.2 Estimation
8	1.2.1	3	1.2.1 Request Component Bids
9	1.2.2	3	1.2.2 Develop Project Schedule
10	1.2.3	3	1.2.3 Draft Technical Details Schedule
11	1.2.4	3	1.2.4 Compile Costs from Component Bids
12	1.3	2	⊟ 1.3 Proposal
13	1.3.1	3	1.3.1 Draft Bid Document
14	1.3.2	3	1.3.2 Meeting to Review the Draft Bid Docu
15	1.3.3	3	1.3.3 Design Presentation
16	1.3.4	3	1.3.4 Edit Proposal Draft Bid Document
17	1.3.5	3	1.3.5 Negotiate Component Work Packages
18	1.3.6	3	1.3.6 Final Review of Bid Document
19	1.3.7	3	1.3.7 Submit Bid

16.6   User Defined WBS Function

There are occasions when information must be presented under a predefined WBS Code structure. This structure could be a company standard, project-specific need, or defined by a client. The **WBS Code Definition** function is a method of tailoring the display of the **Outline Code** in a column titled **WBS**. This does not provide an additional set of codes to organize your project tasks; it only allows an alternate display of the Outline Code.

In a new project, the default WBS code is identical to the Outline Code. The example below displays both the WBS and Outline codes of the OzBuild schedule before doing any tailoring of the WBS code:

	WBS	Outline Number	Outline Level	Task Name
1	1	1	1	⊟ 1 OzBuild Bid
2	1.1	1.1	2	⊟ 1.1 Research
3	1.1.1	1.1.1	3	1.1.1 Bid Request Documents Received
4	1.1.2	1.1.2	3	1.1.2 Bid Strategy Meeting
5	1.1.3	1.1.3	3	1.1.3 Investigate Technical Feasibility
6	1.1.4	1.1.4	3	1.1.4 Document Installation Requirements
7	1.2	1.2	2	⊟ 1.2 Estimation
8	1.2.1	1.2.1	3	1.2.1 Request Component Bids
9	1.2.2	1.2.2	3	1.2.2 Develop Project Schedule
10	1.2.3	1.2.3	3	1.2.3 Draft Technical Details Schedule
11	1.2.4	1.2.4	3	1.2.4 Compile Costs from Component Bids

The WBS Codes structure may be tailored to suit your own requirements. Below is an example of a WBS code that has been tailored using the WBS code function. The Outline sequential numbers may be replaced by user defined sequences of numbers or letters.

	WBS	Outline Number	Task Name
1	OzBuild1	1	⊟ Ozbuild Bid
2	OzBuild1.AA	1.1	⊟ Research
3	OzBuild1.AA-001	1.1.1	Bid Document Received
4	OzBuild1.AA-002	1.1.2	Bid Strategy Meeting
5	OzBuild1.AA-003	1.1.3	Investigate Technical Feasibility
6	OzBuild1.AA-004	1.1.4	Document Installation Requirements
7	OzBuild1.AB	1.2	⊟ Estimation
8	OzBuild1.AB-001	1.2.1	Request Component Bids
9	OzBuild1.AB-002	1.2.2	Develop Project Schedule
10	OzBuild1.AB-003	1.2.3	Draft Technical Details Schedule
11	OzBuild1.AB-004	1.2.4	Compile Costs from Bids
12	OzBuild1.AC	1.3	⊟ Proposal
13	OzBuild1.AC-001	1.3.1	Draft Bid Documents
14	OzBuild1.AC-002	1.3.2	Draft Bid Meeting
15	OzBuild1.AC-003	1.3.3	Design Presentation
16	OzBuild1.AC-004	1.3.4	Edit Proposal Draft
17	OzBuild1.AC-005	1.3.5	Finalise Bid Package
18	OzBuild1.AC-006	1.3.6	Final Bid Meeting
19	OzBuild1.AC-007	1.3.7	Submit Bid

To create your own user defined WBS codes, select **P̲roject**, **W̲BS**, **D̲efine Code...** to open the **WBS Code Definition** form:

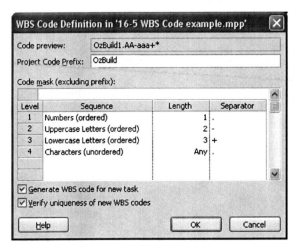

- The **Project Code P̲refix:** is where you enter a text string that will precede all **WBS** codes. See the example on the previous page.

- Each code level is defined in the **Sequence** column. There are four code types. Each is displayed above:
    - ➢ Numbers (ordered)
    - ➢ Uppercase Letters (ordered)
    - ➢ Lowercase Letters (ordered)
    - ➢ Characters (unordered)

    The **Numbers, Uppercase Letters** and **Lowercase Letters** are numbered automatically.

    The **Characters** option will initially define all WBS codes at this level as an * and these may be overwritten with text. Microsoft Project will not renumber them.

- A **Length** of 1 to 10 or "Any" may be selected as the length of the code.

- Check **G̲enerate WBS code for new task** and each new task will be automatically coded when created. When left unchecked, no WBS code is assigned to new tasks.

- Check **V̲erify uniqueness of new WBS codes** to prevent the creation of duplicate WBS codes.

By selecting **All** or **Selected Tasks**, you may renumber the WBS codes. Select **P̲roject**, **W̲BS**, **R̲enumber...** from the menu.

16.7 Creating a Product Breakdown Structure Using Outline Codes

The following example shows how to create a PBS using Outline Codes with Stages identified by Customized Text Column. This example uses Microsoft Project 2003, as at the time of writing this book the Grouping function in 2007 did not display the Outline Code Descriptions in bands. This type of issue is usually fixed with service packs. The steps are:

- Create the Custom Outline **Code** for the PBS in a similar way to the picture on the right by:
  - ➤ Selecting **Tools**, **Customize, Fields…** and selecting a Custom Outline Code.
  - ➤ Renaming the field, and
  - ➤ Adding the codes

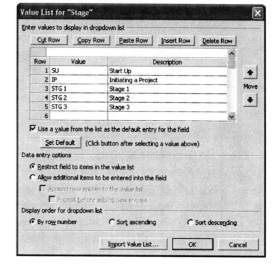

- Create the Custom Fields for the Stage by:
  - ➤ Renaming Text 1 as Stage, and
  - ➤ Adding the Value and Description PBS in a similar way to the picture on the right:

- Assign the PBS and Stage Codes from columns in the Gantt Chart view by:
  - ➤ Adding the columns, and
  - ➤ Selecting the codes from the drop-down list.

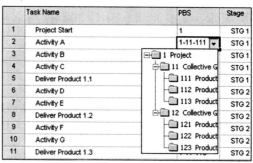

- Group by PBS and Stage, the **Define Group Interval** form should be used to select the level in the Custom Outline Code to be displayed as a band.

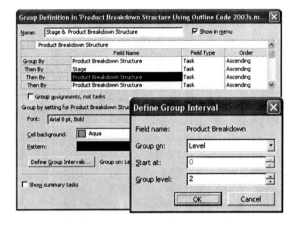

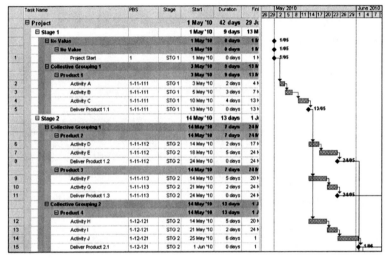

There are a number of issues for a person planning a PRINCE2 project in Microsoft Project to resolve and include but are not limited to:

- It is often difficult to display exactly what one would like to see with Microsoft Project when Products are represented by both Summary and Detailed tasks. The options of not showing Summary tasks in filters and Grouping will result in displaying some but not all the Products.

- Collective Grouping and Stages could be shown as Summary tasks using Outlining. When Products listed under one Collective Grouping are split over one or more Stages then the Collective Grouping will have to be displayed under each Stage.

- Stages may be displayed as Summary tasks or tagging tasks using a Customized Text column and Grouping, or by inserting a vertical bar on the screen or an End Stage indicated by a Milestone.

The least complicated method is usually best. A good starting point is to use Outline Level 1 for the Project, Level 2 for Stages, Level 3 for Products and Level 4 for Activities. Collective Groupings could replace Stages or be added between Stages and Products. Avoid using Outline Codes as they add a level of complexity that is usually best avoided.

WORKSHOP 14

Reorganization of the Schedule

Background

We want to issue another report for comment by management by grouping the activities without float and showing the WBS columns. To simplify this workshop we will revert to the schedule without the detailed activities for the Technical Feasibility Study.

Assignment

1. Grouping – to group tasks without float:
   - Open the **OzBuild No Resources** schedule and save as **OzBuild Grouping Workshop**.
   - Apply the **Entry** table and ensure the **Total Slack** column is displayed between the **Task Name** and **Duration**.
   - Select **Project, Group By, More Groups…** and create a new Group titled **Total Float** and group the tasks by **Total Slack**.
   - Check the **Show in menu** option, do not show summary tasks and apply.
   - All the tasks with zero days' float are grouped at the top under the heading **Total Slack: 0 days**.

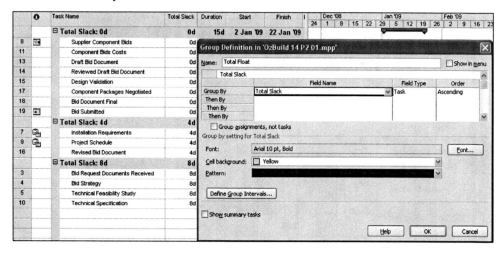

2. Grouping by Responsibility:
   ➢ Remove the Grouping.
   ➢ Rename Text 1 to Responsibility, select **Tools**, **Customize**, **Fields…**.
   ➢ Display the Responsibility (Text 1) column to the right of the Task name, align to the left and assign the Responsibilities in the table below, use copy and paste cells:

ID	Task Name	Responsibility
3	Bid Request Documents Received	David Williams - Account Manager
4	Bid Strategy	Carol Peterson - Bid Manager
5	Technical Feasibility Study	Scott Morrison - Systems Analysis
7	Installation Requirements	Scott Morrison - Systems Analysis
8	Supplier Component Bids	Angela Lowe - Purchasing
9	Project Schedule	Carol Peterson - Bid Manager
10	Technical Specification	Scott Morrison - Systems Analysis
11	Component Bids Costs	Angela Lowe - Purchasing
13	Draft Bid Document	David Williams - Account Manager
14	Reviewed Draft Bid Document	Carol Peterson - Bid Manager
15	Design Validation	Scott Morrison - Systems Analysis
16	Revised Bid Document	Carol Peterson - Bid Manager
17	Component Packages Negotiated	Angela Lowe - Purchasing
18	Bid Document Final	Carol Peterson - Bid Manager
19	Bid Submitted	David Williams - Account Manager

   ➢ Create a Group titled Responsibility: group the tasks by Responsibility showing in the menu but without showing summary tasks:

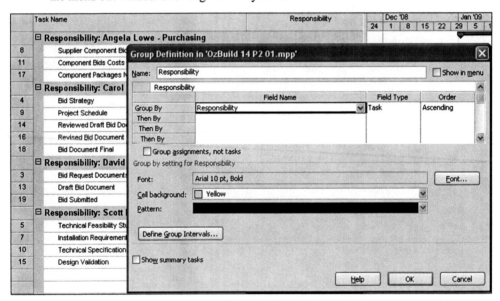

3. Creating a PBS using Custom Outline Codes (This part of the workshop was created using Microsoft Project 2003 as the Grouping Function was not working correctly when the book was written. This issue may be fixed in due course with a service pack.):

➤ Create a Customized Outline Code for this PBS:

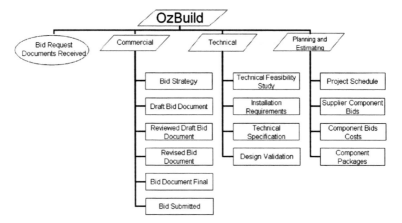

➤ Select **Tools**, **Customize**, **Fields…** and select a Custom Outline Code 1 and rename the field Product Breakdown Structure.

➤ Click on the Lookup… and Edit Mask… button and enter the mask below and click OK:

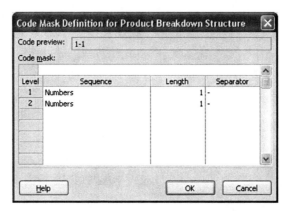

➤ Enter the following PBS Values and Descriptions and close the form:

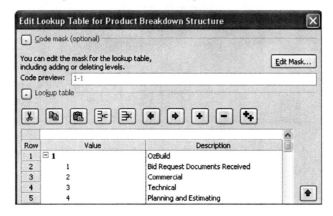

- ➤ Ungroup the project.
- ➤ Replace the Responsibility column with the Product Breakdown Structure column.
- ➤ Assign the PBS as per below:

	Task Name	Product Breakdown Structure
1	⊟ **OzBuild Bid**	
2	⊟ **Research**	
3	Bid Request Documents Received	1-1
4	Bid Strategy	1-2
5	Technical Feasibility Study	1-3
6	⊟ **Estimate**	
7	Installation Requirements	1-3
8	Supplier Component Bids	1-4
9	Project Schedule	1-4
10	Technical Specification	1-3
11	Component Bids Costs	1-4
12	⊟ **Proposal**	
13	Draft Bid Document	1-2
14	Reviewed Draft Bid Document	1-2
15	Design Validation	1-3
16	Revised Bid Document	1-2
17	Component Packages Negotiated	1-4
18	Bid Document Final	1-2
19	Bid Submitted	1-2

- ➤ Create a new Group titled Product Breakdown Structure and Group By **Product Breakdown Structure** on two lines using the $\boxed{\text{Define Group Intervals...}}$ to group the first line by Level 1 and the second line by Level 2:

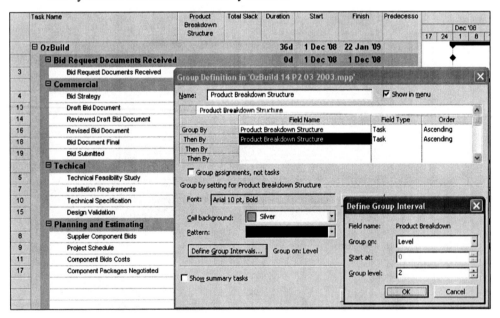

17 OPTIONS

17.1 Options

The **Options** forms allow you to decide how Microsoft Project calculates and displays information. Most of the options are self-explanatory. Under **Tools**, **Options…**, there are ten tabs in Microsoft Project 2007 and there were changes with each version.

Interface	Security		
Schedule	Calculation	Spelling	Save
View	General	Edit	Calendar

There are many options that are not essential for scheduling. Unfortunately, it is often difficult for new users to determine which are important and which are not, which can lead to confusion and large scheduling errors. This chapter will explain most of the functions identified on each Options form tab and indicate the important options.

- **View**   Controls the display of data.

- **General**   Controls the display of software productivity tools and Help, and default resource settings.

- **Edit**   Mainly controls edit and display functions.

- **Calendar**   These options **SHOULD** be understood especially if multiple **Task** calendars are used.

- **Schedule**   These options affect how your schedules calculate and **SHOULD** be understood.

- **Calculation** These options **SHOULD** be understood when progressing a schedule.

- **Spelling**   Controls the spelling check options.

- **Security**   This was a new feature in Microsoft Project 2003 allowing file attributes to be removed on save and security options for the running of macros.

- **Save**   Specifies where and how your files are saved and does not affect how your project calculates.

- **Interface**   This new form has options for the Indicator and Options button settings and the Project Guide, which are intended to assist the user but do not provide further scheduling options.

Some options apply to the current project only and some to all projects:

- Those that apply to the current project have a subheading **Calculation options for 'Project 1'**.

- Those that apply to all projects have a subheading of **Calculation options for Microsoft Office Project**.

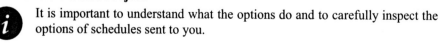 It is important to understand what the options do and to carefully inspect the options of schedules sent to you.

17.2 View

The options in this form control the display of data and not the results of calculation.

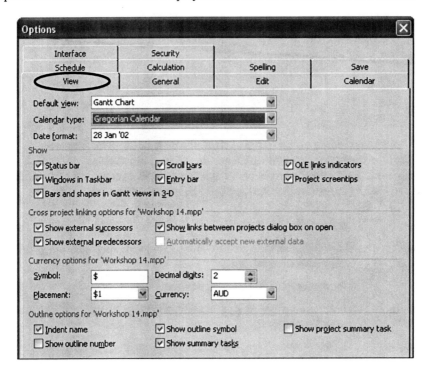

- **Default view:** selects the View applied when a new project is created.

- **Calendar type:** allows the selection of different calendars if the appropriate character set has been loaded. This is new to Microsoft Project 2007.

- **Date format:** provides a selection of date formats from the drop-down box for the display of data in columns. This format is applied to all projects and all views.

  ➤ The date format will be displayed according to a combination of your system default settings and the Microsoft Project Options settings. You may adjust your date format under the system Control Panel, Regional and Language Options. Changing the Control Panel setting will change the options available in the Microsoft Project **Options** form.

  ➤ The dates on the bars are formatted in the **Format, Layout...** option.

  ➤ This date format may be superseded by defining specific dates for each Table in the **Table Definition** form.

 On international projects there can be confusion between the numerical US date style (mmddyy) and the numerical European date style (ddmmyy). For example, in the United States 020710 is read as 07 Feb 10 and in many other countries as 02 Jul 10. You should consider adopting the ddmmmyy style, **28 Jan '02** or mmmddyy style, **Jan 28 '02**.

- **Show** allows each of the display options to be hidden or displayed. The **Bars and shapes in Gantt views in 3-D** is a new function to Microsoft Project 2007.

- **Cross project linking options for 'Project 1'** are options for displaying predecessor and successor task information from other projects. Inter-project relationships are not covered in this book.

- **Currency options for 'Project 1'** allows you to specify the:
  - ➢ Currency sign by inserting a sign into the box next to **Symbol:**,
  - ➢ Placement of the currency sign (before or after the value) as selected from the **Placement:** box, and
  - ➢ The number of decimal places displayed from the **Decimal digits:** box.
  - ➢ The **Currency:** option is new to Microsoft Project 2007 and allows the specification of the currency used in the schedule.

- **Outline options for 'Project 1':**

➢ **Indent name**	Indents the title for each Outline level to the right, see picture below:
➢ **Show outline number**	Shows the Outline Number 1, 1.1, 1.1.1, etc, see picture below:
➢ **Show outline symbol**	Displays the ⊟ and ⊞ sign by the Task Name, see picture below:

	Task Name
1	⊟ **1 OzBuild Bid**
2	⊟ **1.1 Research**
3	1.1.1 Bid Request Documents Received
4	1.1.2 Bid Strategy Meeting

➢ **Show summary tasks**	Uncheck this to hide the summary tasks.
➢ **Show project summary task**	Displays the Project Title as Task displays a Summary bar that spans the duration of the project. This is a virtual task which may not have resources assigned and the default color is grey. The project summary task name is linked to the filed in the **File**, **Properties**, **Summary** tab **Title:** field.

17.3   General

These options control the display of software productivity tools, display of Help, and default resource settings when resources are created.

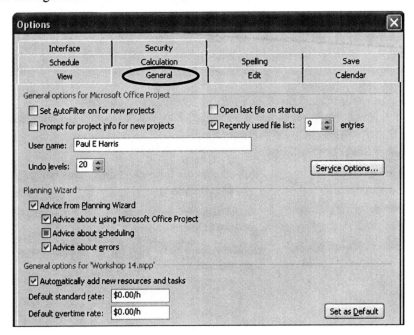

- **General options for Microsoft Project** – These options are self-explanatory and apply to all projects.
  - ➢ **Undo levels** may be increased to 99 in Microsoft Project 2007; other versions have one undo.
  - ➢ Service Options... enables changes to options for customer feedback and document management.
- **Planning Wizard** – These options specify what advice the Planning Wizard will offer you and applies to all projects.
- **General options for 'Project 1':**
  - ➢ **Automatically add new resources and tasks** – This option confirms if a resource exists in the resource pool. If the resource does not exist, a form will ask for confirmation to add the Resource.
  - ➢ **Default standard rate:** – The default standard hourly rate assigned to new resources.
  - ➢ **Default overtime rate:** – The default overtime rate assigned to new resources.
- **Set as Default** – Makes these rules as the default rules for each new project.

17.4 Edit

This form mainly controls the edit and display functions.

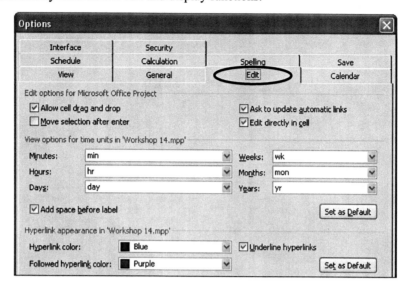

- **Edit options for Microsoft Project** when checked:
  - ➢ **Allow cell drag and drop** – Allows you to select a cell and drag the contents to another location.
  - ➢ **Move selection after enter** – After completing an entry in a cell, pressing the **Enter Key** will result in the cursor moving down a line to the cell below.
  - ➢ **Ask to update automatic links** – On opening a file which has links to other programs such as Excel, you will be asked if you want to refresh the links to the most recent data. To create a link, copy the selected data from another program. Then, in Microsoft Project, select **Edit, Paste Special...**, select the **Paste Link** option, and the data will be placed in the bar chart area.
  - ➢ **Edit directly in cell** – Allows you to edit the data directly in the cell. Otherwise data has to be edited in the **Edit Bar** near the top of the screen.
- **View options for time units in 'Project 1':**
  - ➢ **Minutes:, Hours:, Days:, Weeks:, Months:, Years:** – From the drop-down boxes, select your preferred designators for these units. It is **RECOMMENDED** changing "days" to "d" and "hr" to "h" to make the duration columns narrower.
  - ➢ **Add space before label** – Places a space between the value and the label; this makes the data column wider. It is **RECOMMENDED** to uncheck this to make duration columns narrower.
- **Hyperlink appearance in 'Project 1':**
  - ➢ **Hyperlink color:** and **Followed hyperlink color:** – Select from the drop-down box the color you require for these data items.
  - ➢ **Underline hyperlinks** – Select if you want these data items to be underlined.
- Three phonetics options are available with some Asian operating systems that have IME (Input Method Editor) loaded: Katakana Half, Katakana, or Hiragana.

17.5 Calendar

The title of these options does not clearly indicate their functionality. Options for **Hours per day:**, **Hours per week:** and **Days per month: SHOULD** be understood, especially if multiple Task calendars are used.

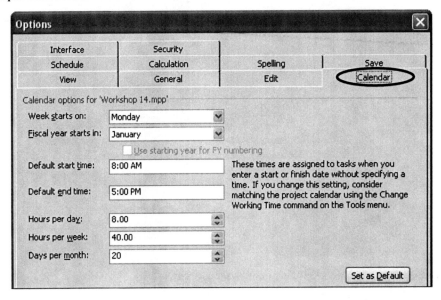

- **Calendar options for 'Project 1':**
  - ➤ **Week starts on:** – Sets the first day of the week. This is the day of the week that is displayed in the timescale. This setting affects the display of the calendar in the Change Working Time form.
  - ➤ **Fiscal year starts in:** – A month other than January may be selected as the first month of the fiscal year for companies that want to schedule projects using their financial years.
  - ➤ **Use starting year for FY numbering** – This option becomes available when a month other than January is selected as a **Fiscal year starts in:**. The year in the timescale may be assigned as the year that the fiscal starts or the year that the fiscal year finishes.

- **Default times:**
  - ➤ **Default start time:** – This is the time of day that tasks are scheduled to start when a start date constraint (without a time) is applied. It is also the default time for an Actual Start when an Actual Start (without a time) date is entered.
  - ➤ **Default end time:** – This is the time of day that tasks are scheduled to finish when a finish date constraint (without a time) is applied. It is also the default time for an Actual Finish when an Actual Finish date (without a time) is entered.

i It is essential to match both of these times with your project calendar normal start and finish times. When the **Default start time:** is set later than the calendar normal start time, a task set with a constraint without a time will appear to finish one day later than scheduled. Therefore a one-day task will span two days and a two-day task, three days.

- The following options need to be understood as they affect how summary durations are displayed. **NOTE: THESE OPTIONS ARE IMPORTANT**. Microsoft Project effectively calculates in hours. Task durations may be displayed in days, weeks and months. These summarized durations are calculated based on the parameters set in **Options, Calendar**. These options work fine when all project calendars are based on the same number of work hours per day. When tasks are scheduled with calendars that do not conform to the **Options, Calendar** settings (e.g., when the **Options, Calendar** settings are set for 8 hours per day and there are tasks scheduled on a 24-hour per day calendar), the results often create confusion for new users.

  ➢ **Hours per day:** – This setting is used to convert the duration in hours to the displayed value of the duration in days. For example, a task entered as a 3-day duration and assigned a 24-hour per day calendar will be displayed in the bar chart as 1-day elapsed duration. This bar chart duration is 1/3 of the duration value since each day is an 8-hour equivalent on a 24-hour calendar and the output is not logical. See Task 1 below.

  ➢ **Hours per week:** – This setting is used to convert the calendar hours to the displayed duration weeks. For example, a task entered as 2 weeks (10 working days) and assigned a 24-hour per day calendar is displayed with a 3-day and 6-hour duration in the bar chart. This is 1/3 of the "normal" duration and again not logical. See Task 2 below.

  ➢ **Days per month:** – This option is used to convert the displayed task duration from days to months. For example, a 0.5-month task on a 24-hour per day calendar is displayed as a 3-day and 6-hour duration in the bar chart and again is not logical. See Task 3 below.

	Duration	Task Calendar	Tue 1 Dec				Wed 2 Dec				Thu 3 Dec				Fri 4 Dec		
			12 AM	6 AM	12 PM	6 PM	12 AM	6 AM	12 PM	6 PM	12 AM	6 AM	12 PM	6 PM	12 AM	6 AM	12 PM
1	3 days	24 Hours															
2	2 wks	24 Hours															
3	0.5 mons	24 Hours															

  ➢ **Set as Default:** – Sets the current calendar settings as the default in the Global.mpt project and is used thereafter as the calendar settings in all new projects.

All the durations displayed in the picture are misleading. It is important that this situation avoided.

Other scheduling software also exhibits the time conversion problem when using multi-calendars. This display can lead to a great deal of confusion. To avoid confusion when using multi-calendars, it is suggested that you only display durations in hours.

This issue was discuss in depth in the **CALENDAR** chapter lease refer to this chapter should multiple calendars be considered for a project schedule.

17.6 Schedule

The options below affect how your schedules calculate and **SHOULD** be understood.

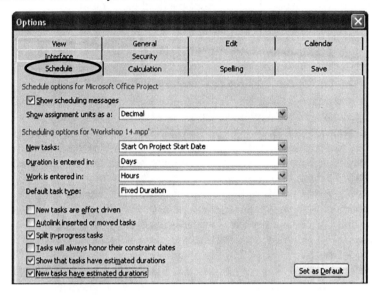

- **Schedule options for Microsoft Project**
  - ➢ **Show scheduling messages** – Uncheck this box to prevent the software from displaying advice on scheduling.
  - ➢ **Show assignment unit as a:** – The options are **Percentage** or **Decimal**. You have the option of assigning and displaying resource assignments as either a percentage, such as 50%, or a decimal, such as 0.5. Both these values would assign a person to work half time on that task.

- **Scheduling options for 'Project 1'**
  - ➢ **New tasks:** – When adding new tasks, you have the option of the new task either:
    - o Scheduled to **Start On Project Start Date** and the task will be scheduled **As Soon As Possible**, or
    - o **Start on Current Date** and the task will be assigned (without any warning dialog box) a **Start No Earlier Constraint** equal to the current date. To have a task assigned a constraint without due reason is not considered good practice and should be avoided, so this option should not be selected.
  - ➢ **Duration is entered in:** – You should select the units you will most frequently use for your task duration units. When "days" are selected, you will only need to type "**5**" in order to enter a 5-day task duration. Similarly, you will have to enter "**5w**" for a task that is 5 weeks long or "**5h**" for a task that is 5 hours long.
  - ➢ **Work is entered in:** – This is similar to the **Durations is entered in:** function, but applies to assigning work to a task. When hours are selected, you will only need to type "**48**" to enter 48 hours of work. If 5 days of work are to be assigned then "**5d**" needs to be entered.

The next two subjects, **Default task type:** and **Effort-Driven**, are **EXTREMELY** important for understanding how resources are used and applied.

➢ **Default task type:** – There is a relationship between the **Duration** of a task, the **Work** (the number of hours required to complete a task) and the **Units per Time Period** (the rate of doing the work or the number of people working on the task). The relationship is:

Duration x Units per Time Period = Work

The three options for the **Default task type:** are:

Fixed Duration – The **Duration** will stay constant if either **Units per Time Period** or **Work** is changed. If you change the **Duration**, then **Work** changes. This is the **RECOMMENDED** option for new users as the duration will not change as resources are manipulated.

Fixed Units – The **Units** stay constant if either **Duration** or **Work** is changed. If you change the **Units per Time Period**, then **Duration** changes.

Fixed Work – The **Work** stays constant if either **Duration** or **Units per Time Period** is changed. Your estimate will not change when you change **Duration** or **Units per Time Period**. If you change the **Work**, then **Duration** changes.

• The six boxes at the bottom of the form:
  ➢ **New tasks are effort driven:** – An **Effort-Driven** task keeps the total work constant as resources are added and removed from a task. When a task is not **Effort-Driven** then the addition of resources to a task will increase the total work assigned to a task. This option is not available with a **Fixed Work** task since, otherwise, it would not be fixed work. New users should consider **NOT** checking this option, so resources may be added independently without affecting the work's other resources.
  ➢ **Autolink inserted or moved tasks:** – With this box checked, new or moved tasks are automatically linked to the tasks above and below in the new or inserted location. Moved tasks that had relationships to tasks immediately above and below in the old location are deleted and the original predecessors and successors are now joined with an FS relationship. This function may confuse you since the logic is changed automatically without warning when you add or move tasks. It is suggested that the option is **NEVER** switched on as dragging an activity to a new location may completely change the logic of a schedule.
  ➢ **Split in-progress tasks:** – This option allows the splitting of in-progress tasks. This option must be checked for the following functions to operate:
    1. **Tools, Tracking, Update Project…, Update work as completed through,**
    2. **Tools, Tracking, Update Project…, Reschedule uncompleted work to start after,** and
    3. **Tools, Options…, Calculation** tab, **Status Date Calculation Options** which are the option found under **Calculation options for 'Project 1'** allowing incomplete or completed parts of tasks to be moved to the Status Date.

➤ **Tasks will always honor their constraint dates:** – This option will make all constraints override relationships. For example, a task with a **Must Start On** constraint, which is prior to a predecessor's Finish Date, will have an Early Start on the constraint date and not the scheduled date. (This is similar to converting all P3 and SureTrak **Must Start On** constraints to **Mandatory** constraints.) When checked, the **Total Slack** may not calculate as the difference between Late Start and Early Start. Examine the following two examples with the option box checked and unchecked:

Tasks will always honor their constraint dates: option box checked.

Start	Finish	Late Finish	Total Float	Constraint Date	Constraint Type	in 06 WTFSS	16 Jan 06 MTWTFSS
10 Jan 06	17 Jan 06	12 Jan 06	-3 days	NA	As Soon As Possible		
18 Jan 06	18 Jan 06	13 Jan 06	-3 days	NA	As Soon As Possible		
14 Jan 06	14 Jan 06	14 Jan 06	-3 days	14 Jan 06	Finish No Later Than		

Note: the third task starts before the predecessor finishes and the total slack of the second task is calculated at –3 days, which is not the difference between the early and late dates. Thus the conventional Total Float calculation is also incorrect.

Tasks will always honor their constraint dates: option box NOT checked.

Start	Finish	Late Finish	Total Float	Constraint Date	Constraint Type	in 06 WTFSS	16 Jan 06 MTWTFSS
10 Jan 06	17 Jan 06	12 Jan 06	-3 days	NA	As Soon As Possible		
18 Jan 06	18 Jan 06	13 Jan 06	-3 days	NA	As Soon As Possible		
18 Jan 06	18 Jan 06	14 Jan 06	-3 days	14 Jan 06	Finish No Later Than		

It is suggested that the option is **NEVER** switched on, as the schedule may appear to be achievable when it is not.

- **Estimated Durations** – These two options do not affect the calculation of projects. A new task is assigned an estimated duration. Once a duration is entered, this assignment is removed. The **General** tab on the **Task** form has a check box which establishes when a task has an estimated duration.

➤ **Show that tasks have estimated durations:** – A task with an estimated duration is flagged with a "?" after the duration in the data columns when this option is checked.

➤ **New tasks have estimated durations:** – When a task is added, it will have the estimated check box checked.

Before entering a Duration and after entering a Duration:

Task Name	Duration	Task Name	Duration
New Task	1 day?	New Task	6 days

17.7   Calculation

The following options **SHOULD** be understood to confidently progress your schedule.

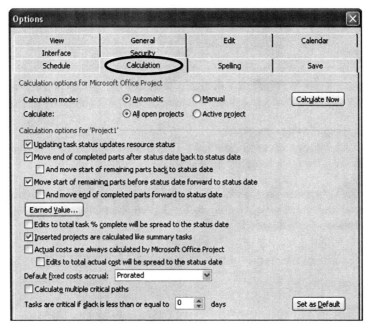

Calculation options for Microsoft Office Project:– Select one of the following two options:

- **Automatic** – This option recalculates the schedule every time a change is made to data. This is the normal option.

- **Manual** – This option requires you to press the **F9 Key** to recalculate the schedule.

- Also, select one of the two following options:
    - ➢ **Calculate all open projects** – Calculates all open projects when the recalculation takes place.
    - ➢ **Calculate the active project** – Calculates only the active project (the one that is displayed on your screen) when recalculation takes place.
    - ➢ Calculate Now – Recalculates the schedule(s) in accordance with the selected option above.

    To recalculate a project when calculation option is set to manual, press **F9**.

Calculate options for 'Project 1'

- **Updating task status updates resource status:** – This option links **% Complete** to **% Work** and in turn **% Work** is linked to **Actual Work**. Therefore when this option is checked:

    Actual Work = % Work x Work and
    Remaining Work = Work – Actual Work

    When unchecked the **% Complete** and **% Work** may have different values and **% Work** or **Actual Work** may have to be entered separately from the **% Complete**.

The example below shows the calculations with this option checked. If you uncheck this option, you may enter actual work and remaining work independently of the **% Complete**. In the example below the % Work is 50% and % Complete, 20%.

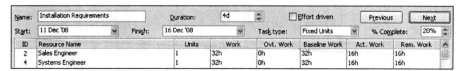

A summary task **% Work** is calculated based on the sum of **Actual Work** divided by the sum of the **Work** and gives an indication of progress based on hours of effort.

Summary Duration % Complete

A Summary Task **% Complete** is calculated by the sum of **Actual Durations** of all the **Detailed Tasks** divided by the sum of the **Durations**.

This option also determines the manner in which a % Complete that is assigned to a Parent Task gets spread to detailed tasks. See the following two examples where 60% is applied to the summary task entitled "Research":

- With the **Updating task status updates resource status** CHECKED.

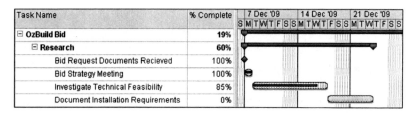

- With the **Updating task status updates resource status** UNCHECKED.

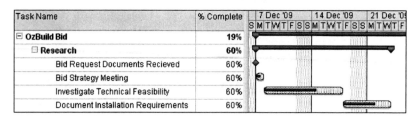

- New functions have been introduced in Microsoft Project 2002, which are intended to assist schedulers to place new tasks in a logical position with respect to the **Status Date**. The following four options were new to Microsoft Project 2002 and are covered in detail in the **Status Date Calculation Options** section of the **TRACKING PROGRESS** chapter.
  - ➢ **Move end of completed task parts after status date back to status date**
  - ➢ **And move start of remaining parts back to status date**
  - ➢ **Move start of remaining parts before status date forward to status date**
  - ➢ **And move end of completed parts forward to status date**

  These functions do not work intuitively and the instructions in the Microsoft documentation do not outline clearly how these functions work. It is recommended that you review these options carefully before applying them.

➢ The <img_1 /> button opens the **Earned Value** form:

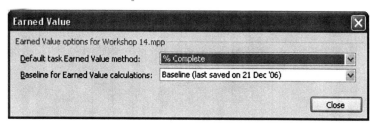

- o The **Default task Earned Value method** (a new field in Microsoft Project 2002) may be set to use the task **% Complete** or the **Physical % Complete** to calculate the Earned Value.

     The **Physical % Complete** is useful when the Earned Value is not progressing in proportion to the duration and may be used for recording the actual progress of the deliverables of a task as opposed to % of the Work (recorded in % Work field) or % of Duration (recorded in the % Complete field).

  - o The **Baseline for Earned Value calculations:** allows the selection of any of the baselines for the calculation of the Earned Value.
- ➢ **Edits to total task % complete will be spread to the status date** – When this option is selected and a **Status Date** is set in the **Project Information** form, and Progress Lines are being viewed then the % Complete is spread from the Actual Start to the Status Date and may be viewed in the **Task** or **Resource Usage** forms. (Right-click to add a % Complete column.)
- ➢ **Inserted projects are calculated like summary tasks** – When checked, an inserted project task's Total Float is calculated to the end of all Projects like a group of related projects. When unchecked, each Project's Total Float is calculated to the end of that Project only.
- ➢ **Actual costs are always calculated by Microsoft Project** – With this option checked, the resource **Actual Cost** is calculated by Microsoft Project from the resource **Work** and **Rates**. When unchecked, you have to directly enter the **Actual Cost** and **Actual Work**.
- ➢ **Edits to total actual costs will be spread to the status date** – When this option is selected and a **Status Date** is set in the **Project Information** form, then Actual Costs are spread from the Actual Start to the Status Date. Actual Costs should not be entered in a time-phased form such as the Task or Resource Usage forms, but the results may be viewed in these forms. **Actual costs are always calculated by Microsoft Project** must be checked for this option to calculate.
- ➢ **Default fixed costs accrual:** – This option sets the default accrual method for **Fixed Costs** (covered in **ASSIGNING RESOURCES AND COSTS TO TASKS** chapter). Fixed cost may be accrued at the **Start**, **End**, or **Prorated** over the duration of the task.
- ➢ **Calculate multiple critical paths** – When checked, Tasks without successors have their Late Dates set to equal their Early Dates, are calculated with zero Total Slack, are indicated critical in the Critical column and displayed as critical in the bar chart. (This is the same function as the Primavera SureTrak and P3 **Open Ends** options.)
- ➢ **Tasks are critical if slack is less than or equal to ? days** – This option will flag tasks as being critical that have **Total Slack** (Total Float) less than or equal to the value as established in this form. Critical tasks may be displayed in the **Critical** column and on bars when the "critical bar" is displayed. This is useful for flagging "near critical" tasks.

17.8   Spelling

The spell check options are self-explanatory and are applied to all projects:

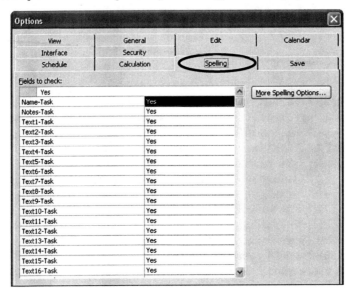

17.9   Security

This is a new feature in Microsoft Project 2003 allowing:

- **Privacy options**. The properties of Author, Manager, Company and Last Saved By are removed from a file when it is saved, and

- **Macro security**. There are security options that may be set to nominate which macros may or may not be used. This is aimed at preventing macros with a virus being activated.

- **Legacy Formats.** These options, new to Microsoft Project 2007, control the notification and opening of legacy file formats such as Microsoft Project 98 format and Microsoft Project 2000 – 2003 mpw files.

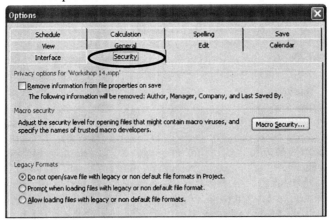

17.10 Save

This Options tab specifies where and how your files are saved. It does not affect how your project calculates.

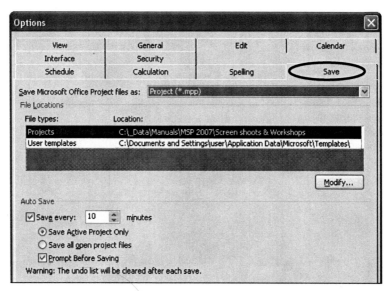

- **Save Microsoft Office Project files as:** – There are several formats that your project may be saved in. The default file type may be defined here but the file type may be changed at the time a project file is saved. This book only covers **Project (*.mpp)** and **Template (*.mpt)** formats in detail:

  ➤ **Project (*.mpp)** – The normal format to save Microsoft Project 2007 files.

  ➤ **Microsoft Project 2000 – 2003 (*.mpp)** will save files in this format as a default.

  ➤ **Template (*.mpt)** – Use this format to save projects that you want to use as project templates. Save them in the **User templates** directory that is specified in the **Tools, Options…, Save** tab.

  Earlier versions of Microsoft Project had some or all of the following options

  ➤ **Microsoft Project 98 (*.mpp)** – This format allows users of Microsoft Project 98 to read your files. If you have Microsoft Project 98, you may save the file in mpx format for transfer to other scheduling programs.

  ➤ **Project Database (*.mpd)** – This is a database format, which allows multiple projects to be saved in one database. It may be used for exporting data to other programs.

  ➤ **Microsoft Access Database (*.mdb)** – A part or all of a project may be saved in Microsoft Assess format and may be read and modified by Access.

  ➤ **ODBC Database** – Your project may be saved as an ODBC compliant database.

- **File Locations** – This is where you set the default locations for your project data files, template files, workgroup templates, and ODBC database files.

- **Auto Save** – These options are self-explanatory.

- **Database save options for 'Project 1'** – Not in Microsoft Project 2007,

  ➤ **Expand time-phased data in the database** – This function creates time-phased data in external databases.

17.11 Interface

This form, new to Microsoft Project 2003, has options for:

- The **Show indicators and Options buttons for:** settings, and

- The **Project Guide settings:**, which are intended to assist the user but do not provide further scheduling options.

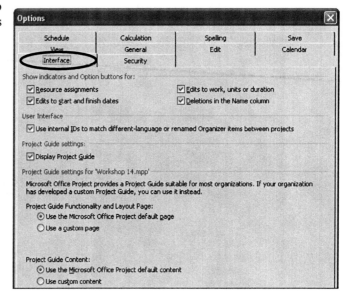

17.11.1 Graphical Indicators

The Indicator buttons give advice to the scheduler when certain functions are used which have more than one potential outcome.

- Below is an example of how the **Show indicators and Option buttons for:** options work when a task description is deleted:

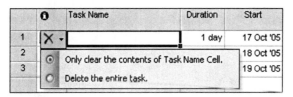

and when a date is edited:

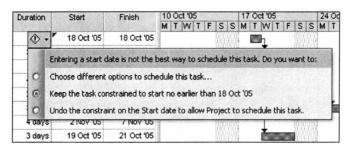

17.11.2 Project Guide

The **Project Guide** is a wizard-type function that assists the user to create a new schedule. It is self-explanatory and not covered in this book.

18 CREATING RESOURCES

A resource may be defined as something or someone that is assigned to a task and is required to complete the task. This includes people or groups of people, materials, equipment and money.

Microsoft Project has a large number of resource functions. Without getting into too much detail, this book will outline the important resource-related functions to enable you to create and assign resources to your schedules, then analyze the resource requirements.

It is recommended that the minimum number of resources be assigned to tasks when it is planned to status a schedule. Avoid cluttering the schedule with resources that are in plentiful supply or are of little importance. Every resource added to the schedule will need to be statused. Therefore the scheduler's workload increases as resources are added to tasks.

Microsoft Project 2007 has introduced a **Cost** resource in addition to the existing **Work** and **Material** resources. This allows the entry of Costs as a resource without requiring a quantity.

When you create your resources, you should consider them within the context of the following headings:

- **Input Resources** – Those that are required to complete the work:
  - ➢ Individual people by name, typically used in a **PRINCE2 Stage Plan** and may be identified in the Project Organisation.
  - ➢ Groups of people by trade or skill, typically used in a **PRINCE2 Project Plan**.
  - ➢ Individual equipment or machinery by name.
  - ➢ Groups of equipment or machinery by type.
  - ➢ Groups of resources such as Crews or Teams made up of equipment and machinery.
  - ➢ Materials or money.
- **Output Resources** – Things that are being delivered or produced:
  - ➢ Specifications completed.
  - ➢ Bricks laid.
  - ➢ Lines of code written.
  - ➢ Tests completed.

After planning your resource requirements the following steps should be followed to create and use resources in a Microsoft Project schedule:

- Create your resources in the **Resource Sheet**.

- Assign the resources to tasks.

- Manipulate the resource calendar if resources have special timing requirements.

This chapter will concentrate on:

- The creation of Resources in the **Resource Sheet**,

- Understanding **Task Type** and **Effort-Driven Tasks**,

- Assigning the Resources to Tasks, and

- Editing **Resource Calendars**.

Resources may be shared between projects using the **Tools**, **Resource Sharing** function.

18.1   Creating Resources in the Resource Sheet

To add resources to the Resource Sheet, select **V**iew, **Resource S**heet.

Resource Name	Type	Material Label	Initials	Group	Max. Units	Std. Rate	Ovt. Rate	Cost/Use	Accrue At	Base Calendar
Clerical Support	Work		CS	Office	200%	$50.00/hr	$30.00/hr	$0.00	Prorated	Standard
Sales Engineer	Work		SAE	Office	100%	$80.00/hr	$0.00/hr	$0.00	Prorated	Standard
Scheduler	Work		SC	Office	200%	$60.00/hr	$0.00/hr	$0.00	Prorated	Standard
Systems Engineer	Work		STE	Office	200%	$80.00/hr	$0.00/hr	$0.00	Prorated	Standard
Bid Manager	Work		BM	Office	100%	$100.00/hr	$0.00/hr	$0.00	Prorated	Standard
Report Binding	Material	Each Folder	BIND			$90.00		$0.00	Prorated	
Contract Consultant	Cost		CC	Consultants					Prorated	

- To add a new resource:
  - Click on the first blank line, or
  - Highlight the line where you would like to insert your resource and select **I**nsert, **N**ew Resources, or
  - Use the **Ins Key**.
- The first column, with a ⓘ in the header, is the indicator column; 📝 is the Notes indicator; and ◈ is the resource over-allocation indicator.
- Enter the **Resource Name**. Microsoft Project allows duplicate Resource Names to be entered into the Resource Table, but this situation should be avoided by visually checking all your Resource Names.
- Enter one of the three Resource **Types**: **Work** or **Materials** or **Cost** (2007 only). They function differently:
  - **Work** resources, such as people, often have a limit to the number that are available. This type of resource may have a maximum number assigned, an overtime rate and may also have a calendar assigned.
  - **Materials** resources have a **Material Label** which is not available with a **Work** resource, have a quantity but do not have a maximum availability, are considered unlimited and do not have a calendar.
  - **Cost** resources have a cost but no quantity or calendar.
- A **Material** resource may be assigned a **Material Label**, which may be the unit of measurement, such as m^3 or feet.
- The **Initials** are filled out by Microsoft Project with the first character of the **Resource Name**. This Initial field should be unique. Because it is displayed in some Views it should be edited so it makes sense to you. For example, you could use a person's initials, log-in name or payroll number.
- You may enter any text in the **Group** field if you want to group, filter or sort your resources by this field. This could be used for Department, Branch or Skill.

- The method of entering the **Resource Units** may be formatted as a percentage or as a decimal. Enter the **Max Units** for **Work** resources only. 100% (or 1.00) would represent one person and 400% (or 4.00) would represent four people. Select the **Tools**, **Options…**, **Schedule** tab to set your option:

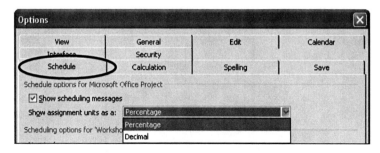

- Edit the **Standard Rate** for **Work** and **Material** resources only, if required. The resource default units are "hours" (hr), but this may be edited to be the cost per:
  - ➤ minute – min
  - ➤ hour – hr
  - ➤ day – day
  - ➤ week – wk
  - ➤ month – mon

- Enter the **Overtime Rate** for the **Work** resources only. A salaried person may not be paid overtime and would have a zero rate for overtime.

- Enter the **Cost per Use** for **Work** and **Material** resources only. This could represent a mobilization cost and is applied each time a resource is assigned to a task. The **Cost per Use** is accrued when an actual start date is entered.

- **Accrue At**:
  - ➤ **Start** – The costs for this resource are incurred when the task commences.
  - ➤ **Prorated** – The costs for this resource are spread over the duration of the task.
  - ➤ **End** – The costs for this resource are incurred when the task is complete.

- **Base Calendar** – This is the calendar assigned to **Work** resources and may be edited to suit each individual resource availability and may be edited for individual holidays.

18.2 Grouping Resources in the Resource Sheet

Resources may be Grouped on any data fields, such as Custom Fields and Custom Outline Codes, using the **Project**, **Group by:** function. The example below shows resources grouped by **Resource Group**:

Resource Name	Type	Material Label	Initials	Group	Max. Units	Std. Rate	Ovt. Rate	Cost/Use	Accrue At	Base Calendar
⊟ **Group: Equipment**				**Equipment**	**7**			**$1,700.00**		
Dozer	Work		DOZER	Equipment	6	$2,500.00/wk	$0.00/hr	$1,000.00	Prorated	Standard
Excavator	Work		EXCAV	Equipment	1	$400.00/day	$0.00/hr	$700.00	Prorated	Standard
⊟ **Group: Material**				**Material**				**$50.00**		
Concrete	Material	m3	CONC	Material		$120.00		$50.00	Prorated	
Crushed Rock	Material	ton	CRCK	Material		$80.00		$0.00	Prorated	
⊟ **Group: Office**				**Office**	**7**			**$0.00**		
Clerical Support	Work		CS	Office	2	$25.00/hr	$30.00/hr	$0.00	Prorated	Standard
Sales Engineer	Work		SALESENGI	Office	1	$40.00/hr	$0.00/hr	$0.00	Prorated	Standard
Scheduler	Work		SC	Office	1	$27.00/hr	$0.00/hr	$0.00	Prorated	Standard
System Engineer	Work		SYSENG	Office	2	$40.00/hr	$0.00/hr	$0.00	Prorated	Standard
Tender Manager	Work		TM	Office	1	$50.00/hr	$0.00/hr	$0.00	Prorated	Standard

18.3 Resources Information Form

The **Resource Information** form is opened by double-clicking on a specific row within the **Resource Sheet** view. The **Working Time** tab in 2000 – 2003 was moved to a new form titled **Change Working Time** (Resources) in 2007. These will not be described in detail:

18.3.1 General

The form on the right is from Microsoft Project 2007.

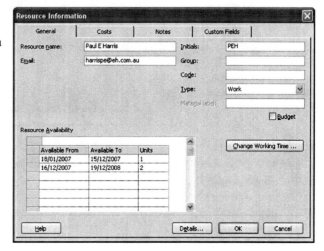

- The **Resource Availability** section of this form allows you to decide the availability of all resources. This would typically be used for Group Resources such as Bricklayers or Testers where their availability will change over time.

- The **Email** field is used in email communication and not covered in this book.

- **Budget** indicates that the resource is being used for budget purposes and the **Resource Availability** features are disabled when a Resource is marked as Budget. This function is new to 2007.

- The [Change Working Time ...] button in 2007 opens the **Change Working Time (Resource)** form or the **Working Time** tab in 2000 – 2003 for editing the resource calendar. Select each resource's **Base calendar** and edit the calendar to suit the resource's availability.

18.3.2 Editing and Using Resource Calendars

Base Calendars are applied to tasks but they may not accommodate specific resource requirements. For example, a base calendar would not reflect when a person goes on vacation or is occupied on another project. Resource Calendars, on the other hand, can be used to schedule this resource-specific nonwork time. Resource Calendars should be used when specific resources have a unique availability.

When a resource is created, a unique resource calendar is created automatically and is a copy of the **Base Calendar** selected when the resource is created. This Resource Calendar may be modified, if required from the **Resource Information** form which may be opened by clicking on a resource in the **Resource Sheet.**

The Resource Calendar may be edited in the same manner as Base Calendars by opening the **Resource Information** form (double-clicking on a **Resource Name** in most forms) and selecting the **Working Time** tab in Microsoft Project 2000 – 2003 or clicking on ⟨ Change Working Time ... ⟩ in the **Resource Information** form in Microsoft Project 2007.

Working Time tab 2000 – 2003   **Change Working Time** form 2007

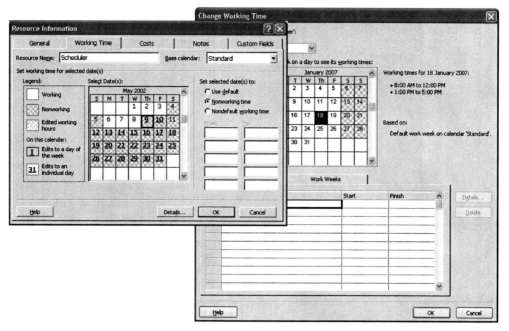

A task will always be calculated using a **Resource Calendar** except when a **Task Calendar** has been assigned. In this case, the **Scheduling ignores resource calendars** option in the **Task Information** form becomes available.

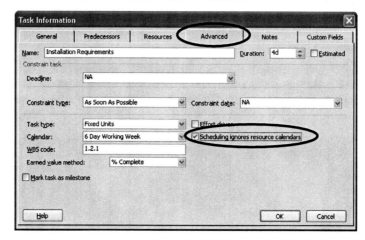

18.3.3   Costs

The **Cost rate tables** allows the adjustment of resource rates over time and assigns up to five different rates to a resource. The rate is assigned in the **Resource Information** form. This form is opened by double-clicking on the **Resource Name** for any assigned resource in either the **Resource Sheet, Task Usage** view or the **Resource Usage** view.

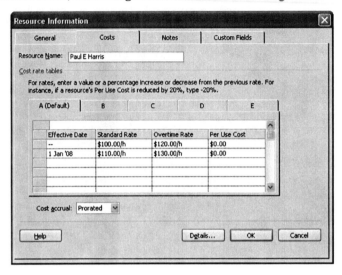

18.3.4   Notes

This is where notes are made about the resource.

18.3.5   Custom Fields

Custom Fields are for assigning user-defined information to resources and are not covered in detail in this book.

- Custom Resources fields may be created in the **Customize Fields** form by selecting **Tools, Customize, Fields...**.

- After the fields have been defined in the **Customize Fields** form, these fields appear in the **Resource Information** form and may be used to assign custom-defined costs and other information to resources from the **Custom Fields** tab of the **Resource Information** form.

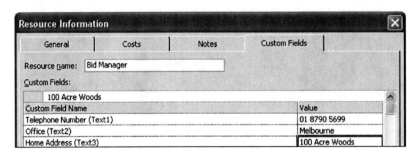

WORKSHOP 15

Defining Resources

Background

The resources must now be added to this schedule. Since we have statused our project, we need to revert to the un-statused schedule that we saved prior to statusing the current schedule.

Assignment

1.   Save and close your current project.
2.   Open the **OzBuild No Resources** project and save it as **OzBuild With Resources**.
3.   Select **Tools**, **Options...** from the menu. From the **Schedule** tab, set **Show assignment Units as a: Decimal**.
4.   Open the **Resource Sheet** view and add the following resources to the project:

Resource Name	Type	Material Label	Initials	Group	Max. Units	Std. Rate	Ovt. Rate	Cost/Use	Accrue At	Base Calendar
Clerical Support	Work		CS	Office	2	$50.00/hr	$0.00/hr	$0.00	Prorated	Standard
Sales Engineer	Work		SAE	Office	1	$80.00/hr	$0.00/hr	$0.00	Prorated	Standard
Scheduler	Work		SC	Office	2	$60.00/hr	$0.00/hr	$0.00	Prorated	Standard
Systems Engineer	Work		STE	Office	2	$80.00/hr	$0.00/hr	$0.00	Prorated	Standard
Bid Manager	Work		BM	Office	1	$100.00/hr	$0.00/hr	$0.00	Prorated	Standard
Report Binding	Material	Each Folder	BIND			$90.00		$0.00	Prorated	
Contract Consultant	Cost		CC	Consultants					Prorated	

Microsoft Project 2000 - 2003 users should create the Contract Consultant as a Work Type resource with a cost of $0.00 per hour and $10,000 per use.

5.   Save your project file.

19 ASSIGNING RESOURCES AND COSTS TO TASKS

Microsoft Project has the following types of resources:

- **Work resources** that are used for people or equipment. The **Work** (quantity) is usually measured in hours and the **Work** resource components are linked to the Task Duration. These resources may be assigned a **Rate** to calculate their cost.

- **Material resources**, which have a quantity but the quantity is not linked to the task duration.

- Microsoft Project 2007 introduced a **Cost resource**, which is a resource that does not have a quantity and is not affected by the task duration.

- **Fixed Costs**, which are costs assigned to tasks without assigning a resource.

The **PRINCE2** process **PL4 – Estimating** may be completed in Microsoft Project using Resources or Fixed Costs.

When a **Work** resource is assigned to a task it has three principal components:

- **Quantity**, in terms of **Work** or **Material** required to complete the task,

- **Units**, which represents the number of people working on a task, and

- **Cost**, calculated from the **Standard Rate**, **Overtime Rate** and **Cost per Use**.

The **Units per Time Period** of a **Work** resource may be entered against a task and the **Work** (Quantity) will be calculated, or the **Work** entered and the **Units** calculated. The resource cost is calculated from the resource **Work** times the resource **Rate**.

Method	Menu Command
• **Fixed Costs** assignment	Display the **Fixed Costs** and **Fixed Costs Accrual** columns.
• **Resource Assignment** form	Click on the **Assign Resource** icon 💲. You may assign **Units** only.
• **Task Information** form	Double-click on a **Task** name or click on the **Task Information** icon 📅. You may assign **Units** only.
• The **Resource Task Details** forms	In the bottom window, select the **Task Details Form**, **Task Form** or **Task Name Form**, and then select the appropriate option from the **Format**, **Details** option. Each form has different options.
• The **Resources Names** and **Resource Initials** columns	Insert appropriate columns by right-clicking on the column heading where you want to insert a column and then assign a Resource.
• **Contoured** Resource assignment	Open the **Assignment Information** form by: • Double-clicking on a resource in the **Task Usage** or **Resource Usage** view, or • Right-clicking on a resource and selecting **Assignment Information** from the menu.
• **Shared Resources**	Select **Tools**, **Resource**, **Share Resources...** to share resources with other projects.

19.1   Task Type and Effort-Driven

The **Task type** and **Effort-driven** options operate after the first **Work** resource has been assigned to a task. The relationship amongst the following four variables are controlled by these options:

- The number of different **Resources**, i.e., painters and testers are two different resources.

- The **Task duration**.

- The resource **Units per Time Period**, i.e., two testers would be 2 Units per Time Period.

- The amount of **Work** to be performed, i.e., the total number of hours.

The **Task type** and **Effort-driven** functions control which variable changes when one of these four parameters is changed or when **Work** resources are added or removed from a task. These options may be set in a number of forms including the **Task** and the **Task Details** form. **Material** resources, **Cost** resources and **Fixed Costs** do not change values after they have been assigned.

19.1.1   Task Type – Fixed Duration, Fixed Units, Fixed Work

There is a relationship between the **Duration** of a task, the **Work** (the number of hours required to complete a task) and the **Units per Time Period** (the rate of doing the work or number of people working on the task). The relationship is:

Duration x Units per Time Period = Work

There are three options for the **Default task type:** which decide how this relationship operates. They are:

- **Fixed Duration**   The **Duration** stays constant when either the **Units per Time Period** or **Work** are changed. If you change the **Duration**, then the **Work** changes.

- **Fixed Units**   The **Units per Time Period** stay constant when either the **Duration** or **Work** is changed. If you change the **Units per Time Period**, then the **Duration** changes.

- **Fixed Work**   The **Work** stays constant if either **Duration** or **Units per Time Period** are changed. Therefore your estimate will not change when you change **Duration** or **Units per Time Period**. If you change the **Work**, then the **Duration** changes.

19.1.2   Effort-Driven

Once a resource has been assigned to a task, the **Task Effort** is the combined number of hours of all resources assigned to a task. The **Effort-driven** option decides how the effort is calculated when a resource is added or when a resource removed to a **Fixed Units** or **Fixed Duration** task. There are two options:

- **Effort-driven**   When a resource is added or removed from a task, the **Task Effort** assigned to a task remains constant. Adding or removing resources leaves the total effort assigned to a task as a constant unless all resources are removed.

- **Non Effort-driven**   When a resource is added to or removed from a task, the **Resource Effort** or **Work** of other resources remains constant. Adding or deleting resources increases or decreases the total task effort.

You may also wish to consider setting your default options to:

- The **Default task type:** as **Fixed Work** in the **Tools**, **Options…**, **Schedule** tab.

- This will make new tasks as Effort-Driven. The **New tasks are effort driven** box in the **Tools**, **Options…**, **Schedule** tab appears gray.

Click on the [Set as Default] icon and all new projects will have these options set as the default. With this scenario:

- When you change the durations of your tasks your estimate of hours and cost of labor resources will not change, and

- You will be able to enter resources against a task and allocate hours against each resource as you assign the resource.

- You may then change tasks to different options as required by exception.

19.2   Fixed Costs

Fixed costs are a function where you may assign costs to a task without creating resources. It is a useful function if you require a cash flow only and will not progress the schedule.

- A fixed cost is assigned using the **Fixed Cost** column.

- The fixed cost may be accrued at the **Start**, **End** or **Prorated** over the duration of the task. This option is selected from the **Fixed Cost Accrual** column. The default for the **Fixed Cost Accrual** is set in the **Tools**, **Options…**, **Calculation** tab:

Task Name	Duration	Fixed Cost	Fixed Cost Accrual	1 March M	T	W	T	F
⊟ **Summary**	**5 days**	**$0.00**	**Prorated**	$240.00	$40.00	$40.00	$40.00	$240.00
$200.00 Fixed cost accrued at Start	5 days	$200.00	Start	$200.00				
$200.00 Fixed cost Prorated	5 days	$200.00	Prorated	$40.00	$40.00	$40.00	$40.00	$40.00
$200.00 Fixed cost accrued at End	5 days	$200.00	End					$200.00

- Fixed Costs will not be displayed in the **Resource Sheet** or **Resource Usage** views but are available in the **Task Usage** view and in a **Report**. The **Cash Flow** report will only give you the cash flow in weeks but may be exported to Excel.

- Fixed Costs are added to resource costs and the total of the two is shown in the **Cost** column.

Task Name	Fixed Cost	Fixed Cost Accrual	Resource Initials	Cost
⊟ **Summary**	**$0.00**	**Prorated**		**$8,800.00**
$200.00 Fixed cost accrued at Start	$200.00	Start		$200.00
$200.00 Fixed cost Prorated	$200.00	Prorated		$200.00
$200.00 Fixed cost accrued at End	$200.00	End		$200.00
Activity With Resources Only	$0.00	Prorated	PEH	$4,000.00
Activity With Costs & Resources	$200.00	Prorated	PEH	$4,200.00

When both **Fixed Costs** and **Resource Costs** are assigned to a task, there is no column to display only total **Resource Costs**. It is therefore recommended that only either Fixed Costs or Resource Costs be assigned to a task.

When a Baseline is set, the Fixed costs and the Resource costs are added together in the Baseline costs value.

19.3   Assigning Resources using the Resource Assignment Form

Highlight one or more tasks that you want to assign resources. Click the **Assign Resources** icon ⬛ on the **Standard** toolbar to display the **Assign Resources** form.

The **Units** may be the number of people working on a task and may be displayed as **Units** shown in the picture on the left, or as a **Percentage** shown on the right. 1.00 is the same value as 100%. This option may be changed in the **Schedule** tab of the **Options** form.

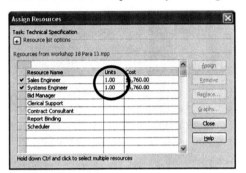
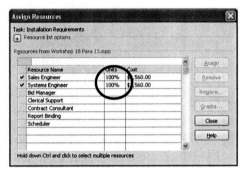

- Select the **Resource** from the form.
  - ➢ Type in the number of resources you want to assign under **Units**. This may be in % or whole numbers depending on how your options are set.
  - ➢ Click on the ⬚ **Assign** button to assign a resource to a task.

- You may then assign another resource to a task.

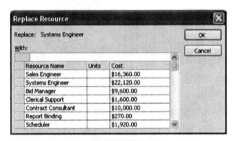

- Select a resource and click on the ⬚ **Remove** button to remove a resource.

- Select a resource and click on the ⬚ **Replace...** button to open the Replace Resource form to replace a resource.

- The **Resource list options** at the top of the screen allows the resource list to be reduced by the use of filters and is very useful when there is a large number of resources and new resources to be created from your address book.

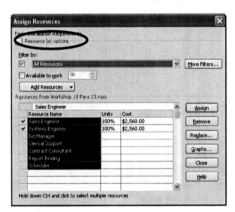

- The ⬚ **Graphs...** option is new to Microsoft Project 2007 and displays a small resource graph or one or more selected resources in the **Graphs** form. This function is cover in more detail in the **RESOURCE HISTOGRAMS, TABLES, S-CURVES AND LEVELING** chapter.

19.4   Assigning Resources Using the Task Details Form

Open the bottom window displaying the
Task Detail Form, **Task Form** or **Task
Name Form**. Then select the appropriate
option from the **Format**, **Details** option or
by right-clicking in the form. See the picture
on the right:

The table below lists the resource
component options available in these forms:

Form	Assignment Option
• **Resources & Predecessors**	**Units** and **Work**
• **Resources & Successors**	**Units** and **Work**
• **Resource Schedule**	**Work** only
• **Resource Work**	**Units** and **Work**
• **Resource Cost**	**Units** only with calculated **Costs**

The **Task Entry** form with the **Resource Work** details form is displayed below.

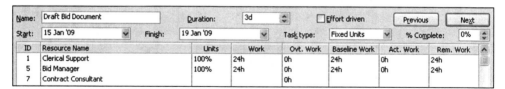

- Select the required resource in the drop-down box under the **Resource Name** heading.

- Enter the number of resources under **Units**, or

- Enter the amount of **Work** – the number of hours may be entered under this heading.

- **Ovt. Work** – Overtime Work may be assigned to reduce the duration of the task. The
  Work remains the same, but the **Overtime** value represents the amount of work being
  done on overtime.

 When **Overtime** work is assigned and costs are being calculated if an
Overtime Rate is not entered the cost will decrease as more overtime is
assigned.

- **Baseline Work** is copied from **Work** when a **Baseline** is set.

- **Act. Work** – **Actual Work** is entered when work is in-progress.

- **Rem. Work** – **Remaining Work** is calculated by subtracting **Actual Work** from
  Work.

19.5 Assigning Task Information Form

Double-click on a **Task** name or click on the **Task Information** icon 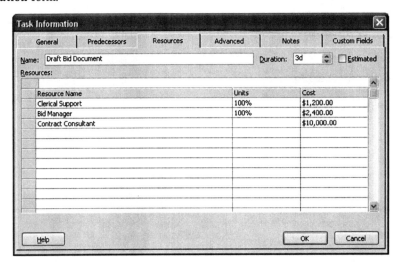 to open the **Task Information** form.

Double-click on a **Task** name or click on the **Task Information** icon to open the **Task Information** form.

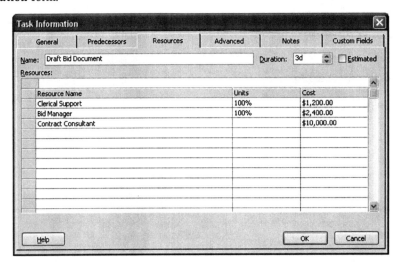

- Select the required resource from the drop-down box.
- Type in the number of required resources in the **Units** box.

19.6 Assignment of Resources to Summary Tasks

Summary tasks may be assigned **Fixed Costs**, **Work Resources** and **Material Resources**.

You must also be aware that when a Work resource is assigned to a summary task the task type is set to **Fixed Duration** and that setting may not be changed. Thus, any change in duration of a summary task due to rescheduling of associated detailed tasks will result in a change to the work assignment and the calculated costs of a Summary task.

 It is recommended that unless a Summary task Work resource assignment is required to vary in proportion to the Summary task duration, then Work Resources should not be assigned to a Summary task. You should consider using Fixed Costs, Cost resource or a Material resource if appropriate.

19.7 Sharing Resources with Other Projects

Microsoft Project allows resources to be shared with multiple projects. This feature is not covered in detail in this book. Select **Tools**, **Resource**, **Share Resources...** to open the **Share Resources** form, select the project to share resources from and set calculation options for leveling.

19.8   Rollup of Costs and Hours to Summary Tasks

The task **Cost** and **Work** fields are calculated from the sum of the costs and work assigned to the related detailed tasks and those of the summary task.

It becomes difficult for a scheduler to check the total cost of a Summary task after costs and work have been assigned to both the Summary task and associated Detailed tasks. It is recommended that you consider only assigning costs and work to Detailed tasks.

Summary Tasks have the costs and work rolled up to give you a cost at any Outline level.

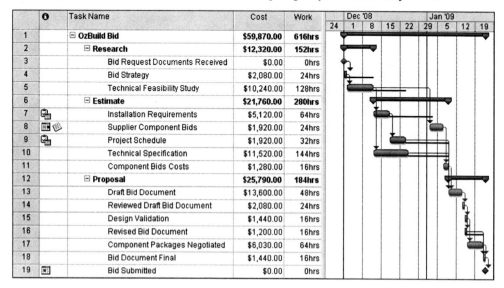

	❶	Task Name	Cost	Work
1		⊟ OzBuild Bid	$59,870.00	616hrs
2		⊟ Research	$12,320.00	152hrs
3		Bid Request Documents Received	$0.00	0hrs
4		Bid Strategy	$2,080.00	24hrs
5		Technical Feasibility Study	$10,240.00	128hrs
6		⊟ Estimate	$21,760.00	280hrs
7		Installation Requirements	$5,120.00	64hrs
8		Supplier Component Bids	$1,920.00	24hrs
9		Project Schedule	$1,920.00	32hrs
10		Technical Specification	$11,520.00	144hrs
11		Component Bids Costs	$1,280.00	16hrs
12		⊟ Proposal	$25,790.00	184hrs
13		Draft Bid Document	$13,600.00	48hrs
14		Reviewed Draft Bid Document	$2,080.00	24hrs
15		Design Validation	$1,440.00	16hrs
16		Revised Bid Document	$1,200.00	16hrs
17		Component Packages Negotiated	$6,030.00	64hrs
18		Bid Document Final	$1,440.00	16hrs
19		Bid Submitted	$0.00	0hrs

The Baseline Costs and Work are copied from the Cost and Work fields at the time that the Baseline is set and are not calculated from their child tasks. Thus, when tasks are added, deleted or moved to different Summary tasks then the Baseline Costs and Work are no longer the sum of their child tasks.

There is a function titled **Summary Task Interim Baseline Calculation**, which is covered in the **STATUSING PROJECTS WITH RESOURCES** chapter. This will allow the Summary Tasks Baseline Dates and Costs to be recalculated.

19.9 Contour the Resource Assignment

A Resource Assignment may be assigned to a task with a non-linear profile. This function is titled **Work Contour** and is similar to the Resource Curve function in Primavera software. To assign a contour to a resource assignment:

- Open the **Assignment Information** form by:
  - ➢ Double-clicking on a resource in the **Task Usage** or **Resource Usage** view, or
  - ➢ Right-clicking on a resource and selecting **Assignment Information** from the menu.
- The picture below shows the Sales Engineer being assigned as **Back Loaded**.

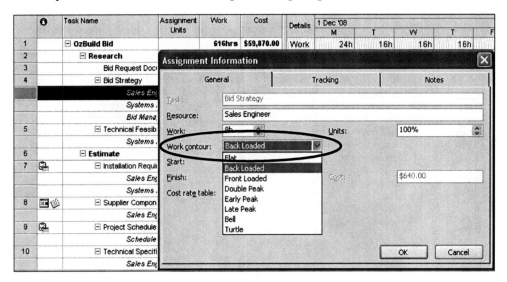

- From the **Work contour:** drop-down box, select the **Work Contour** type.
- The picture below is the **Resource Usage** form. It shows one task titled **Example Task** with six resources. Each resource name has been made the same as the assigned **Work** contour. The picture shows:
  - ➢ The effect of the assignment for each of the **Work Contour** types, and
  - ➢ The icon displayed in the **Task Information** column as a graphical representation of the contour.

		Task Name	Work	Details	10 June				
					M	T	W	T	F
1		Example Task	320 hrs	Work	39.68h	95.27h	68.1h	78.27h	38.68h
		Flat	40 hrs	Work	4h	25h	0h	8h	3h
		Back Loaded	40 hrs	Work	1.67h	5h	8.33h	11.67h	13.33h
		Front Loaded	40 hrs	Work	13.33h	11.67h	8.33h	5h	1.67h
		Double Peak	40 hrs	Work	6h	12h	4h	12h	6h
		Early Peak	40 hrs	Work	6h	16h	10h	6h	2h
		Late Paek	40 hrs	Work	2h	6h	10h	16h	6h
		Bell	40 hrs	Work	2.4h	9.6h	16h	9.6h	2.4h
		Turtle	40 hrs	Work	4.28h	10h	11.43h	10h	4.28h

The **Flat** option allows you to type in any value into each of the cells. A resource assignment is automatically set to **Flat** when one manual entry is made in the table.

WORKSHOP 16

Assigning Resources to Tasks

Background
The resources must now be assigned to their specific tasks.
Assignment
Open the **OzBuild With Resources** project and complete the following steps:

1. Select the **Gantt Chart** view.
2. Split the pane by selecting **Window**, **Split**.
3. Display the **Task Details Form** in the lower pane window, select **Format**, **Details**, and choose **Resource Work**.
4. Using the **Resources Work** and the **Assign Resources** form assign the following resources:

Notes: Once you have entered the **Resource Name** in the **Resources Work** form and assigned the **Units**, Microsoft Project will calculate the worked hours automatically after you click out of the form. Ensure the tasks are **NOT Effort-Driven** as you enter resources, otherwise the Total Work may stay constant as you add additional resources. As resources are assigned to tasks 6 and 9 the task calendars will be ignored and these tasks will end a day later, but as they are not on the Critical Path they will not change the project end date.

Task No	Task Name	Resource	Units	Work
4	Bid Strategy	Sales Engineer	1	8 hrs
		System Engineer	1	8 hrs
		Bid Manager	1	8 hrs
5	Technical Feasibility Study *After assigning this resource check that the task duration is still 8 days.*	System Engineer	2	128 hrs
7	Installation Requirements	Sales Engineer	1	32 hrs
		System Engineer	1	32 hrs
8	Supplier Component Bids	Sales Engineer	1	24 hrs
9	Project Schedule	Scheduler	1	32 hrs
10	Technical Specification	Sales Engineer	1	72 hrs
		System Engineer	1	72 hrs
11	Component Bids Costs	Sales Engineer	1	16 hrs
13	Draft Bid Document	Clerical Support	1	24 hrs
		Bid Manager	1	24 hrs
		Contract Consultant Assign at $10,000.00		
14	Reviewed Draft Bid Document	Sales Engineer	1	8 hrs
		System Engineer	1	8 hrs
		Bid Manager	1	8 hrs

continued over…

WORKSHOP 16 CONTINUED

5. Use the **Task Information** form to assign the remaining resource to each task. You may display this form by double-clicking the Task Name item on your Gantt Chart.

Task No	Task Name	Resource	Units	Work
15	Design Validation	System Engineer	1	8 hrs
		Bid Manager	1	8 hrs
16	Revised Bid Document	Clerical Support	1	8 hrs
		Bid Manager	1	8 hrs
17	Component Packages Negotiated	Sales Engineer	1	32 hrs
		Bid Manager	1	32 hrs
		Report Binding	3 Folders	
18	Bid Document Final	System Engineer	1	8 hrs
		Bid Manager	1	8 hrs

6. Insert the **Resource Names** and **Resources Initials** columns to the right of the Task Name. Align the data in the columns to the left.

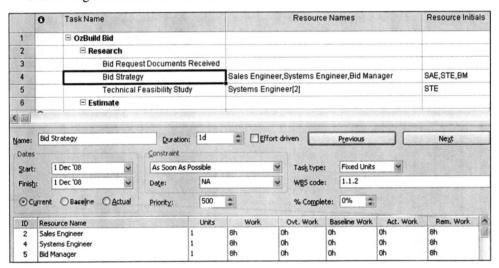

7. Now display the **Task Usage** view, insert the **Assignment Units** and **Costs** columns and check that your data matches the table below and the data in the table above.

20 RESOURCE HISTOGRAMS, TABLES, S-CURVES & LEVELING

This chapter will briefly cover the following topics:

- **Resource Histograms** – Allow the display of each resource on a time-phased vertical bar graph. These are termed **Resource Graphs** in Microsoft Project.

- **Resource Tables** – Allow the display of one or more resource requirements in a table on a time-phased basis. This information is displayed by the **Task Usage** and **Resource Usage** views.

- **S-Curves** – Allow the display of the planned, earned or actual consumption of resources or costs as a line graph. A single S-Curve may be produced for one or selected resource costs or hours using the Resource Graph View. The display of multiple S-Curves showing the Planned, Actual and Earned cost or hours of resources is not possible. It is also not possible to display Fixed Costs on the S-Curves, but the source data for resources may be exported to a spreadsheet where multiple S-Curves may be readily created.

- **Leveling** – There are several techniques available for smoothing resource peaks or overloads in resource requirements.

Function	Command Menu
- To display a small resource graph in the resource graph form	Select one or more resources and then select ⬚ Graphs... from the **Assign Resources** form to display the **Resource Graph** form.
- To display a **Resource Graph**	Select the **Resource Graph** View.
- To display a **Resource Table**	Select the **Task Usage** or **Resource Usage** Views.
- To print a **Resource Profile** or **Resource Table**	Select the appropriate **View**, make the view active and use the normal print commands.
- Export data to Excel	Display the **Analysis** toolbar.

20.1   Resource Graph Form

The **Resource Graph** form is a new feature to Microsoft Project 2002 and is the simplest way to display a small graph showing resource utilization. Select ⬚ Graphs... from the **Assign Resources** form to display the **Resource Graph** form.

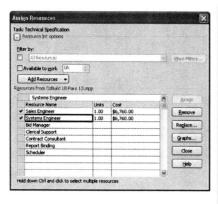
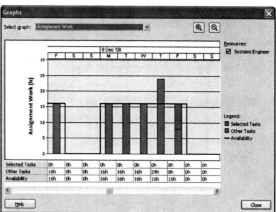

20.2 Resource Graph View

A **Resource Graph** may be displayed with the **Resource Graph** view. Only the resources assigned to the highlighted activity will be displayed.

- The **Resource Graph** may be viewed in the top or bottom pane. The view below displays the Gantt Chart in the top pane and Resource Graph in the bottom pane and shows the Sales Engineer is overloaded:

To be able to view all resources click on the **Select All** button:

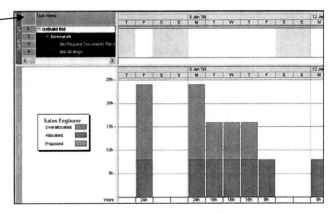

- Only one resource is displayed at a time. You may scroll through the resources by:
  - ➤ Striking the **Page Up** and **Page Down Keys,** or
  - ➤ Clicking on the scroll bar in the lower left-hand side of the **Resource Graph** view.

- The **Resource Graph Units** options may display the vertical scale by using any of the units shown in the gray box on the right. The **Units** to be displayed may be selected by:
  - ➤ Selecting **Format, Details,** or
  - ➤ Right-clicking in the graph area of the screen.

- The **Resource Graph** gridlines and colors may be formatted by opening the **Bar Styles** form and:
  - ➤ Selecting **Format, Bar Styles…** when the **Resource Graph** is the active pane, or
  - ➤ Right-clicking in the graph area of the screen and selecting the **Bar Styles** option.
- The **Timescale** of the graph is adopted from the timescale setting. You will find the **Zoom** icons 🔍🔍 useful for changing the timescale.

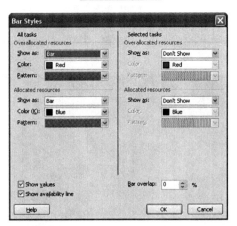

20.3   Resource Tables View

Resource tables are displayed using the **Task Usage** or **Resource Usage** views.

- The **Task Usage View** organizes the schedule by **Task** and then by **Resource**:

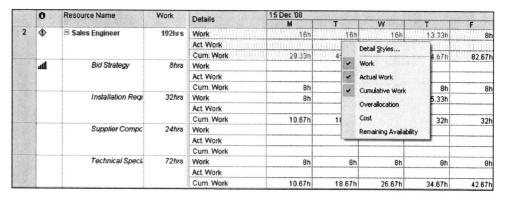

	🛈	Task Name	Assignment Units	Work	Cost	Details	1 Dec '08				
							M	T	W	T	F
1		⊟ OzBuild Bid		616hrs	$59,870.00	Work	19h	10.33h	16h	16h	16h
2		⊟ Research		152hrs	$12,320.00	Work	19h	10.33h	16h	16h	16h
3		Bid Request Doc	0hrs	$0.00	Work						
4		⊟ Bid Strategy		24hrs	$2,080.00	Work	19h	5h			
	📶	Sales Enç	100%	8hrs	$640.00	Work	3h	5h			
		Systems .	100%	8hrs	$640.00	Work	8h				
		Bid Mana	100%	8hrs	$800.00	Work	8h				
5		⊟ Technical Feasib		128hrs	$10,240.00	Work		5.33h	16h	16h	16h
		Systems .	200%	128hrs	$10,240.00	Work		5.33h	16h	16h	16h
6		⊞ Estimate		280hrs	$21,760.00	Work					
12		⊞ Proposal		184hrs	$25,790.00	Work					

- The **Resource Usage** view organizes the schedule by **Resource** and then by **Task**. Note the Sales Engineer is overloaded as indicated by the icon in the indicators column:

	🛈	Resource Name	Work	Details	15 Dec '08				
					M	T	W	T	F
2	◈	⊟ Sales Engineer	192hrs	Work	16h	16h	16h	13.33h	8h
				Act. Work					
				Cum. Work	29.33h	4		4.67h	82.67h
	📶	Bid Strategy	8hrs	Work					
				Act. Work					
				Cum. Work	8h			8h	8h
		Installation Reqı	32hrs	Work	8h			5.33h	
				Act. Work					
				Cum. Work	10.67h	1		32h	32h
		Supplier Compc	24hrs	Work					
				Act. Work					
				Cum. Work					
		Technical Speci	72hrs	Work	8h	8h	8h	8h	8h
				Act. Work					
				Cum. Work	10.67h	18.67h	26.67h	34.67h	42.67h

Menu shown over the table:
- Detail Styles...
- ✔ Work
- ✔ Actual Work
- ✔ Cumulative Work
- Overallocation
- Cost
- Remaining Availability

- When these views are displayed in the top **Pane** they display all resources and all tasks.

- When these views are displayed in the bottom **Pane** they display values for resources or tasks that have been selected in the top **Pane**.

- More than one line of data may be displayed by right-clicking in the display and selecting from the menu as shown above.

20.4   Detailed Styles Form

This form may is opened from the **Resource Usage** and **Task Usage** forms and allows further options for formatting these forms.

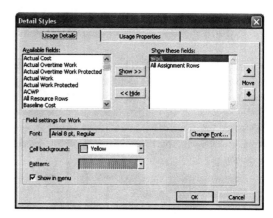

20.5 Creating an S-Curve from Microsoft Project

A single S-Curve may be created graphically and displayed by Microsoft Project. The example below is produced by:

- Displaying the **Resource Sheet** in the top pane and selecting all the resources,

- Displaying the **Resource Graph** in the bottom pane,

- Right clicking and displaying the **Cumulative Costs** and

- Right clicking, open the **Bar Styles...** form and formatting as displayed below:

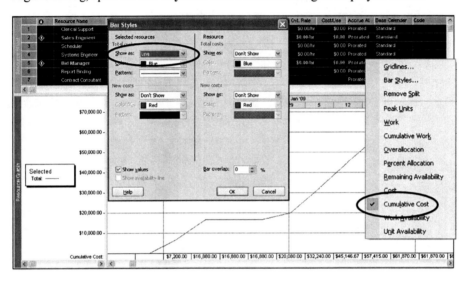

20.6 Printing Resource Profiles and Tables

To **Print** a **Task Usage**, **Resource Usage**, or **Resource Graph**, make the appropriate **Pane** active and use the print functions as described in the **PRINTING AND REPORTS** chapter.

20.7 Creating Table, S-Curves and Histograms in a Spreadsheet

Tables, S-Curves and histograms may be created for displaying:

- Planning information, such as the number of people required or a project cash flow,

- Progress in terms of hours spent or cost to date, and

- Performance, say comparing planned and actual hours or costs to date.

Earned Value (EV) also know as **Earned Value Performance Measurement (EVPM)** is a well document technique used for the management of projects. This technique requires the results output in a number of formats which Microsoft Project is not able to reproduce. Spreadsheets or specialists software will produce these outputs from data exported from Microsoft Project. There are many good Earned Value reference documents that may be used to assist in the establishment of an Earned Value Performance Measurement system including:

- The Australian Standard "AS 4817-2005 Project performance measurement using Earned Value", and

- The Project Management Institute Practice "Standard For Earned Value Management"

Excel is often used to create S-Curves and Histograms for the following reasons:

- The ability to easily record and display period information, this may be hours consumed or dollars spent per week or per month.

- The ability to simply record and enter actuals at a summary level in Excel. It is simpler to record cost and hours at project or at WBS component than at a detailed task level.

- The superior graphical output of Excel and flexibility compared to Microsoft Project; such as the ability to display both tabular and graphical information on a single printout.

Many people are familiar with exporting or copying and pasting tabular data from one software program to another and are also comfortable with creating S-Curves and Histograms in spreadsheets which are titled charts in Excel. This section of this book will cover the basics of transferring the data from Microsoft Project to a spreadsheet for the creation of S-Curves and Histograms.

20.7.1 Export Time Phased Data Using Analysis Toolbar or Visual Reports

The **Analysis** toolbar is designed to allow the export time-phased data to Excel where Charts may be created. This is a Wizard-style function and the instructions will step you through the process which results is the data being available in tabular format in Excel.

In Microsoft Project 2007 this export function was moved to the **Report, Visual Reports…, Visual Reports - Create** form. Reports like the **Cash Flow Report** and the **Earned Value Over Time Report** are intended to be used to display time phased data but you may find them difficult to use.

20.7.2 Export Using Time Phased Data Copy and Paste

A data table may be highlighted, copied, and then pasted into spreadsheets to create S-Curves. The Microsoft Project headings are not copied, and the data on the left-hand side of the **Pane** and the data on the right-hand side of the **Pane** have to be copied separately and aligned with manually created headings in Excel.

To transfer the data into Excel by copy & paste:

- Type the column headings from both sides of the pane into the top row of your spreadsheet.

- Organize the **Task Usage** or **Resource Usage** view and **Details** so it displays the rows, columns, units and timescale you require in your graph.

- Highlight the rows on the left-hand side of your Pane that you want to copy to the spreadsheet. Position the cursor under the spreadsheet heading and paste. If your headings do not line up, move either the data or the headings so that they do line up.

- Follow the same process with the data on the right-hand side of the Pane.

You may now create your S-Curves in the spreadsheet using its built-in graphing function.

This process is not as simple as using the Analysis Toolbar but the precise data may be copied from a Table in Microsoft Project and pasted directing into a spread sheet.

20.7.3 Creating S-Curves in Excel

Earned Value Performance Measurement (EVPM) data may be calculated in Microsoft Project (an example is shown at the end of the **STATUSING PROJECTS WITH RESOURCES** chapter) or in Excel. The table below is a simple example of EVPM data and this data may be displayed at any level such as at Project, Phase, WBS Node or task.

- The **Planned Value** is usually exported from Microsoft Project when the schedule is Baselined.

- The **Earned Value** could be calculated either:
  - ➢ In Microsoft Project after the project has been updated and transferred to Excel, or
  - ➢ Calculated in Excel from the original Baseline Costs multiplied by the % Complete.

- The **Actual Costs** could be calculated either:
  - ➢ Outside Microsoft Project and entered into Excel, or
  - ➢ Calculated in Microsoft Project by entering the detail cost information against each task in Microsoft Project and exporting the rolled up cost into Excel each period.

- The **Estimate To Complete** is displayed in an EVPM graph and is best generated in Microsoft Project after the schedule, resources and costs have been revised and the Estimate To Complete exported to Excel at the required level.

	Jan	Feb	Mar	Apr	May	Jun	Jul	Aug
Planned or BCWS	$ -	$ 6,000	$15,000	$30,000	$43,000	$50,000	$ -	$ -
Earned or BCWP	$ -	$ 4,000	$10,000	$20,000	$ -	$ -	$ -	$ -
Actual or ACWP	$ -	$ 8,000	$20,000	$40,000	$ -	$ -	$ -	$ -
Estimate At Completion	$ -	$ -	$ -	$40,000	$55,000	$65,000	$70,000	$75,000

The Excel S-Curve Chart below may be created by highlighting the data in Excel, selecting **Insert, Chart…**, selecting a **Line** Chart Type and following the Wizard instructions. Histograms are created in a similar way by selecting a different Chart Type.

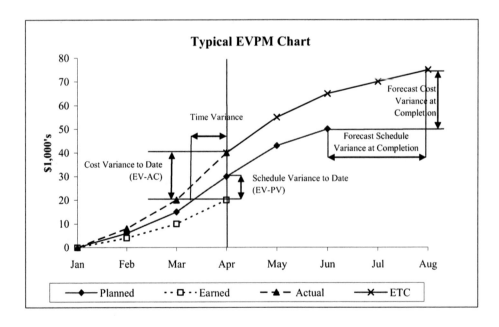

20.8   Resolving Resource Overloading

Resource overloading may be solved either by:

- Leveling the schedule which delays and/or splits activities until resources become available, or

- Using other techniques to reduce peaks in requirement, overloading or uneconomical use of resources which may be due to demobilization and remobilizing of crews.

20.8.1   Methods of Resource Leveling

After resource overloads or inefficient use of resources have been identified with Histograms and Tables the schedule may now have to be leveled to reduce peaks in resource demands. The process of leveling is defined as delaying activities until resources become available. There are several methods of delaying activities and thus leveling a schedule

- **Turning off Automatic Calculation and Dragging Activities**. This option does not maintain a critical path and reverts back to the original schedule when recalculated. This option should not be used when a contract requires a critical path schedule to be maintained as the schedule will no longer be calculating correctly.

- **Constraining Activities**. A constraint may be applied to delay an activity until the date that the resource becomes available from a higher priority activity. This is not a recommended method because if the higher priority activity is delayed the schedule may become unleveled.

- **Sequencing Logic**. Relationships may be applied to activities sharing the same resource(s) in the order of their priority. In this process a resource-driven critical path will be generated. If the first activity in a chain is delayed then the chain of activities will be delayed. But the schedule will not become unleveled and the Critical Path maintained. In this situation a successor activity may be able to take place earlier and the logic will have to be manually edited.

- **Leveling Function**. The Leveling function will level resources by delaying activities without the need for Constraints or Logic and will find the optimum order for the activities based on nominated parameters. Again, as this option does not maintain a critical path it should not be used when a contract requires a critical path schedule to be maintained. The Leveling function may be used to establish an optimum scheduling sequence and then Sequencing Logic applied to hold the leveled dates and to create a critical path.

20.8.2   Other Methods of Resolving Resource Peaks and Conflicts

Other methods of resolving resourcing problems that are not strictly under the definition of leveling are:

- **Revising the Project Plan**. Revise a project plan to mitigate resource conflicts such as changing the order of work, contracting work out, prefabricating instead of site fabrication, etc.

- **Duration Change**. Increase the task duration to decrease the resource requirements, so a 5-day activity with 10 people could be extended to a 10-day task with 5 people.

- **Resource Substitution**. Substitute one resource with another available resource.

- **Increase Working Time**. Accelerate the working time of a project task, which may release the resource for other tasks.

20.8.3   Resource Leveling Function

Microsoft Project has a basic resource leveling function that is accessed through the **Resource Leveling** form by selecting **Tools, Level Resources….**

When one or more resources are selected in a resource view, such as the **Resource Sheet**, the **Level Now** function will open the **Level Now** form and allow the option of leveling all or selected resources.

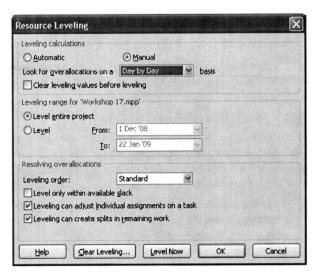

- **Leveling calculations**
  - ➤ **Automatic/Manual**. When manual is selected, the **Level Now** button in the **Resource Leveling** form is used to level the project or the **Level Now** button may be added to a toolbar by right-clicking in the toolbar area and selecting **Customize…** from the menu.
  - ➤ **Look for overallocations on a … basis** – considers the average allocation in the time period selected and only levels when average exceeds the available, thus allowing for short periods of overloading.
  - ➤ **Clear leveling values before leveling** – un-levels the schedule and then re-levels.
- **Leveling range for…**allows for the whole project or a time portion of a schedule to be leveled, such as a Stage or Phase.

- **Resolving overallocations**
  - ➤ **Leveling order:** allows three options for the order that tasks are prioritized for leveling. One option is the task **Priority** field which may be set in a column or in the **General** tab of the **Task Information** form. A **Priority** of 0 is the lowest priority and 1000 is the highest and tasks that must not be delayed should be set at 1000.
  - ➤ **Level only within available slack** will not delay the end date of the project but will attempt to level the schedule in the available total slack (float).
  - ➤ **Level can adjust individual assignments on a task** allows one resource assigned to a task to be delayed in relation to others assigned to the same task, thus allowing other resources to work as scheduled. This will in effect increase the duration of a task and may result in a split task. This function works in conjunction with the **Level Assignments** field that may be displayed in a column and individual tasks may or may not be allowed to have their resource assignments adjusted. This function has a similar effect to the Primavera Activity Type Independent.
  - ➤ **Leveling can create splits in remaining work** allows leveling to split or not to split tasks during leveling.
- **Clear Leveling…** allows the option of clearing leveling for selected task or all tasks and returns the schedule to the unleveled state.

WORKSHOP 17

Histograms and Tables

Background
We will create a copy of our current project file for this workshop, then use Tables and Histograms to isolate the resources that are overallocated and level the schedule.

Assignment
1. Save your OzBuild Bid project file and then resave as **OzBuild Leveling**.
2. Display the **Gantt Chart** view in the top pane and the **Resource Sheet** view in the bottom pane.
3. Click on **Select All** button to display all resources. The overloaded resources are highlighted in red.
4. Display the **Resource Usage** view in the bottom pane, right-click in the bottom pane and display both the Work and Overallocation resources. The overallocated resources are highlighted in red and the overallocated lines of data show by how much:

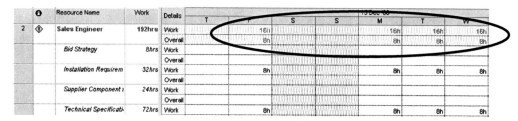

5. Display the **Resource Usage** form in the bottom pane and check the Histograms for the resources. See again the overallocated resources:

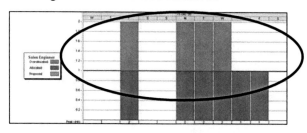

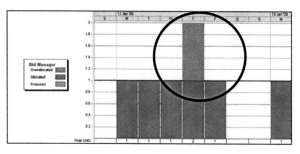

6. Set the Baseline and display the Baseline bars using the Gantt Chart Wizard so we are able to see the delay to the project from leveling.

7. Use the Zoom 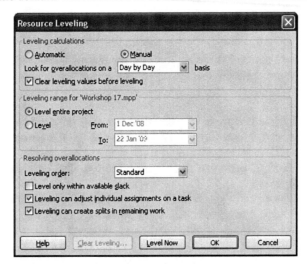 button to set the scale to weeks.

8. Now level the schedule, select **Tools**, **Level Resources…** to open the **Resource Leveling** form:

9. Accept the defaults which should be as below and click on Level Now :

10. Select **Entire Pool** if requested, your answer should look like this:

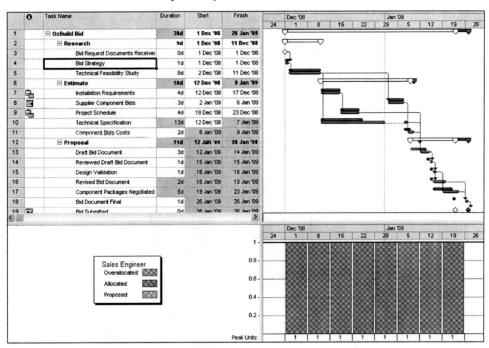

21 STATUSING PROJECTS WITH RESOURCES

Statusing a project with resources uses a number of features that are very interactive. It is suggested that after you have read this chapter and before you work on a live project that you create a simple schedule with a couple of tasks and assign two or three resources against each task. Set the **Options** to reflect the way you want to enter the information and how you want Microsoft Project to calculate. Go through the statusing process with dummy data and then check that the results are as you expected. The options to consider are:

- Have you linked **% Complete** and **% Work** with the **Updating task status updates resource status:** option? If unlinked, the **% Work** may be different from **% Complete**.

- How is the measure of progress at the summary task level displayed? The summary **% Work** is based on hours of efforts, which is more meaningful than the summary **% Complete**, which is based on durations.

- Does Microsoft Project calculate the resource **Actual Costs** with this option checked: **Actual costs are always calculated by Microsoft Project**?

- Are your tasks scheduled to start after a date using the **Reschedule uncompleted tasks to start after:** in conjunction with the **Split** task option?

Statusing a project with resources takes place in two distinct steps:

- The dates are statused using the methods outlined in the **TRACKING PROGRESS** chapter, and

- The resources' hours and costs are updated.

This chapter covers the following topics:

- Understanding **Baseline Dates** (Target Dates), **Baseline Costs** (Budget) and **Baseline Work**.

- Understanding the **Status Date, Work After Date** and **Current Date** with respect to resources.

- Information Required to Update a Resourced Schedule.

- Updating Resources.

- Splitting Tasks.

- Summary Task Interim Baseline Calculation.

Microsoft Project does not provide the capability of producing multiple S-Curves. The data may be exported or copied and pasted to products such as Excel where S-Curves may be created.

21.1 Understanding Baseline Dates, Duration, Costs and Hours

Baseline Dates are also known as Target Dates and are normally the original Project Early Start and Early Finish dates. These are the dates against which project progress is measured.

Baseline Duration is the original planned duration of a task.

Baseline Costs are also known as Budgets and represent the original project cost estimate. These are the figures against which the expenditures and Cost at Completion (or Estimate at Completion) are measured.

Baseline Work is also known as Budgeted Quantity and represents the original estimate of the project quantities. These are the quantities against which the consumption of resources are measured.

The **Baseline Costs** and **Work** of resources are **NOT** automatically recorded in the Baseline fields of each resource as the resource is assigned to a task. All **Baseline** information **(Dates, Costs** and **Work)** is saved when the project or selected Tasks have the Baseline set.

If resources have been assigned then the Baseline Costs and Work are recorded at the same time as the Baseline dates.

Setting the **Baseline Dates** is covered in the **TRACKING PROGRESS** chapter.

Baseline Dates may be displayed by using the following methods:

- Baseline Date Start and Finish columns, or

- Bar Chart Bars, or

- Dates on the Bars, or

- In forms such as the **Task Details** form.

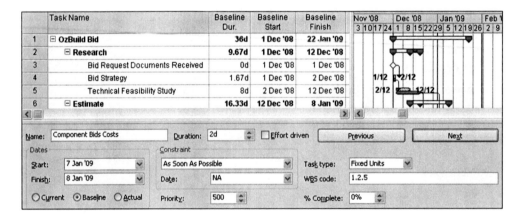

21.2   Understanding the Data Date

The **Data Date** is a standard scheduling term. It is also known as the **Review Date, Status Date, As of Date** and **Update Date**.

- The **Data Date** is the date that divides the past from the future in the schedule. The **Data Date** is not normally in the future but is often in the recent past due to the time it may take to collect the information to status the schedule.

- **Actual Costs** and **Quantities/Hours** or **Actual work** occur before the data date.

- **Costs** and **Quantities/Hours To Complete** or **Work to Complete** occur after the Data Date.

- **Remaining duration** is the duration required to complete a task. It is calculated forward from the **Data Date**.

Microsoft Project has four dates associated with updating a schedule. These are covered in the **TRACKING PROGRESS** chapter. In summary, these date fields are:

- **Current Date** – This date is set to the computer's system date each time a project file is opened. It is used to calculate **Earned Value** data when a **Status Date** has not been set.

- **Status Date** – By default this is blank. After assigning this date it will not change (the **Current Date** does) when the project is saved or reopened at a later date. When set, this date overrides the **Current Date** for calculating **Earned Value** data.

- **Update work as completed through:** – When a project is updated using the **Update Project** form (the project is statused as if it were progressed exactly according to plan), the **Status Date** is set to the same date as **Project Update Date**.

- **Reschedule uncompleted work to start after:** date – This function is used to move the **Incomplete Work** of **In-Progress** tasks into the future.
  - ➤ **In-Progress** tasks must be able to **Split** for this function to operate. The option to split tasks is found on the **Tools, Options…, Schedule** tab.
  - ➤ The **Status Date** is **NOT** set to the **Reschedule uncompleted work to start after:** date when this function is invoked.
  - ➤ This function will not move the incomplete portions of tasks back in time when a task is completed ahead of schedule. This causes the task's **Remaining Duration** to occur sometime in the future and not immediately after the selected date. The example below shows a schedule with the **Reschedule uncompleted work to start after:** date set to 10 June. The top task's Remaining Duration commences on 11 June, the task is split and the Remaining Duration occurs immediately after 10 June. The lower task's Remaining Duration does not commence until 18 June. This is not realistic and manual intervention is required to correct this.

% Comp.	Act. Dur.	Rem. Dur.	3 June							10 June							17 June						
			M	T	W	T	F	S	S	M	T	W	T	F	S	S	M	T	W	T	F	S	S
10%	1 day	9 days																					
90%	9 days	1 day																					

NEITHER the **Current Date** nor the **Status Date** is used to calculate the **Early Finish** of an **In-Progress** task when a schedule is calculated using **F9**, or when the **Calculation options for Microsoft Project**'s option of **Automatic Scheduling** is enabled. The end date of an in-progress task in Microsoft Project is normally calculated from the **Actual Start Date** plus the **Duration**. This is a different method of calculation than employed by some other scheduling software, which normally calculate the end date of a task from a single **Data Date** plus the **Remaining Duration**.

21.3 Formatting the Current Date and Status Date Lines

To format the display of the **Current Date** and **Status Date** lines on the Bar Chart, select **Format**, **Gridlines…** to display the **Gridlines** form:

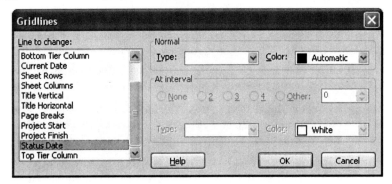

- These **Options** allow the selection of colors and line types for all sight lines as shown in the **Lines to Change** box on the left of the example above.

- All other sight lines may also be formatted in this form.

21.4   Information Required to Update a Resourced Schedule

A project schedule is usually updated at the end of a period, such as each day, week or month. One purpose of updating a schedule is to establish differences between the plan and the current schedule and if necessary take action to bring the project back on track.

Microsoft Project may calculate task **Actual Costs** from the rates entered in the **Resource Table** or the Costs may be entered manually. This option is set in the **Options Calculation** tab. If the **Actual Costs** are to be calculated by Microsoft Project then the **Actual Costs** do not need to be collected.

The following information is required to status a resourced schedule:

Tasks completed in the update period:

- **Actual Start** date of the task.

- **Actual Finish** date of the task.

- **Actual Costs** spent, **Actual Resource Hours** spent, and/or **Actual Material Quantities**.

Tasks commenced in the update period:

- **Actual Start** date of the task.

- **Remaining Duration** or **Expected Finish** date.

- **Actual Costs** and **Actual Resource Hours** and/or **Actual Material Quantities**.

- **Hours** or **Quantities** to complete. Costs to complete are always calculated using the resource rates in the Resource Table.

- **Suspend** and **Resume** dates for tasks that have had their work suspended. These are used for splitting tasks.

Tasks Not Commenced:

- Changes in Logic or date constraints.

- Changes in estimated **Costs, Hours** or **Quantities**.

The schedule may be updated once this information is collected.

You have the option of allowing Microsoft Project to calculate many of these fields from the **% Complete** by selecting the appropriate option found in the **Tools, Options...**, **Calculation** tab.

21.5   Updating Dates and Percentage Complete

The schedule should be first updated as outlined in the **TRACKING PROGRESS** chapter. In summary, this is completed by entering:

- The **Actual Start** and **Actual Finish** dates of **Complete** tasks.

- The **Actual Start**, **% Complete** and **Remaining Duration** or **Expected Finish** of **In-Progress** tasks.

- Adjust Logic and **Durations** of **Un-started** tasks.

Before you do this, you should set the **Tools**, **Options…**, **Calculation** tab to ensure that the actual costs and hours calculate the way you want.

A simple process to update a project is to:

- Use **Tools**, **Tracking**, **Update Project…** and select **Update work as complete through:** to update the project through to the data date.

- Adjust the **Actual Start** and **Actual Finish** dates for **Complete** tasks.

- Adjust the **Actual Start** dates of **In-Progress** tasks and drag the **% Complete** to the required value.

- Drag the finish date of **In-Progress** tasks to the required date.

The option of **Tools**, **Tracking**, **Update Project…** will only work when the following Project Options are enabled. Then, Microsoft Project calculates **Work** and **Costs**.

- **Updating task status updates resource status**, and

- **Actual costs are always calculated by Microsoft Project.**

21.6   Entering a % Complete Against Summary Tasks

A **% Complete** may be entered against a summary task and all the child tasks and their resources will be updated automatically to reflect the Summary % Complete. Full details of this function are outlined in the **TRACKING PROGRESS** chapter. In the picture below 50% was entered against the **Research** task and the Actual and Remaining work have been calculated:

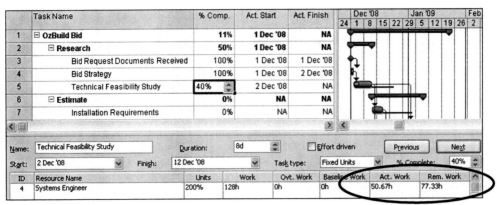

21.7   Updating Resources

There are many permutations available in the **Tools**, **Options...** form for calculating resource data. Due to the number of resource options and numerous forms available in Microsoft Project, it is not feasible to document all the combinations available for resource calculation.

This book, therefore, outlines some typical scenarios and examples of entering the status data that you may want to try on your projects.

Material and **Cost** resources are updated in the same way as **Work** resources and are not covered separately.

21.7.1   Updating Tasks with Fixed Costs Only

A project with fixed costs only is the simplest option for managing costs. The example below displays:

- A 10-day **Duration** task which is 40% Complete.

- A **Baseline Cost** of $1000.00 which was created by an original **Fixed Cost** of $1000.00 when the **Baseline** was set.

- A **Fixed Cost** of $800.00 representing a revised estimate that has reduced the original estimate by $200.00 to $800.00.

- An **Actual Cost** of $320.00 and **Remaining Cost** of $480.00, which are calculated from the 40 % Complete.

- The **Current Bar** (the upper bar in the picture below) shows that the task started two days late and is scheduled to end two days late as compared to the **Baseline Bar** (the black lower bar).

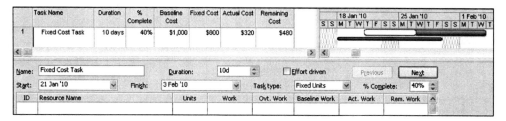

You will notice that the **Task Details** view with the **Resource Cost** details form does not show any resources or costs when **Fixed Costs** are used.

The disadvantage of fixed costs is that they are always linked to the % Complete and an independent Actual Fixed Cost may not be entered. Microsoft Project 2007 introduced Cost resources which has resolved this problem.

21.7.2 Forecasting Resource Hours

The next level of complexity usually occurs when a schedule is used for the management of resource hours but not costs.

One or more resources may be applied to a task and you may want to enter both the **Actual Work** and the **Remaining Work** independently. In this situation you will need to unlink **% Complete** and **Actual Work** with the **Updating task status updates resource status:** option in the **Tools**, **Options…**, **Calculation** tab. Now the **% Work** field will be linked to the **Work, Actual Work** and **Remaining Work** fields and will now operate independently of the **% Complete** field.

The example below uses the **Task Details** form.

- A 10-day **Duration** task which is 40% Complete.

- The task's **Baseline Work** of 240 hours is from the addition of the two resource allocations when the **Baseline** was set.
  - ➤ The **Bid Manager** was originally assigned at 100%, or full-time, giving a **Baseline Work** of 80 hours.
  - ➤ The **Clerical Support** was originally assigned at 200%, or 2 full-time people, giving a **Baseline Work** of 160 hours.

- The task's **Actual Work** of 90 hours is the addition of the two resources' **Actual Work** of 20 hours and 70 hours.

- The task's **Remaining Work** of 220 hours is the addition of the **Remaining Work** of 70 hours and 150 hours.

- The **% Work** of 29% is calculated by dividing the **Actual Work** by the **Work**. This is different than the **% Complete**, which represents the elapsed time.

- Again, the **Current Bar** shows the task started two days late and is scheduled to end two days late.

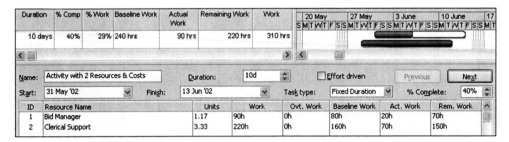

- The **Actual Work** and **Remaining Work** were entered manually and have not been calculated by Microsoft Project from the **% Complete**.

- The duration of the task is still 10 days long because it is a **Fixed Duration** task. The **Units** have increased from 1 to 1.17 and 2 to 3.33 for the Bid Manager and Clerical Support, respectively, as the **Work** is now greater than the **Baseline Work** due to the increase in the number of hours required to complete the task.

21.7.3   Forecasting Resource Hours and Costs Form

The example below is similar to the previous example, but it now displays the **Resource Costs** (not the **Work**) calculated by Microsoft Project with **% Complete** and **Actual Work** unlinked.

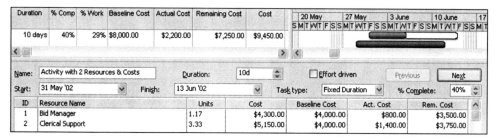

The next level of complexity occurs usually when a schedule is used for the management of resource hours and costs.

You may want to enter both the **Actual Work** and **Actual Costs** separately. For example, you may want to take the costs and hours from a timesheet and/or an accounting system that may have a different resource rate than your schedule. Input your data in the lower pane of the window, which is known as the **Resource Details** form.

In this situation you will need to:

- Unlink **% Complete** and **Actual Work** with the **Updating task status updates resource status:** option in the **Tools, Options…, Calculation** tab, and

- Unlink the **Actual Work** and **Actual Costs** by disabling the **Actual costs are always calculated by Microsoft Project** option in the **Tools, Options…, Calculation** tab.

The example below shows how the costs are calculated with:

- **Work** and **Costs** unlinked, and

- Updated hours as per the previous example.

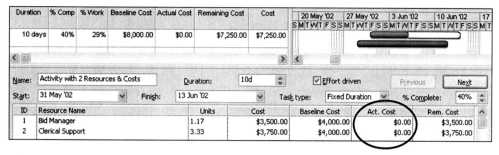

The **Actual Costs** have not been calculated by Microsoft Project and remain at zero. The **Remaining Costs** are based on the resources' **Standard Rate**. The **Actual Costs** should be entered by the user to update the schedule.

Now that the Actual Costs and Actual Work are unlinked, you may type in the **Actual Costs** per resource in the lower pane of the window (i.e., the **Resource Details** form) without affecting the **Actual Work.**

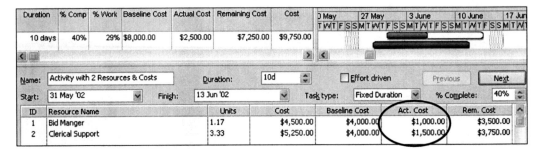

21.7.4   Using the Task Usage and Resource Usage Views

The **Task Usage** and **Resource Usage** forms allow the most flexibility when entering resource quantities and costs to used date, e.g. **Actual Work** and **Actual Cost**. The picture below is the **Task Usage** form from the OzBuild workshops showing the **Work**, **Actual Work** and **Baseline Work** rows. Additional rows of information may be obtained by right-clicking to display a menu or selecting **Format, Details**.

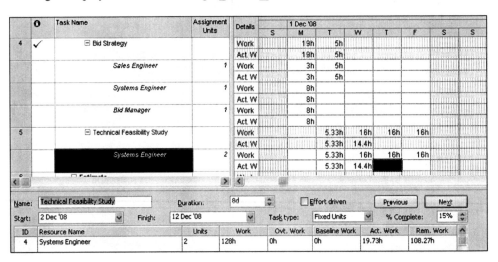

A timesheet-style view may be created with the **Resource Usage** view. This view may be printed or used by team members to directly update their hours to-date in the **Act. Work** (Actual Work) rows and their estimated hours in the **Work** rows. The advantage of this view is that all activities are grouped together in one band under each name. The Systems Engineer's hours for Thu 4 Dec 08 could be typed into the highlighted square above.

Calculated fields that may not have data entered into them are shaded, such as the task rows in the picture above.

21.8 Splitting Tasks

When the **Split in-progress tasks** option is enabled, a task may be **Split** by:

- Dragging the incomplete portion of a task in the bar chart, or

- Clicking on the [icon] icon and then moving your cursor over the point on the task bar where you want a split and dragging the task, or

- Using the **Tools, Tracking, Update Project…, Reschedule uncompleted work to start after:** function, or

- Commencing a task before its predecessor finishes.

In the picture below the upper task was split using the [icon] icon and the lower task was split because it commenced before its predecessor.

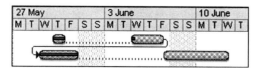

A **Split** may be reversed by dragging the split portion back in the bar chart if there is no predecessor pushing the split out. The first task in the example below has been dragged back. The second task may not be dragged back due to the FS relationship. The relationship could be removed.

Once a task is **Split**, then the resources are not scheduled to work during the split period. This concept is demonstrated in the **RESOURCE HISTOGRAMS, TABLES, S-CURVES AND LEVELING** chapter.

21.9   Summary Task Interim Baseline Calculation

Microsoft Project 2002 introduced a new function titled **Summary Task Interim Baseline Calculation** that enables the Baseline dates and costs of summary activities to be recalculated when tasks are added, deleted or moved. The date aspect of this function is covered in the **TRACKING PROGRESS** chapter.

There are a number of permutations that may be used with this option and a little experimentation with a simple schedule, such as the one below, will enable you to understand this function.

Often it is required to recalculate the Baseline Costs Summary Tasks based on the Original Baseline Costs after activities have been moved to different Summary Tasks. This function may recalculate the Summary Task Baseline Costs from the detailed tasks Baseline Costs when the costs for a project have been revised and are showing a forecast with a deviation from the Baseline. The example below demonstrates this process:

- Original schedule with Baseline Costs and Dates, the Baseline bar being the lower bar:

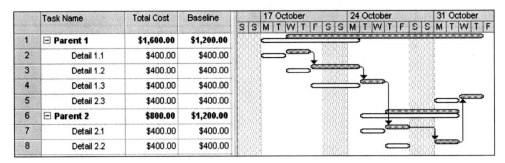

- After the project has been delayed and the task Child 1.3 moved under Parent 1:

You will observe that neither the summary bars nor the Baseline Costs of Parent 1 or Parent 2 are now correct.

- Now highlight only the parent tasks and then select **Tools Tracking, Save Baseline…** and select the options shown in the Save Baseline form below:

You will see from the picture below that now both the Baseline Dates displayed as the lower bar and the Baseline Costs are recalculated from the original baseline data.

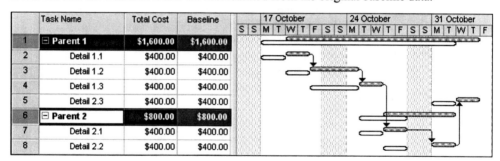

This topic is covered in more detail in the **TRACKING PROGRESS** chapter.

21.10 Summary Tasks and Earned Value

Actual Costs and **Work** may be summarized at any level in the same way as **Work** and **Costs**. The picture below is showing the **Earned Value** table. The costs have been summarized up to the Project Level:

	Task Name	Planned Value - PV (BCWS)	Earned Value EV (BCWP)	AC (ACWP)	SV	CV	EAC	BAC	VAC
1	☐ OzBuild Bid	$14,880.00	$16,147.20	$16,880.00	$1,267.20	-$732.80	$62,587.05	$59,870.00	-$2,717.05
2	☐ Research	$12,320.00	$12,320.00	$12,320.00	$0.00	$0.00	$12,320.00	$12,320.00	$0.00
3	Bid Request Docur	$0.00	$0.00	$0.00	$0.00	$0.00	$0.00	$0.00	$0.00
4	Bid Strategy	$2,080.00	$2,080.00	$2,080.00	$0.00	$0.00	$2,080.00	$2,080.00	$0.00
5	Technical Feasibili	$10,240.00	$10,240.00	$10,240.00	$0.00	$0.00	$10,240.00	$10,240.00	$0.00
6	☐ Estimate	$2,560.00	$3,827.20	$4,560.00	$1,267.20	-$732.80	$25,926.42	$21,760.00	-$4,166.42
7	Installation Require	$1,280.00	$2,560.00	$2,560.00	$1,280.00	$0.00	$5,120.00	$5,120.00	$0.00
8	Supplier Compone	$0.00	$0.00	$0.00	$0.00	$0.00	$1,920.00	$1,920.00	$0.00
9	Project Schedule	$0.00	$0.00	$0.00	$0.00	$0.00	$1,920.00	$1,920.00	$0.00
10	Technical Specifica	$1,280.00	$1,267.20	$2,000.00	-$12.80	-$732.80	$18,181.82	$11,520.00	-$6,661.82
11	Component Bids C	$0.00	$0.00	$0.00	$0.00	$0.00	$1,280.00	$1,280.00	$0.00
12	☐ Proposal	$0.00	$0.00	$0.00	$0.00	$0.00	$25,790.00	$25,790.00	$0.00

The terminology below is used by a large number of companies and organizations. It provides standard terms to describe Earned Value calculations, which many people understand. Below are some of the terms that are in common use:

- AC or ACWP   Actual Cost or Actual Cost of Work Performed
- EV or BCWP   Earned Value or Budget Cost of Work Performed
- PV or BCWS   Planned Value or Budget Cost of Work Scheduled
- BAC   Budget At Completion
- C/SCSC   Cost/Schedule Control Systems Criteria (CS^2)
- CV   Cost Variance to date, BCWP – ACWP
- EAC   Estimate At Completion
- ETC Time   Estimate To Complete expressed in Time
- ETC   Estimate To Complete
- FAC $ Forecast at Completion
- FC CV   Forecast Cost Variance at Completion (Budget – Forecast)
- FC SV   Forecast Schedule Variance at Completion (Baseline End Date – Scheduled End Date)
- FTC CT   Forecast To Complete Calendar Time
- SV   Schedule Variance to date, BCWP – BCWS
- VAC   Variance At Completion

The **Physical % Complete** field may be used to calculate the Earned Value (Budget Cost of Work Performed) independently from the value in the task **% Complete** field. The **Physical % Complete** function is useful for measuring the progress of work that is not progressing linearly. This may be set for each individual task in the **General** tab of the **Task Information** form. The default for new tasks may be set with the [Earned Value...] button in the **General** tab of the **Options** form, where the Baseline to be used for the Earned Value calculations may be selected.

The method that Microsoft Project uses to calculate the Earned Value data is documented in the Help file and should be read carefully, as different versions of Microsoft calculate these fields differently. Should different Earned Value calculations be required then Custom Data Fields should be considered as an alternative.

WORKSHOP 18

Updating a Resourced Schedule

Background

We need to status the tasks and resources.

Assignment

Note: If your settings are not exactly the same as the computer on which this exercise was undertaken or you enter data in a different order you may end up with different results.

Open your OzBuild with Resources project file and complete the following steps:

1. We will initially allow Microsoft Project to calculate costs and hours from the % Complete. Adjust the options using **Tools**, **Options...**, **Calculation** tabs to:
   - ➤ **CHECK** the **Updating task status updates resource status** option. This will link % Complete and Actual Work. (This option also needs to be checked to allow Summary % Completes to be spread correctly to detailed tasks.)
   - ➤ **CHECK** the **Actual costs are always calculated by Microsoft Project** option. With this option checked the resource Actual Cost is calculated by Microsoft Project from the resource Work and Rates.
   - ➤ **UNCHECK** both **Move end of completed task parts after status date back to status date** and **Move start of remaining parts before status date forward to status date** options.
   - ➤ Select the **Schedule** tab and **UNCHECK** the **Split in-progress tasks** option. This will prevent the splitting of tasks.

2. Save the Baseline using **Tools, Tracking, Save Baseline...**.

3. Split the screen. Display the **Gantt Chart** with **Tracking** table in the upper screen and the **Task Details Form** with **Resource Work** details form in the lower screen.

4. Format the bars by selecting **Format, Gantt Chart Wizard...**, using a Custom Gantt Chart display the **Baseline** without text and display logic links lines.

5. Format the Timescale to **Weeks 28 Jan '02** and **Days M,T,W,...** at 100%.

6. Display the Status Date by selecting **Format, Gridlines...**.

Continued Over...

WORKSHOP 18 CONTINUED

7. We are recording progress as of the end of the second week, so we will set the **Status Date** as Saturday 13 December 2008. The time will default to the end of the work day:
    > Update the project using **Tools, Tracking, Update Project...**, as per the picture below:

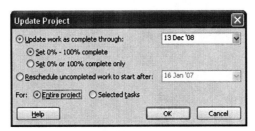

> Check the **Status Date** in the **Project Information** form. It should be 13 Dec 08 and the Status Date should be displayed on the Gantt Chart.
> The **Physical % Complete** has not been updated. This is an optional field that may be used for entering the progress. It is not linked to the durations and may be used for calculating the Earned Value. Hide the **Physical % Complete** column.
> Enter 20% Complete against the summary task **6 Estimate** and observe how the % Complete fields of the Detailed Tasks of **6 Estimate** are calculated.
> Select task **7 Installation Requirements** and look at the **Resource Work** and then open the **Resource Cost** forms in the lower pane. Observe how the resource work and costs have been updated.
> Enter 50% Complete against task **7 Installation Requirements** and enter an Actual Start Date of 11 Dec 08. Task **9 Project Schedule** should start earlier as its predecessor is scheduled to finish earlier. Press F9 if required.
> Enter 1d Actual Duration against task **10 Technical Specification,** the % Comp should equal 11.

Your schedule should look like this:

	Task Name	Act Start	Act Finish	% Comp	Act Dur	Rem. Dur.	Act Cost	Act Work
1	⊟ OzBuild Bid	1 Dec '08	NA	29%	10.29d	25.71d	$16,160.00	200hrs
2	⊟ Research	1 Dec '08	11 Dec '08	100%	9d	0d	$12,320.00	152hrs
3	Bid Request C	1 Dec '08	1 Dec '08	100%	0d	0d	$0.00	0hrs
4	Bid Strategy	1 Dec '08	1 Dec '08	100%	1d	0d	$2,080.00	24hrs
5	Technical Fea	2 Dec '08	11 Dec '08	100%	8d	0d	$10,240.00	128hrs
6	⊟ Estimate	11 Dec '08	NA	14%	2.45d	15.55d	$3,840.00	48hrs
7	Installation Re	11 Dec '08	NA	50%	2d	2d	$2,560.00	32hrs
8	Supplier Com	NA	NA	0%	0d	3d	$0.00	0hrs
9	Project Sched	NA	NA	0%	0d	4d	$0.00	0hrs
10	Technical Spe	12 Dec '08	NA	11%	1d	8d	$1,280.00	16hrs
11	Component B	NA	NA	0%	0d	2d	$0.00	0hrs

8. Now enter the hours and costs to date and hours to go. To prevent Microsoft Project from calculating the costs, open the **Tools, Options...** form, **Calculation** tab and:
    > **UNCHECK** the **Updating task status updates resource status**. This option is to prevent the updated % Complete from calculating **Actual Work** and **Remaining Work**.
    > **UNCHECK** the **Actual costs are always calculated by Microsoft Project**. This option is to prevent Microsoft Project from calculating the **Actual Costs** from the **Actual Work**.

WORKSHOP 18 CONTINUED

➢ Update task **10 Technical Specification** with the following information:
    72 hours of **Remaining Work** against the **Sales Engineer**, and
    72 hours of **Remaining Work** against the **System Engineer**.
➢ Click the **OK** button to accept the changes.

The task duration extends. This is because the task is **Fixed Units**, so the **Units** stayed the same and duration was extended. Your schedule should look like this:

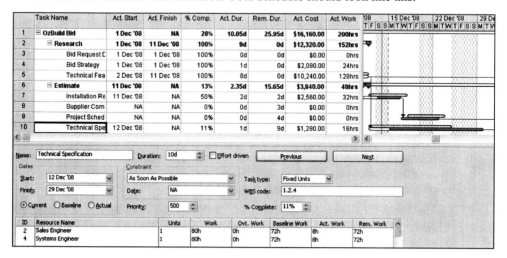

9. Apply the **Resource Cost** details form:
➢ Update task **10 Technical Specification** with the following information:
    Actual Cost of $1,000.00 against the **Sales Engineer**, and
    Actual Cost of $1,000.00 against the **System Engineer**.
➢ Click the **OK** button to accept the changes.
➢ The **Remaining Costs** will always be calculated by Microsoft Project and your schedule should look like this:

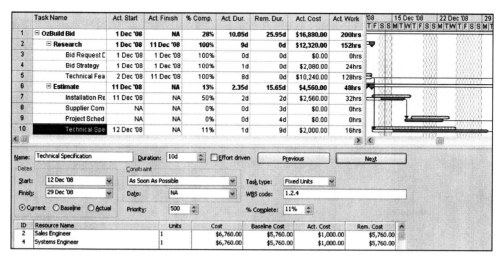

WORKSHOP 18 CONTINUED

10. Now apply the **Earned Value** table. Your answer may vary as alternate versions of Microsoft Project calculate differently. The VAC column does not calculate vertically as Microsoft Project calculates the EAC horizontally using the formula EAC = ACWP + (Baseline cost X - BCWP) / CPI:

	Task Name	Planned Value - PV (BCWS)	Earned Value - EV (BCWP)	AC (ACWP)	SV	CV	EAC	BAC	VAC
1	⊟ OzBuild Bid	$14,880.00	$16,147.20	$16,880.00	$1,267.20	-$732.80	$62,587.05	$59,870.00	-$2,717.05
2	⊟ Research	$12,320.00	$12,320.00	$12,320.00	$0.00	$0.00	$12,320.00	$12,320.00	$0.00
3	Bid Request Docur	$0.00	$0.00	$0.00	$0.00	$0.00	$0.00	$0.00	$0.00
4	Bid Strategy	$2,080.00	$2,080.00	$2,080.00	$0.00	$0.00	$2,080.00	$2,080.00	$0.00
5	Technical Feasibilit	$10,240.00	$10,240.00	$10,240.00	$0.00	$0.00	$10,240.00	$10,240.00	$0.00
6	⊟ Estimate	$2,560.00	$3,827.20	$4,560.00	$1,267.20	-$732.80	$25,926.42	$21,760.00	-$4,166.42
7	Installation Require	$1,280.00	$2,560.00	$2,560.00	$1,280.00	$0.00	$5,120.00	$5,120.00	$0.00
8	Supplier Compone	$0.00	$0.00	$0.00	$0.00	$0.00	$1,920.00	$1,920.00	$0.00
9	Project Schedule	$0.00	$0.00	$0.00	$0.00	$0.00	$1,920.00	$1,920.00	$0.00
10	Technical Specifica	$1,280.00	$1,267.20	$2,000.00	-$12.80	-$732.80	$18,181.82	$11,520.00	-$6,661.82
11	Component Bids C	$0.00	$0.00	$0.00	$0.00	$0.00	$1,280.00	$1,280.00	$0.00
12	⊞ Proposal	$0.00	$0.00	$0.00	$0.00	$0.00	$25,790.00	$25,790.00	$0.00

11. To demonstrate the splitting of tasks, assume that the data date is 24 Dec 08 and no more work will continue until after the New Year, and ensure that **Split in-progress tasks** is checked in the **Tools**, **Options…**, **Schedule** tab.

12. Use the **Tools**, **Tracking**, **Update Project…** to reschedule all incomplete work after 01 Jan 09, to allow for any scheduling conflicts. Your schedule should look like the following:

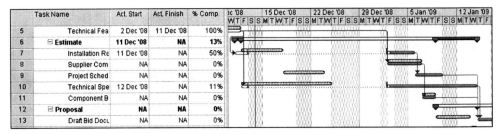

13. Add the Negative Float bar as per the picture below. You will notice there will be negative float on Submit Bid which is generated by the Must Finish By constraint.

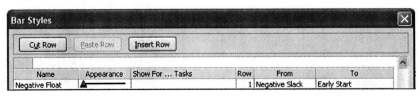

	Task Name	Act. Start	Act. Finish	% Comp.	
12	⊟ Proposal	NA	NA	0%	
13	Draft Bid Docu	NA	NA	0%	
14	Reviewed Dra	NA	NA	0%	
15	Design Valida	NA	NA	0%	
16	Revised Bid D	NA	NA	0%	
17	Component P	NA	NA	0%	
18	Bid Document	NA	NA	0%	
19	Bid Submitted	NA	NA	0%	

22 TOOLS AND TECHNIQUES FOR SCHEDULING

22.1 Understanding Menu Options

You will find that the menu options change as you select rows, cells, all rows and cells, or views. Therefore, not all menu options are always available. The following topics will be covered in this chapter:

- Menu items sometimes found under **Edit**:
  - ➤ **Cut, Copy** and **Paste Task**
  - ➤ **Cut, Copy** and **Paste Cell**
  - ➤ **Copy Picture**
  - ➤ **Fill**
  - ➤ **Clear**
  - ➤ **Find...** and **Replace...**
  - ➤ **Go To...**
- **Insert, Recurring tasks...**
- **Splitting** a Task
- **Copy, Cut** and **Paste** from Spreadsheets
- **Unique Task, Resource** and **Assignment ID**
- **Organizer**

22.2 Cut, Copy and Paste Row

This function allows you to select one or more consecutive or non-consecutive tasks (using Ctrl-click) and either copy them, or cut them and paste as a group to a new location that you select with your mouse. Any inter-task relationships are also copied but external relationships to unselected tasks are not copied.

22.3 Cut, Copy and Paste Cell

You may cut or copy information and then paste into one or more cells from:

- One cell, or
- Adjacent cells by dragging in rows and/or columns, or
- A non-contiguous group of cells by Ctrl-clicking.

This function operates in a similar way to Excel's cut-and-paste operation:

- Highlight the cell(s) you want to copy or cut.
- Select **Edit, Copy Cell** or **Ctrl+C** to copy a cell or **Edit, Cut Cell** or **Ctrl+X** to cut a cell.
- Position the mouse where you want to paste the data and select **Edit, Paste** or **Ctrl+V**.

This is an interesting function since it allows you to copy from one column to another when the format is compatible. This function may also be used for transferring and/or updating your schedule from other software such as Excel and is covered later in this chapter.

22.4   Copy Picture

This allows a section or total screen to be copied to the clipboard and then either pasted into a document or saved as a **gif** file. Select **Edit**, **Copy Picture...** in Microsoft Project 2000 – 2003 and **Report**, **Copy Picture** in Microsoft Project 2007 to open the **Copy Picture** form:

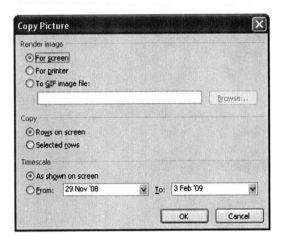

The options are self-explanatory and when pasted into a document the picture looks like the example below in Microsoft Project 2007.

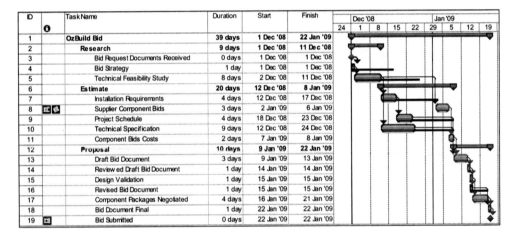

22.5   Fill

The **Edit**, **Fill** command allows you to select one cell or a range of cells and then copy them up, down, left, or right without the need to copy and paste.

22.6 Clear

The **Edit, Clear** command allows you to clear the following data from a task:

- **All** – This clears all information from the cell you have highlighted.

- **Format** – This sets the formats back to the default.

- **Notes** – Clears the Notes contents on a task.

- **Contents** – This clears the contents of the highlighted cells but leaves the formatting.

- **Entire task** – This deletes the entire task but leaves blank rows.

22.7 Find and Replace

The **Edit, Find…** and **Edit, Replace…** functions allow you to find any task by matching data with your defined criteria. This will also allow you to find the data and then replace it with another piece of information.

22.8 Go To

The **Edit, Go To…** function allow you to quickly find a date and move the timescale horizontally to that date or to a task if you know the Task ID number:

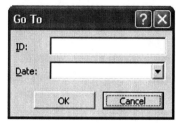

22.9 Insert Recurring Task

The **Insert, Recurring tasks…** function allows the insertion of more than one task that occurs on a regular basis. Select **Insert, Recurring Task…** to display the **Recurring Task Information** form. The options are self-explanatory. These activities use the Rollup bars in the **Bars Styles** form.

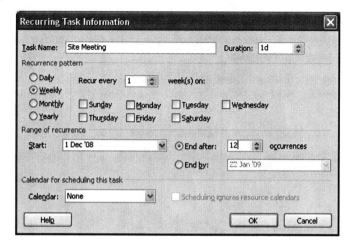

22.10 Splitting a Task

A task may be manually split by clicking on the ⬚ icon, moving your cursor over the point on the task bar where you want a split, and dragging the task. Splitting a task effectively increases the duration of the task but work associated with a split task is scheduled intermittently.

The Tools, Options, Schedule **Split in-progress tasks** option must be checked to allow the splitting of a task.

An in-progress task may also be split by:

- Dragging the incomplete portion of a task in the bar chart, or

- Using the **Tools, Tracking, Update Project…, Reschedule uncompleted work to start after:** function, or

- Commencing a task before its predecessor finishes as shown by the second task in the diagram below:

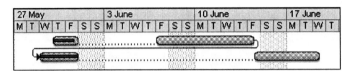

22.11 Copy or Cut-and-Paste to and from Spreadsheets

Microsoft Project will allow **Copy** or **Cut**-and-**Paste** to and from spreadsheets and other software packages. This may be useful for a number of purposes:

- Importing Tasks from other applications,

- Assigning Codes and Resources to Tasks,

- Statusing a schedule, and

- Exporting Data to other packages.

The **Copy** or **Cut** function copies the task data from highlighted columns and rows in the schedule to the Windows clipboard. These may then be pasted into another software package:

- Highlight the data in your schedule that you want to transfer to another software package and cut or copy the data.

- Move to the spreadsheet application and paste the task information. You will find the column headers are **NOT** pasted into the application; only data from the schedule is pasted.

- The data may be edited or updated in the application, as required.

- The tasks may be selected and pasted back into the schedule to update it with the normal copy and paste functions.

22.12 Paste Link – Cell Values in Columns

A cell may be copied, and the paste linked to another cell or an external application. Thus when the copied cell is updated the linked cell is also updated with the same value. This could be used to update a number of activities that have the same % Complete. A linked cell has a small triangle in the corner and the linking may be removed by overtyping the cell value.

22.13 Unique Task, Resource and Assignment ID

The Task IDs change for all tasks below an inserted task. There are many contractual and management reasons to be able to identify each task by a unique task number.

22.13.1   Task Unique ID

When a new task is added to a blank schedule, it is assigned a **Unique ID** commencing with the number 1. When tasks are deleted these numbers are not re-used and any new task is assigned a new sequential number. This **Unique ID** number may be displayed in a column titled **Unique ID**. It is also possible to display the **Unique Predecessor** and **Unique Successor** columns:

	Unique ID	Task Name	Unique ID Predecessors	Unique ID Successors
1	18	⊟ OzBuild Bid		
2	17	⊟ Research		
3	2	Bid Document Received		3
4	3	Bid Strategy Meeting	2	4
5	4	Investigate Technical Feasibility	3	5,6,8
6	5	Document Installation Requirements	4	7,9
7	19	⊟ Estimation		
8	6	Request Component Bids	4	9

22.13.2   Resource Unique ID

A resource **Unique ID** is created for each resource. Again, when a resource is deleted, the resource **Unique ID** is not re-used. This number may be displayed in the **Resource Sheet** or **Resources Usage** view column titled, **Unique ID**.

22.13.3   Resource Assignment Unique ID

When a resource is assigned to a task, the assignment is given a unique **Assignment ID**. This number may be displayed in the **Resource Sheet** or **Resources Usage** view column titled **Unique ID**:

	❶	Task Name	Unique ID
1		⊟ OzBuild Bid	18
2		⊟ Research	17
3		Bid Document Received	2
4		⊟ Bid Strategy Meeting	3
		Sales Engineer	*2097170*
		System Engineer	*2097181*
		Tender Manager	*2097169*
5		⊟ Investigate Technical Feasibility	4
		System Engineer	*2097171*
6	🗐	⊟ Document Installation Requirements	5

22.14 Organizer

The **Global.mpt** file holds the schedule's default settings such as **Tables** and **Views**, which are inherited from new projects and not created from a template. The **Organizer** function is also used to copy information between projects or to update the **Global.mpt**.

Select **Tools**, **Organizer…**to open the **Organizer** form:

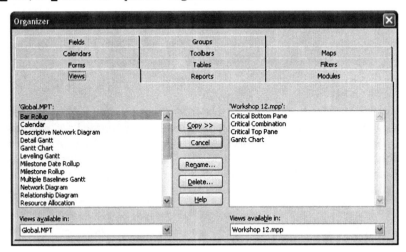

Except for the **Global.mpt** project, the projects you want to copy settings to and from will have to be opened in order to copy data.

- The Organizer function is used for renaming and deleting most items such as **Tables**, **Views and Calendars**.

- The two tab titles above that are self-explanatory are:

  ➤ **Maps** – These are predefined tables for exporting data, and

  ➤ **Modules** – These are Visual Basic Macros.

23 WHAT IS NEW IN MICROSOFT PROJECT

23.1 WHAT IS NEW IN MICROSOFT OFFICE PROJECT 2007

As with most Microsoft releases there are many enhancements. This section is aimed at listing the main changes since Microsoft Project 2000.

23.1.1 New File Format

There have been several changes in the file types Microsoft Project 2007 will work with:

- A new file format, mpp (2007), has been introduced with Microsoft Project 2007. Microsoft Project 2007 will save to the 2003/2002/2000 format but will not save to mpp (98), the Microsoft Project 98 format, so those who wish to create an mpx file for exporting to other planning software will need to keep a version of 98, a version of 2000 – 2003, as well as running 2007.

- The Microsoft Access format available in Microsoft Project 2000 – 2003 is not available in Microsoft Project 2007.

- The Project Database (*.mpd) database format that may be used for exporting data in Microsoft Project 2000 – 2003 and was intended to replace the mpx format in Microsoft Project 2000 – 2003 is not available in Microsoft Project 2007.

See the **CREATING PROJECTS AND SETTING UP THE SOFTWARE** chapter for more detail.

23.1.2 Notes on Calendar Exceptions and Repeating Nonwork Periods

Microsoft Project 2007 has two new calendar functions that now allows:

- Notes to be added to calendar exceptions, and

- Repeating Nonwork periods.

As a result the interface for creating calendars and editing the nonwork times has changed significantly between the 2000 – 2003 versions and 2007 version. See the **DEFINING CALENDARS** chapter for more details.

23.1.3 Multiple Undo

Multiple Undo is now available, allowing a default of 20 **Undos** and **Redos**. This number may be increased to 99 in the **Tools**, **Options**, **General** tab.

23.1.4 3-D Bars

The default display of bars in Microsoft Project 2007 is in 3 dimension. Should you prefer the traditional display or wish to match existing report formats then select **Tools**, **Options**, **View** tab and uncheck the **Bars and shapes in Gantt view in 3-D** option.

Microsoft Project 2007   Microsoft Project 2000 – 2003

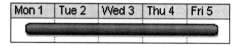

23.1.5 Format Fonts

The **Format, Font...** function allows you to format any selected text in rows or columns. This function has been enhanced with Microsoft Project 2007 and now allows a **Background Color** and **Background Pattern** that was not available in earlier versions.

- Select all the rows by clicking on the **Select All** button, box above row number 1, or

- Select one or more rows or columns by Ctrl-clicking or dragging, then

- Select **Format, Font...** to open the **Font** form:

- You may select the **Font, Font style, font Size, Color** of the text, **Background Color** and **Background Pattern** from the **Font** dialog box.

- Once formatted, the selected font style and type will be applied to the data column or task row in any table.

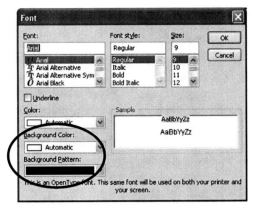

23.1.6 Highlighted Changed Fields

This function highlights all the fields that will change when another field has been changed.

- The menu **View, Show/Hide Change Highlight** or clicking on the 🖺 icon will hide/display the highlighting.

- Remove the shading as a result of the last change by pressing the **F9** key to recalculate the project, by saving the project or by entering a value into a changed cell twice.

- Select **Format, Text Styles...** and select **Changed Cells** from the **Item to change** list.

This is a very good feature as it highlights changes in date and duration fields of all tasks as a result of a change, thus making it simpler to see what tasks have moved as a result of the change.

	ⓞ	Task Name	Dur	Start	Finish	Total Slack	Dec '08					Jan '09			
							24	1	8	15	22	29	5	12	19	26
1		⊟ OzBuild Bid	36d	1 Dec '08	22 Jan '09	0d									
2		⊟ Research	10d	1 Dec '08	12 Dec '08	2d									
3		Bid Request Documents Received	0d	1 Dec '08	1 Dec '08	2d									
4		Bid Strategy	1d	1 Dec '08	1 Dec '08	2d									
5		Technical Feasibility Study	9d	2 Dec '08	12 Dec '08	2d									
6		⊟ Estimate	16d	13 Dec '08	8 Jan '09	0d									
7	🗗	Installation Requirements	4d	13 Dec '08	17 Dec '08	3d									
8	🗗🖉	Supplier Component Bids	3d	2 Jan '09	6 Jan '09	0d									
9	🗗	Project Schedule	4d	18 Dec '08	22 Dec '08	3d									
10		Technical Specification	9d	15 Dec '08	29 Dec '08	7d									
11		Component Bids Costs	2d	7 Jan '09	8 Jan '09	0d									

23.1.7   Schedule Currency

The **Currency:** option found under the **Tools**, **Options**, **View** tab allows the specification of the currency used in the schedule.

23.1.8   Cost Resource

There is now a cost resource, thus estimates may more easily be entered as cost resources. See the **RESOURCES** chapters for more detail.

23.1.9   General

The form on the right is from Microsoft Project 2007. **Budget** indicates that the resource is being used for budget purposes and the **Resource Availability** features are disabled when a Resource is marked as Budget

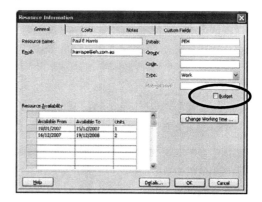

23.1.10   Reports Menu and New Reports

A new **Report** menu item includes the following options:

- **Visual Reports…** – These are a new set of graphical reports in Microsoft Project 2007 which allow reports to be exported to Excel or Visio.

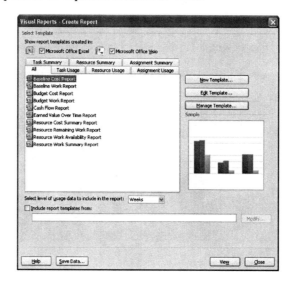

- **Copy Picture…** – This function has been move from the **Edit** to **Reports** menu in Microsoft Project 2007 but the functionality has not been changed.

- **Reports…** – This item has been moved from the **View** to **Reports** menus in Microsoft Project 2007.

23.1.11 Task Drivers

A task may not be on the Critical Path and may have more than one predecessor. A **Driving Relationship** is the predecessor that determines the Early Start of a task. Microsoft Project 2000 – 2003 does not identify the difference between **Driving** and **Non-driving Relationships,** which often makes analyzing a schedule difficult. In earlier versions of Microsoft Project often the simplest way to determine the driving relationship for tasks not on the critical path and with more than one predecessor was to delete the relationships until the task moved. Primavera products have always displayed the driving predecessors and successors in the Predecessor and Successors.

Microsoft Project 2007 introduced a **Task Drivers** form that indicates which is the driving predecessor and whether the schedule has been Resource Leveled. It will also display the effects of leveling.

Select the Task Drivers icon on the Standard Toolbar to open the **Task Drivers** pane:

- The picture below shows that task 10 is the driving predecessor of task 13.

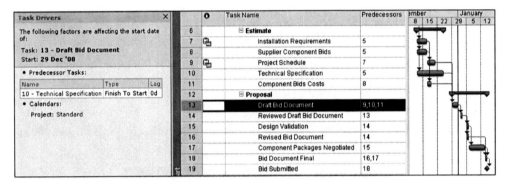

- The picture below shows that task 11 has been delayed by leveling:

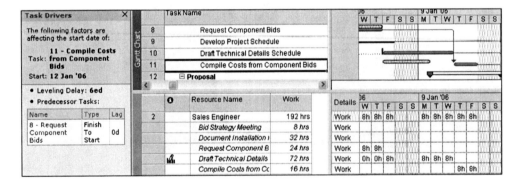

23.1.12 Security

Legacy Formats. These options, new to Microsoft Project 2007, control the notification and opening of legacy file formats such as Microsoft Project 98 format and Microsoft Project 2000 – 2003 mpw files.

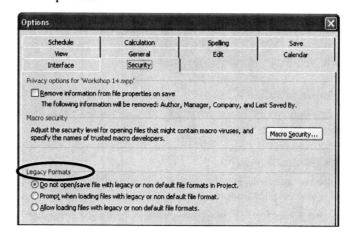

23.2 WHAT WAS NEW IN MICROSOFT PROJECT 2003 STANDARD

There were very few changes made in functionality of Microsoft Project 2003 and for the benefit of users upgrading from Microsoft Project 2000 I have kept the new features from 2002 to 2003 in separate sections.

Earlier versions of Microsoft Project 2003 did not function correctly and it was not possible to outdent some tasks. A Hotfix Package (software patch) and service packs are available from the Microsoft website to correct this problem.

23.2.1 Copy Picture to Office Wizard

There is a new function available on the **Analysis** toolbar that runs a wizard to copy a picture to PowerPoint, Word or Visio.

23.2.2 Print a View as a Report

There is a new wizard available for displaying views and printings. Display the **Project Guide** toolbar and click on the Reports tab to run this function.

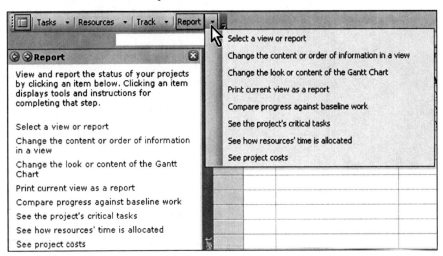

23.2.3 Options

In Microsoft Project 2000 there was an Option Titled **Workgroup;** this was replaced with **Collaborate** in 2002 and then removed in 2003 Standard.

Microsoft Project 2003 had a new option added titled **Security** allowing:

- The properties of Author, Manager, Company and Last Saved By to be removed from a file when it is saved, and

- Security options set to nominate which macros may be used or not used. This is aimed at preventing macros with a virus from being activated.

23.3 WHAT WAS NEW IN MICROSOFT PROJECT 2002 STANDARD

There were many features added or amended in the release of Microsoft Project Standard 2002. The following is a list of important features added that are considered to be useful for planning and scheduling projects.

23.3.1 Timescale

The timescale, such as in Gantt Chart, may be displayed with one, two or three tiers with each tier displaying a different unit of time. By default, the timescale is shown in two tiers. The timescale may be adjusted by double-clicking the timescale or selecting **Format, Timescale…..**

23.3.2 Smart Tags

This feature provides information about your scheduling results as well as some ease of use features to change your results.

23.3.3 Multiple Baselines

Microsoft Project 2002 can save 11 Baselines over the course of a project. To save a baseline, select **Tools, Tracking**, and then **Save Baseline….**

23.3.4 Status Date Calculation Options

The Calculation Options form has additional options that allow user to automatically adjust where actual and remaining work of new in-progress activities are placed with respect to the **Status Date**. These options are found under **Tools, Option…, Calculation** tab.

23.3.5 Earned Value

There is an additional field titled **Physical % Complete** which may be used for calculating the **Earned Value** of the Project based on any of the Baselines. Select **Tools, Option…,** select the **Calculation** tab and click on the [Earned Value…] button.

23.3.6 Project Guide

The Project Guide allows user to define project parameters such as tasks, tracks, project calendar, resource, and report, etc., using a guide steps wizard. The Project Guide is activated by default and you may disable this features under the **Tools, Option…, Interface** tab.

23.3.7 Summary Task Baseline Recalculation

The baseline of Summary Tasks may not be valid when tasks are added, deleted or moved to another Summary Task. There are options found under **Tools, Tracking, Save Baseline…** to recalculate baseline data for the associated summary tasks.

23.3.8 Resource Graph Form

The **Resource Graph** form is a new feature to Microsoft Project 2007 and is the simplest way to display a small graph showing a resources utilization. Select [Graphs…] from the **Assign Resources** form to display the **Resource Graph** form.

24 ITEMS NOT COVERED IN THIS BOOK

The following subjects are not covered in this book. This list is not exhaustive but is intended to give a guide to the other functions available in Microsoft Project.

- **File, Save As Workspace…** – Saves and opens more than one file at a time 2003 and earlier.

- **File, Send To** – Emails your data to other people.

- **Edit, Paste Special…** – Allows options for pasting data or graphics into the schedule.

- **Edit, Paste as a Hyperlink** – Pastes data as a hyperlink that can be pasted into the Hyperlink columns.

- **Edit and Insert Objects** – Incorporates pieces of information from another application that may be displayed on the bar chart using OLE, Object Linking and Embedding.

- **Insert, Hyperlink…** – Allows you to save a hyperlink to another file. The link need not be to another Microsoft Project file. You may click on the hyperlink icon in the **Task Information** column, and the function will take you to the file by opening the associated application to view the data. You may right-click on the hyperlink to access the Hyperlink menu to edit, copy, etc.

- **Insert, Drawing** – Used to draw lines and other common geometrical objects (commonly found in graphics drawing software packages) on a Gantt Chart.

- **Format, Drawing** – Formats your drawings.

- **Tools, AutoCorrect Options…** – Specifies how the Spelling AutoCorrect function operates.

- **Tools, Import Outlook Tasks…** – Imports a list of tasks from Outlook.

- **Tools, Resource Sharing** – Shares resources with other projects.

- **Tools, Link Between Projects…** – Creates a link between two different projects.

- **Tools, Macro** – This function allows you to store a number of keystrokes and invoke them in one action. This is useful when executing repetitive keystroke operations. You may need to understand the Visual Basic programming language to fully implement this feature.

- **Collaborate** – These options are mainly used in conjunction with Project Server which is beyond the scope of this book

- **Help, Detect and Repair…** – Fixes problems with Microsoft Project 2003.

- The **Analysis** toolbar has three options:
  - ➤ **Adjust Dates** – To change the start date of the project and associated task constraint dates.
  - ➤ **Analyze Timescale Data in Excel…** – Allows you to export time-phased data to Excel.
  - ➤ **PERT Analysis** –Functions like a Monte Carlo Simulation. **PERT Analysis** also has its own toolbar.

Details of all these topics may be found in the User Manual and Help.

25 APPENDIX 1 – SCREENS USED TO CREATE VIEWS

Microsoft Project has a complex method of accessing the data on screen.

- The screen may be split with an **Upper** and **Lower Pane**.
  - ➢ The **Upper Pane** displays all project information, except when a filter is applied.
  - ➢ The **Lower Pane** displays information about the task or tasks that are highlighted in the upper pane.
- A **View** may be created and edited. A **View** is based on a **Screen**.
  - ➢ A **Combination View** sets the view for both the Upper and Lower Pane.
  - ➢ A **Single View** may be applied to either the **Upper** or **Lower Pane** as long as the **Screen** may be displayed in that **Pane**.
- There are 14 **Screens**, most of which may be applied to the **Upper** or **Lower Panes** through **Views**.
  - ➢ There are some restrictions. For example, the **Calendar** screen may not be applied to the bottom pane.
  - ➢ Some **Screens** are not useful when displayed in the incorrect pane. It is better to display the **Task** form in the bottom **Pane** and leave a **Gantt Chart** in the **Upper Pane**.
  - ➢ Some **Screens** are very similar to each other, such as the **Task** screen and the **Task Details** screen.
- Some **Screens** have **Details** forms where the content of a **View** may be changed. An example of this is a **Task Usage** view, which may be formatted to show **Work** or **Costs** and **Cumulative** or **Period**.
- Some Screens are split vertically and have a left-hand side and a right-hand side such as the **Gantt Screen**. Other **Screens** do not split vertically, like the **Task Screen** and the **Task Details Screen**, which are used in the **Task Form** view and the **Task Details Form** view.

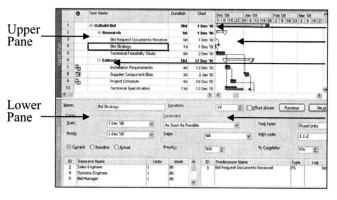

Upper Pane

Lower Pane

Gantt Screen, this is split vertically here.

RHS of Gantt Screen

LHS of Gantt Screen

Task Form Screen that has many Details forms but not split vertically.

The following table summarizes the **Screen**, **View** and **Details** options:

	Screen Name	Panes	Split Verti-cally	Details Form Options	Format Column Options
1	Calendar	Upper Only	No	None	Right-click Format Options Go To… Timescale… Gridlines… Text Styles… Bar Styles… Zoom… Layout… Layout Now Split
2	Gantt Chart	Best in Upper	Yes	Bars and Columns may be formatted	Yes
3	Network Diagram	Best in Upper	No	Task Boxes may be edited	No
4	Relationship Diagram	Either	No	None	No
5	Resource Form	Best in Lower	No	Hide Form View ✓ Schedule Cost Work Notes Objects	No
6	Resource Graph	Best in Lower	No	Gridlines… Bar Styles… Remove Split ✓ Peak Units Work Cumulative Work Overallocation Percent Allocation Remaining Availability Cost Cumulative Cost Work Availability Unit Availability	No
7	Resource Name Form	Best in Lower	No	Hide Form View ✓ Schedule Cost Work Notes Objects	No
8	Resource Sheet	Either	No	None	Yes

	Screen Name	Panes	Split Vertically	Details Form Options	Format Column Options
9	Resource Usage	Either	Yes	Detail Styles... / ✓ Work / Actual Work / Cumulative Work / Baseline Work / Cost / Actual Cost	No
10	Task Details Form	Best in Lower	Yes	Hide Form View / ✓ Resources & Predecessors / Resources & Successors / Predecessors & Successors / Resource Schedule / Resource Work / Resource Cost / Notes / Objects	No
11	Task Form	Best in Lower	No	Hide Form View / Resources & Predecessors / Resources & Successors / ✓ Predecessors & Successors / Resource Schedule / Resource Work / Resource Cost / Notes / Objects	No
12	Task Name Form	Best in Lower	No	Hide Form View / Resources & Predecessors / Resources & Successors / Predecessors & Successors / Resource Schedule / ✓ Resource Work / Resource Cost / Notes / Objects	No
13	Task Sheet	Best In Upper	No	None	Yes
14	Task Usage	Best in Lower	Yes	Detail Styles... / ✓ Work / Actual Work / Cumulative Work / Baseline Work / Cost / Actual Cost	Yes

The following table displays the Screens and provides some background on each:

Screen Name	Note and/or Screen Dumps
1. Calendar	May be displayed in top pane only. 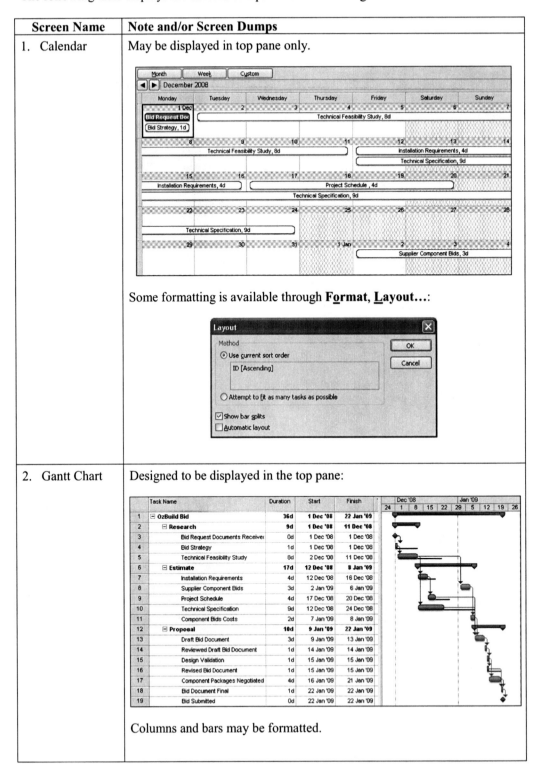 Some formatting is available through **Format, Layout…**:
2. Gantt Chart	Designed to be displayed in the top pane: Columns and bars may be formatted.

Screen Name	Note and/or Screen Dumps
3. Network Diagram	Designed to be displayed in the top pane: 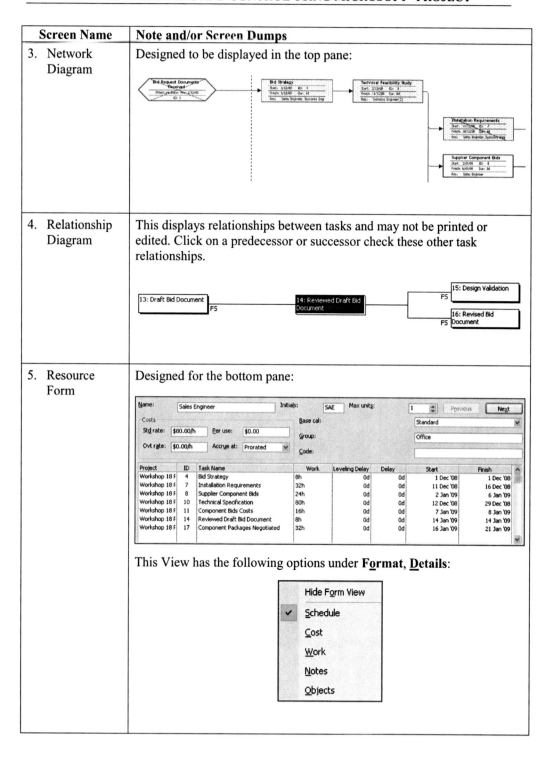
4. Relationship Diagram	This displays relationships between tasks and may not be printed or edited. Click on a predecessor or successor check these other task relationships.
5. Resource Form	Designed for the bottom pane: This View has the following options under **Format**, **Details**:

Screen Name	Note and/or Screen Dumps
6. Resource Graph	This View is designed to be displayed in the bottom pane: 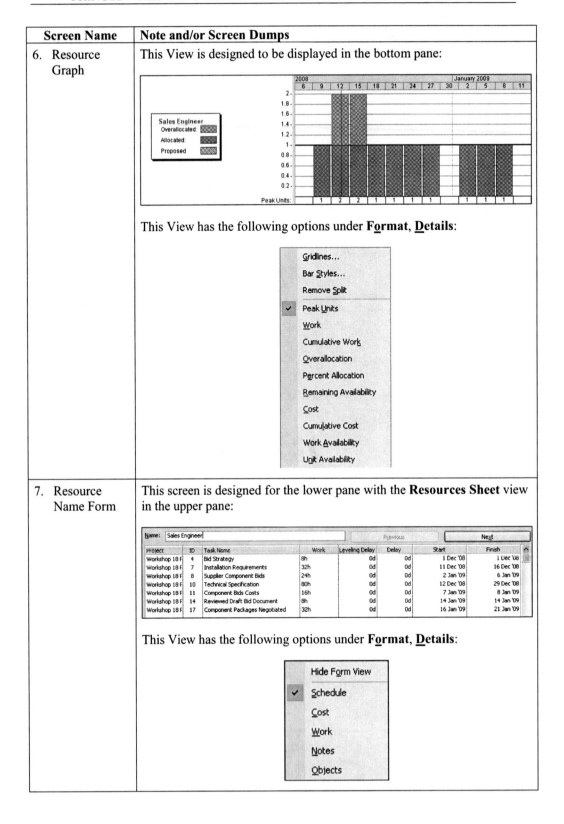 This View has the following options under **Format, Details**:
7. Resource Name Form	This screen is designed for the lower pane with the **Resources Sheet** view in the upper pane: This View has the following options under **Format, Details**:

Screen Name	Note and/or Screen Dumps
8. Resource Sheet	This screen may be used in the top or bottom pane and the columns may be formatted with the **Table and Columns** functions: 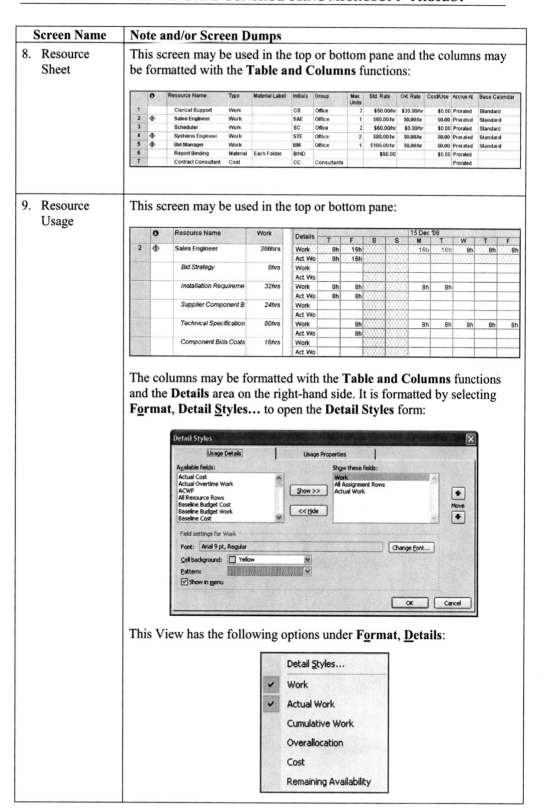
9. Resource Usage	This screen may be used in the top or bottom pane:

The columns may be formatted with the **Table and Columns** functions and the **Details** area on the right-hand side. It is formatted by selecting **Format, Detail Styles...** to open the **Detail Styles** form:

This View has the following options under **Format, Details**:

Screen Name	Note and/or Screen Dumps
10. Task Details Form	This form is best displayed in the bottom pane and displays information about the task highlighted in the top pane: 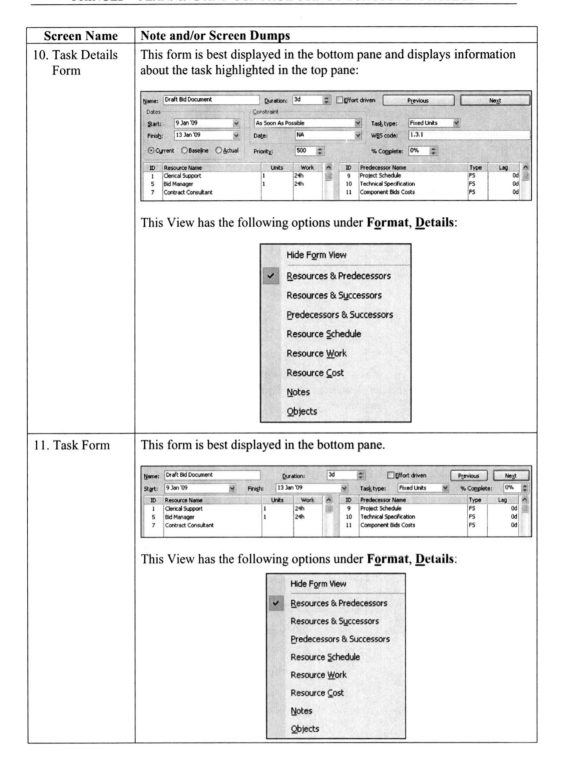 This View has the following options under **Format**, **Details**:
11. Task Form	This form is best displayed in the bottom pane.

Screen Name	Note and/or Screen Dumps
12. Task Name Form	This form is best displayed in the bottom pane. 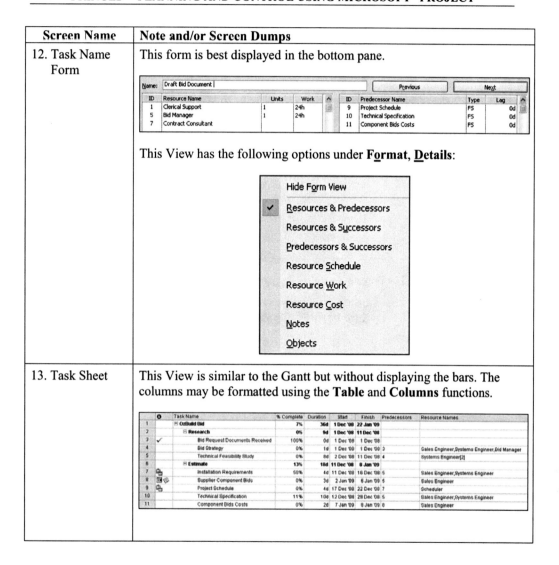 This View has the following options under **Format**, **Details**:
13. Task Sheet	This View is similar to the Gantt but without displaying the bars. The columns may be formatted using the **Table** and **Columns** functions.

Screen Name	Note and/or Screen Dumps
14. Task Usage	This view displays the tasks in the columns and the resources and work on the right-hand side:  The columns may be formatted using the **Table** and **Columns** functions. The information displayed on the right-hand side of the screen may be set by selecting **Format**, **Details**: 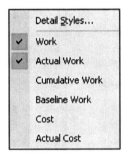 The formatting of the right-hand side of the screen may be changed by selecting **Format, Detail Styles…** to open the **Detail Styles** form: 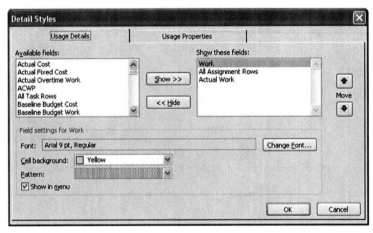

26 INDEX

Excel, 3-2, 14-10, 20-4
  Pivot Table, 3-2
Exception Plan, 1-5, 1-7
Exception Report, 2-11
Executing a Work Package, 1-14
Expected Finish Constraint, 11-2
Exporting, 22-4
eXtended Markup Language, 3-2
External dependencies, 2-8
External Logic, 9-2
External Products, 2-4, 2-5, 10-2
FAC, 21-14
File Locations, 17-15
File Types, 3-1
  mdb, 3-1
  mpd, 3-1, 23-1
  mpp, 3-1
  mpp 98 Format, 3-1
  mpt, 3-1
  mpx, 3-1
  xml, 3-2
Filter
  And/Or, 12-5
  And/Or Filters, 12-7
  AutoFilter, 12-1
  Calculated, 12-6
  Create, 12-4
  Criteria, 12-5
  Definition Form, 12-4
  Edit, 12-4
  Interactive, 12-8
  Multiple And/Or, 12-8
  Show in menu, 12-4
  Show related summary rows, 12-4
  Value(s), 12-6
  Wild Cards, 12-5
Find and Replace, 22-3
Finish Constraint, 11-1
Finish No Earlier Than Constraint, 11-2
Finish No Later Than Constraint, 11-1,
  11-2
Finish Variance, 15-25
Finish-to-Finish Relationship, 9-3
Finish-to-Start Relationship, 9-3
First Day of the Week, 17-6
First page number, 14-4
Fiscal
  Year, 8-12, 17-6
  Year Starts On, 17-6

Fixed
  Costs, 19-3
  Duration Task Type, 17-9, 19-2
  Units Task Type, 17-9, 19-2
  Work Task Type, 17-9, 19-2
Float, 2-9, 2-10
  Bars, 8-6
  Calculations, 10-7
  Free Float, 2-10
  Positive, 8-6
  Total, 8-6
  Total Float, 2-10, 9-10
Font Formatting, 8-10, 23-2
Forecast
  At Completion, 21-14
  To Complete, 21-14
Form
  Box Styles, 13-10
  Cell Layout, 13-10
  Change Working Time, 5-8
  Change Working Time (Resource), 18-4
  Column Definition, 8-4
  Customize Fields, 16-1, 16-2
  Data Template Definition, 13-10
  Data Templates, 13-10
  Define Group Interval, 16-6
  Detailed Styles, 20-3
  Edit Lookup Table For Products, 12-10
  Filter Definition, 12-2
  Format Bar, 8-5, 8-7, 8-15
  Format Box, 13-12
  Group Definition, 16-6
  Layout, 8-8, 8-15
  Level Now, 20-8
  More Filters, 12-4
  More Groups, 16-6
  More Views, 13-1
  Print, 14-9
  Project Statistics, 15-23
  Reports, 14-11
  Resource Graph, 20-1, 23-7
  Resource Information, 18-4, 18-5
  Resource Usage, 19-8
  Tables, 13-8
  Task Dependency, 9-8
  Task Details, 11-4
  Task Information, 6-5, 9-7, 19-6
  Text Styles, 8-11
  Timescale, 8-12
  Update Project, 15-19
  View Definition, 13-6

P2WORLD

A PRINCE2 PLANNING TOOL

P2WORLD is a software tool designed to assist project managers using the "Product-based planning" technique defined as part of the PRINCE2™ Project Management Method. Project data may be simply imported and exported to Microsoft Project.

BACKGROUND

The PRINCE2 approach to project management is used by about 30,000 qualified project managers in the UK, but up until now there has been a desperate shortage of easy-to-use software tools to help those managers using the vitally important "Product Based Planning" technique, which is at the heart of what makes PRINCE2 so effective.

P2WORLD addresses the need to support project managers by automating the key elements of the 'Product Based Planning' technique

FEATURES

P2WORLD has an intuitive "click, drag and type" graphical user interface, which project managers can use to easily create and maintain all the important diagrams and text required in the Planning (PL) process within PRINCE2.

Each **P2WORLD** project has its own:

Product Breakdown Structure diagram (PBS);

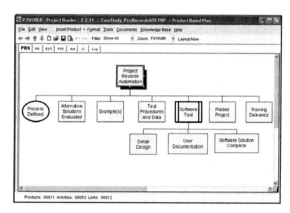

Product Descriptions for each product on the PBS;

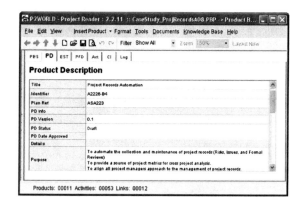

Note:

This software product supports PRINCE2 Product Based Planning and PMBOK® Guide

EASTWOOD HARRIS

Eastwood Harris Pty Ltd   Web: www.eh.com.au   Email: harrispe @eh.com.au   Fax: +61 (0)3 9856 7700

P2WORLD
A PRINCE2 Planning Tool

Features Continued…

Product Flow Diagram for all the products identified on the PBS;

Project Activities to structure the work needed;

Project **Daily Log**;

Product Description reports and **Project Activity** reports; and

Stage PBSs and PFDs as the project progresses.

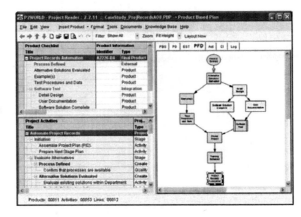

Many potential errors are automatically prevented because these are all consistently merged into a single "PBP container".

Documents can be exported in various formats, including DHTML, PDF, Excel, Word.

Most importantly, P2WORLD will create project plans for instant import into MS Project!

BENEFITS OF P2WORLD

Reduces the amount of project manager time needed to create and maintain consistent Product Based Plans.

Provides **interactive tracking** of all these project elements and the relationships between them, thus reducing time to find information within the plan.

Includes **help files and integrated tutorials** to show how to use the toolset.

Provides **example projects** to demonstrate an integrated view of a Product Based Plan.

Provides valuable support in **learning and applying the underlying PRINCE2 methods**.

Eases the creation of plans for Microsoft Project.

Provides a **Visual Status** mechanism to highlight incomplete products in ongoing projects.

PRODUCT ENVIRONMENT

P2WORLD can be installed on windows based PCs running Windows 98 or later, as a standalone application or as a Microsoft Project Add-in.

AVAILABILITY

P2WORLD is available through Eastwood Harris Pty Ltd at www.eh.com.au, download your trial version now.